Strictly Parenting

Dr Michael Carr-Gregg is one of Australia's most high-profile psychologists and an internationally recognised authority on child and adolescent behaviour. He is currently a consultant psychologist to many schools and national organisations, including ReachOut and beyondblue. Carr-Gregg has been a regular on Melbourne radio 3AW, and is the resident parenting expert on Channel 7's *Sunrise* and *Morning Show*. He is the author of numerous bestselling books on parenting and is the 'Agony Uncle' for *Girlfriend* magazine. He has won many awards for his work.

Strictly Parenting

Everything you need to know about raising school-aged kids

Michael Carr-Gregg

VIKING
an imprint of
PENGUIN BOOKS

VIKING

UK | USA | Canada | Ireland | Australia
India | New Zealand | South Africa | China

Penguin Books is part of the Penguin Random House group of companies whose addresses can be found at global.penguinrandomhouse.com.

First published by Penguin Group (Australia), 2014

Cover design by John Canty © Penguin Group (Australia)
Text design by John Canty © Penguin Group (Australia)
Illustrations by Ron Tandberg
Cover photographs – Vans & Tie © Penguin Group (Australia), Yo Yo: Stockbyte/Getty Images, Pencil: Sezer yadigar/Getty Images, Tennis Ball: jclegg/Getty Images, Basketball: spxChrome/Getty Images
Typeset in Adobe Garamond Pro 12/16pt by Penguin Group (Australia)
Printed and bound in Australia by Griffin Press, an accredited ISO AS/NZS 14001 Environmental Management Systems printer.

National Library of Australia Cataloguing-in-Publication data:

Carr-Gregg, Michael, author.
Strictly parenting / Michael Carr-Gregg.
9780143206286 (paperback)
Subjects: Parenting. Parent and child.

306.874

penguin.com.au

To my wife, Therese, and our boys, Christopher and Rupert.

CONTENTS

YOU HAVE A GIFTED CHILD?

OH YES, WE GIVE HIM EVERYTHING HE WANTS

TANDBERG

INTRODUCTION

I got the idea for this book after a visit to the dentist. It's not often that I gain any great insights from going to see my dentist, but this particular visit was different. I was quietly waiting my turn for my annual check-up when a mother walked in with her 6-year-old son, whom I'll call Elvis (not his real name).

Beautifully dressed in designer clothes, Elvis made a beeline for the toys that were neatly stacked away in a corner of the waiting room. After a few minutes of screeching and wild play, he proceeded to hurl them all over the room, narrowly missing an elderly lady sitting near me.

Elvis's mother was the picture of insouciance, completely absorbed in the tiny characters on her smart phone and ignoring the larger than life character who was now creating quite a commotion.

After what seemed like an eternity, Elvis was summoned by the receptionist to see the dental hygienist. The receptionist said in a reasoned, kind voice, 'Now before you go in, do you mind just putting the toys away?'

This tricky situation hit critical mass when Elvis turned on the receptionist and in a loud, rude voice said, 'Why should I? They aren't mine!'

Showing some Mary MacKillop–like qualities, the receptionist replied patiently, 'Well, you were playing with them and it would be nice if you'd put them back where you found them.'

'You can't make me! Do it yourself!' he replied.

With this, Elvis strode off towards the hygienist – leaving those of us in the waiting room open-mouthed with disbelief.

'Never mind, I'll do it,' said Elvis's mother, obviously embarrassed by our amazement, and then dutifully scuttled around the room, hastily collecting the toys and placing them neatly back in the corner.

Chatting with the receptionist long after Elvis had left the building – presumably with sparkling teeth – I learnt that similar scenes were often repeated in the waiting room and that she was seriously considering ditching the toys. Many of the parents who brought their children to her office exhibited levels of compliance and indulgence that defied imagination.

Elvis's story is a parenting parable for our age. The impact of this type of parenting is everywhere. On a reality TV show, a 16-year-old girl planning her birthday wants a major road blocked off so a marching band can precede her grand entrance onto a red carpet. Talentless young people audition for talent shows and are inconsolable when a judge tells them they are hopeless. Five times as many Australians undergo plastic surgery and cosmetic procedures as ten years ago, and high school students post YouTube videos of themselves beating up their classmates to get attention.

In thirty years of clinical practice and ten years of research for my segments on Channel 7's *Sunrise*, I have been exposed to every style of parenting on this planet. From the father in North Carolina who shot his daughter's computer and posted the video on YouTube after he found one of her Facebook posts offensive, to the Townsville mother who punished her son by making him wear a pair of Shrek ears and sit in public wearing a sign that read, 'Do not trust me. I will steal from you, as I am a thief' while his family ate lunch nearby.

Or the parent who called for advice after her child attended a 'slumber' party with nine other 10-year-olds. She'd assumed that when she picked him up the next day he'd be a bit tired, perhaps, but otherwise fine. She was surprised and a little annoyed to find that none of the kids had slept but was unaware that they had been subjected to an MA 15+ horror movie marathon. She discovered this only after the child had a series of terrifying nightmares and developed such severe anxiety that he required therapy.

Aside from the fact that a 10-year-old needs *at least* eight and a half hours sleep a night for normal brain and body development, MA 15+ classified material is 'legally restricted to persons 15 years and over' because it contains strong violence and/or explicit sex or drug references. How could these parents think it was okay to show this stuff to their own kids, let alone to *other people's children*? This in my opinion is truly crap parenting.

How did it get like this?

If you google the word 'parent' you will get 192 million results in just 0.17 seconds, thousands upon thousands of pages of parenting advice on the websites and blogs of health departments, educational organisations and self-proclaimed parenting gurus. How does a bewildered mum or dad sort through this tidal wave of advice that is often contradictory, lacking an evidence base or just plain quackery?

Indeed, many of the parenting practices I have observed over the last decade fly in the face of a mountain of sound research. We know what children need to help them grow into happy, healthy and resilient adults – to feel safe, valued and 'heard', to be given opportunities to solve their own problems, to have boundaries to push against and to experience the consequences of failure – yet I'm seeing large numbers of Australian parents hesitant to set limits or boundaries, to use moral language or to enforce consequences when their kids make bad choices. Their mantra has become 'you can be anything you want to be', and their children are coddled, coached and told they are magnificent when they are mediocre at best. Accustomed to receiving rewards divorced from actual effort and accomplishment, these children arrive in the real world equipped only with a heightened sense of entitlement and soon become anxious and depressed when they discover that life isn't what they were promised.

Sometimes children need to feel badly – it's how they learn to cope. This doesn't mean that we stand aside and tell them to get over it. (As a schoolkid, if I or my fellow students complained about something, our teacher – ironically named Mr Cherry – would say, 'You'll live. If not, you'll die. Either way, problem solved.') We support them by acknowledging how they feel and letting them know that we're there to help if they need us. Protecting them from failure and never allowing them to 'miss out' means we remove the capacity for them to develop resilience by overcoming adversity. The result will be a generation of young people incapable of assuming adult responsibility, with no idea how to handle the routine challenges of life, making them risk-averse, psychologically anaemic and riddled with anxiety.

Want proof? The latest Mission Australia Youth Survey of 14,461 young Australians aged 15–19 contains some discouraging news: 50 per cent of girls and 22 per cent of boys say that coping with stress is a major personal concern. Recent statistics from the Australian Institute of Health and Welfare show that young women aged 15–24 are being admitted to hospital after self-harming at more than twice the rate they were ten years ago and experts are at a loss to explain why. Perhaps this is a by-product of this generation's inability to cope with stress.

Few people realise that 75 per cent of all mental health problems in human beings begin prior to the age of 25. Current ABS data suggests that 1 in 7 primary school students and 1 in 4 secondary school student have a diagnosable mental illness, but 70 per cent of these children will not get help. Those in their late adolescence are not faring any better. Despite reporting generally good health, in a recent survey by the Young and Well Cooperative Research Centre, it was found that 15 per cent of young men report 'high' to 'very high' psychological distress, while 28 per cent report 'moderate' psychological distress. Even more alarming, nearly 1 in 5 young men in the past 12 months have felt that life is hardly worth living. Nearly 1 in 10 young men have thought about taking their own lives, while 4 per cent reported making plans, and 2 per cent reported an attempt. Suicidal ideation increased with age and significant predictors were unemployment and psychological distress.

The truth is that there will never be enough funding for youth mental health services – that is, to assist young people after their emotional problems become severe enough to interfere with the quality of their lives. Instead, there not only needs to be reconsideration of existing service delivery models but also a concentrated investment in prevention, i.e. parent education. My colleagues and I are expensive ambulances at the bottom of a cliff – all the evidence suggests that children need a robust fence at the top (or at least, the sense to keep away from the edge). That's what this book is about.

In Part 1, I encourage you to think about your own style of parenting and how adopting a developmental perspective is the key to avoiding crappy parenting. In Part 2, I take you through my top parenting strategies for encouraging healthy emotional and social development in your kids. These are evidence-based approaches I have used for the past thirty years in my work with children and their families.

In Part 3, I answer the most common questions I'm asked by parents – everything from 'Should I let my daughter get a tattoo?' to 'How do I get my son to do his homework?' to 'What do I do when my kids won't stop fighting?'

My hope is that by reading this book, parents will have the knowledge, skills and strategies to help their children become resilient, confident and considerate human beings.

PART 1

A DEVELOPMENTAL PERSPECTIVE

Raising children is widely acknowledged as one of the toughest jobs around. Yet parenting is also one of life's richest experiences. It must be, otherwise we wouldn't keep making families. Yet it's a job most of us can get quite easily, without any experience, skills or qualifications. American author Michael Levine once wrote that having children makes you no more a parent than having a piano makes you a pianist.

In this section I'm hoping to inspire you to have a good hard look at the way you are parenting. This might sound confrontational, but it is not meant to be an exercise in blame or criticism. The Australian Childhood Foundation reports that substantial numbers of parents lack confidence in their parenting, which makes sense given that most of us are doing it without any training and often with very little support from extended families. None of us are perfect but we can all do better.

So what are you doing well? What could do with some improvement? As a starting point, I describe some of the parenting styles that have evolved over the past couple of decades and explain why they are less than ideal. If you see yourself in some of these examples, don't panic. My job is to help you rethink your strategies so that they reflect a developmental perspective. In other words, to help you understand what your children *really* need from you to ensure their healthy physical, mental, emotional and social development.

In order to do this, you first need to understand how the brain develops and how this impacts on your children's behaviour, how it will change *drastically* over the eighteen or so years they are in your care, and that you will be able to better provide for those needs with this new understanding. It means you will understand why they do the things that they do. You will know when to step in to help, and you will know when to let them fight their own battles. The idea, of course, is that good parents make themselves redundant, and our children learn to parent themselves.

IS RAISING KIDS MORE DIFFICULT THAN CLIMBING MOUNT EVEREST?
WHY DO YOU THINK I'M CLIMBING MOUNT EVEREST?
TANDBERG

Chapter 1

What's Your Parenting Style?

While it is quite the fashion these days to have a trial marriage, there's no such thing as a trial child.

If you're reading this, chances are you're the type of parent who has reflected on your style of parenting (by 'style' I mean the approach you take to the job of raising your children). There's far less chance that you might answer such a question with, 'Whaddya mean? I just do what my parents did, and I turned out all right.'

Broadly speaking, raising kids is a delicate balancing act between support and control; between discipline and affection. So depending on the particular balance, there are four main parenting styles:

- Autocratic ('Do what I say because I'm bigger and stronger than you.')
- Neglectful ('Do whatever you want because I don't care.')
- Laissez-faire ('Do whatever you want because I'm too scared or too lazy to set limits.')
- Authoritative ('Here are the guidelines. I'm here to help you follow them.')

AUTOCRATIC

In this style of parenting, control is high and affection is low. The parental rule is law and failure to follow the rules usually results in punishment. Although these parents might insist that they love their children, they rarely show affection, and are very obedience- and status-oriented. My dad grew up in a family that operated on the principle that children should be seen and not heard. There was minimal expression of love and quite a lot of whacking, which was great for short-term control and revenge fantasies. I'm forever grateful that my mum was able to bring a supportive balance to our family when I was growing up – otherwise I might not be the well-balanced, charming, charismatic chap that I am today.

NEGLECTFUL

Neglectful parenting is also referred to as uninvolved, detached, dismissive or hands-off parenting. This kind of parenting is low in control *and* affection. The parents may (or may not) provide for their children's basic needs, but don't seem to care at all about their children's lives. They offer little or no supervision, virtually no discipline, no communication and little warmth, love or affection. They tend to be absent from school events and parent–teacher nights and are often too overwhelmed by their own problems to deal with their children. Children parented this way have an increased risk of substance abuse and of developing other serious problems later in life and, ultimately, of replicating this parenting style.

LAISSEZ-FAIRE

Laissez-faire is a French term meaning 'let them do as they please'. Applied to parenting, the term refers to a permissive style in which parents avoid providing guidance and discipline – the tail truly wags the dog. Now this kind of parenting is usually high in affection and low in control. These parents are nurturing and understanding, but make few demands on their children in terms of setting boundaries or enforcing them. They want to be friends with their children, rather than authorities. Unfortunately, research by Diana Baumrind and her colleagues has shown that the children of permissive parents tend to be impulsive, disobedient, rebellious, demanding and dependent on adults. As adolescents, many have poor self-control, poor school performance and a high rate of drug use.

AUTHORITATIVE

Authoritative parents establish clear rules and guidelines, but when children fail to meet expectations, these parents are supportive rather than punitive – allowing their children to experience the consequences of their own actions while being nurturing, forgiving and accepting. These parents are willing to listen to what their children have to say. They know their role is to support their child, not save them, so they are assertive, flexible and democratic. The research by Baumrind found that the best-adjusted and most academically competent children had authoritative parents who were neither too lenient nor too strict; these parents set reasonable limits for their children, were warm and responsive, and did not use harsh methods of punishment.

TAKE THE QUIZ

Before we go any further, I want you to take a short quiz. It's only ten questions, but it will get you thinking about your overall approach to parenting, as well as alert you to any uncertainties you might have. If you're not sure of the answers to some of them now, don't worry – you will be able to answer them easily once you've read the book.

1. On which *one* of the following issues is it most important to stand your ground with your 14-year-old?
   a) bedtime
   b) curfews
   c) homework
   d) purple hair

2. Which of the following is the most appropriate response when your 12-year-old (during an argument) says that they wish their sibling were dead?
   a) Nothing. Ignore the behaviour and it will eventually go away.
   b) 'Don't say that! Your brother/sister has some wonderful gifts.'
   c) 'You sound angry. Tell me about it.'
   d) 'I know what you mean! Sometimes I want to kill him/her myself!'

3. You discover that your Year 8 son was drinking without your permission with a group of other boys. What should you do?
   a) Tell him, 'You'd better stop or you'll end up like your father/grandad/Auntie Shirl.'
   b) Sit him down and give him enough to drink so that he vomits and understands the consequences.
   c) Ground him for a month, but explain why.
   d) Organise a meeting with those involved.

4. Which of the following statements about bullying is true?
   a) Boys tend to bully with physical behaviours while girls bully with words.
   b) Girls tend to bully with physical behaviours while boys bully with words.
   c) Boys and girls bully in exactly the same way.
   d) Both boys and girls use a combination of physical and verbal bullying.

5. What should you do if sibling rivalry gets physical between your 8-year-old and 9-year-old sons?
   a) Let them fight it out.
   b) Break it up without taking sides.
   c) Strongly state a 'no violence' rule.
   d) Buy them both a first-aid kit.

6. You and your partner are invited to stay in the country overnight. What arrangements do you make for your children, who are in years 8 and 9?
   a) Take them with you, as it's wrong to leave them behind.
   b) Leave them home alone to show you trust them.
   c) Arrange supervision by a trusted adult.
   d) Buy them a pit bull.

7. Your Year 10 daughter is going to a party with her Year 11 boyfriend. They are taking public transport to get there. You want her home at a reasonable hour. What do you do?
   a) Set a non-negotiable time.
   b) Ask her what she thinks is fair.
   c) Discuss a reasonable consequence if she's late.
   d) Ask her boyfriend to sign a contract and leave a deposit.

8. You are chatting with a friend and your 5-year-old starts whacking you to get attention. Which of the following is the most appropriate initial response?
   a) Say, 'I'm talking. Please wait until I'm finished.'
   b) Shout at him to stop.
   c) Ignore him.
   d) Hit him back.

9. What is the most appropriate response when your 16-year-old daughter comes home with a tongue stud?
   a) Invite her to take it out, or find somewhere else to live.
   b) Take her to your doctor to have it removed.
   c) Get one yourself.
   d) Tell her that she must be really pleased with it, but you'd like to discuss your concerns, including the health risks.

10. What should you do if you hear that your 8-year-old daughter is being bullied at school?
    a) Move her to another school.
    b) Speak to the principal.
    c) Tell her that it's not her fault, she's not alone, she doesn't deserve it and that together you can do something about it.
    d) Talk to the bully's parents.

MY DAD'S ALWAYS THERE WHEN I NEED HIM
GRAMMAR
TANDBERG
MY DAD'S ALWAYS THERE

Chapter 2

The Unfortunate Rise of Crap Parenting

If you want to land your kids in therapy, then by all means give them everything under the sun.

In this chapter I want to examine in more detail some of the dysfunctional, over-involved parenting styles that have emerged over the past two decades. While it is admirable that parents do want to be involved (I'm thinking of the harsh, neglectful practices of the 'children should be seen and not heard' era), the pendulum has swung too far in the other direction. Some readers may be offended by the term 'crap', arguing that parenting is hard enough without psychologists slagging them off for being incompetent. But the truth is that they *are* crappy, and sometimes it requires a zap to the circuitry to stop the merry-go-round. At some point we have to say, 'I am the grown-up and it's up to *me* to change this!' Blaming our own parents for the mistakes we make is a national pastime, and it simply won't help our children become the best people they can be.

So what are some of the hallmarks of well-meaning but over-involved parenting?

THE HELICOPTER

This is an idiomatic term coined by child and adult psychiatrist Foster Cline for a parent who 'hovers', that is, one who pays particularly close attention to a child's or children's experiences and problems, particularly during the school years, higher education and even the working world. These parents will swoop down *a la* Superman and intervene if they see their offspring in any distress or facing any sort of challenge.

These parents are the ultimate micro-managers of their children's lives. No one really knows what started this craziness, although one academic, University of Georgia Professor Richard Mullendore, says the rise of helicopter parenting is attributable to the increased use of mobile phones – calling them 'the world's longest umbilical cord'.

Is this just a passing fad? Sadly, no. A 2012 study from the Queensland University of Technology suggests that this so-called form of parenting is actually spreading like a cancerous growth, with more than 90 per cent of school psychologists and counsellors regularly encountering over-involved parents. Examples include one mother who made her 16-year-old take a special plate of food to parties because he was a picky eater, and another who dressed her 10-year-old (the child could not dress himself when he went to school camp). Others requested their children be placed in the same class as a friend, or in a sports house that matched their favourite colour. Still others contest the disciplinary action taken by the school in response to their poorly behaved child.

Just to recap, a helicopter parent:

- is knee-deep in every issue of their child's school and home life
- does not allow their child to make mistakes (and therefore learn from them) so will finish their child's homework for them

- overly protects their child from experiencing pain or disappointment, so will confront another parent if their child is not invited to a party or will buy a present for their child on a sibling's birthday
- constantly checks on their child to see what they are doing at home, or when out with friends
- cleans and tidies up after their child
- accompanies their child on school trips or puts a GPS tracker on their phone.

These parents are easily recognised, as they will visit the school three or four times a week, ostensibly to bail their child out, or to deliver forgotten clothing, lunch or assignments. But their involvement is not always so benign – some of these parents are so aggressive in their desire to protect their child at schools that Dr Timothy Hawkes, headmaster of The King's School in North Parramatta, refers to them as 'helicopter gunship parents'. Bellicose and belligerent, this new breed of over-involved parent forced one Japanese primary school to stage a version of Snow White with no dwarfs, no wicked stepmother and twenty-five Snow Whites.

So what impact does this type of parenting have? In an online survey, which was conducted by the University of Mary Washington in the US and involved 297 American graduate students aged 18–23, participants were asked to describe their mothers' parenting behaviours and to rate their own perceptions of their autonomy, competence and how well they get along with other people. The researchers chose to measure perceptions of mothers' behaviours because most of the research shows that it is nearly always the mother who remains overly involved in her offspring's life. Participants were also asked to rate their overall satisfaction with life, their level of anxiety, and whether or not they suffered depressive symptoms. They found that young people with helicopter parents are more likely to be depressed or anxious, have problems getting along with others, and to feel less competent and less able to manage life and its stressors. Research demonstrates that children who are protected from grappling with difficult tasks are denied what psychologists call 'mastery experiences', which help people to become optimistic, decisive and independent.

This style of 'uber-parenting' is helping to produce a generation of anxious children who lack resilience, have poor life skills and are high on sense of entitlement and low on sense of responsibility.

However, it is important to point out that helicopter parents are not malevolent beings, rather a product of good intentions gone awry – the play of culture on natural parental fears. Helicopter parenting is the confusion of over-involvement with stability. Our job as parents is to protect, but we also need to teach our children how to protect themselves.

These parents have to ask themselves how a young person can learn to become an independent adult if their parents continue to make all the choices for them. How do they learn about making their own way in the world if mum or dad is remote controlling them? Most importantly how do they learn to take responsibility if they are never really given any?

THE HOT-HOUSER

Hot-housing is a contentious form of parenting focused on the intense enrichment of a child's mind. Advocates have an almost pathological desire for their offspring to flourish intellectually, so they do everything in their power to push them into learning much earlier than is suitable for children of their cognitive age.

This can occur in any stage of development. For example, preschool gymnastics and baby swimming classes attempt to accelerate gross motor skill development ('gross' refers to movements involving larger muscles, like those in the arms, legs, feet or the entire body, used for walking, jumping and so on). It has long been known that the development of gross motor skills encourages both cognitive and fine motor skill development (fine motor skills involve smaller muscles, like those in the hands, wrists and fingers, used for holding a crayon or toy). 'Baby media' educational programs for computers and tablets, specialised books and toys, flashcards and DVDs purport to accelerate cognitive development and language learning.

It all started in 1997 when the first Baby Einstein video appeared and many mimics followed. Overnight the baby media industry became a huge commercial success. Exaggerated assertions have been made for the educational value of these products, but children are usually introduced to this 'genius-making merchandise' at times of speedy development (almost all 2-year-olds have a rapid expansion in vocabulary) and so parents often mistakenly attribute these language growth spurts to the products. They then turn round and provide glittering endorsements on the web regarding their usefulness.

Some hot-house parents may insist that their strategies are important because they believe their child is gifted. However, there is a critical difference between gifted children and hot-housed children. While both learn material more quickly and earlier than most children their age, the gifted or talented child's learning has come from within – it comes from the child, not the parent.

One example of hot-housing is when parents try to teach toddlers the 3Rs. They believe that young children can learn anything if it is properly taught, so they provide every type of enrichment for their child, beginning in the womb! These parents play classical music for their unborn child, and may even use flashcards to prepare their infant for reading and maths. You can easily spot a hot-house parent because shortly after conception, they have placed their child on waiting lists for the 'best' kindergartens, primary schools and secondary colleges; classical music is played in the nursery; and by age three or four, their child is learning piano, violin or Japanese. For the hot-house parent, proof of good parenting means that by the age of four, their child has a black belt in karate, is tri-lingual and is a dab hand in the kitchen.

In summary, a hot-house parent:

- is very caring and attentive to the child
- schedules in more than four after-school activities a week for their child

- buys thousands of dollars' worth of educational toys, which the child never has time to play with
- completes the child's homework
- lobbies for the child to be assigned to certain classes.

At first glance hot-housing might seem attractive. After all, if the learning environment for the infant is benign and supportive, then what's the problem? Don't all kids enjoy learning when they are being treated kindly? What's wrong with the hot-housing claim that children have the potential for mastering academic material?

But there is a reason to be concerned. These terribly well-meaning parents are ignoring the developmental constraints in the child that preclude the mastery of academic material. The human brain is not designed for abstract thinking at age three! Trying to create the next Beethoven by piping music into their crib simply doesn't work, nor does teaching your son how to play chess at 12 months – it is really a waste of time and he may swallow one of the chess pieces.

In 2010, a study published in the lead journal of the American Psychological Association evaluated the validity of a best-selling baby DVD specially designed to hasten vocabulary learning in seventy-two infants aged 12–18 months. There were four experimental settings. In one, parents simply presented the video to their infants; in the second, parents interacted with their babies throughout the viewing; in the third, parents imparted the same words on the video verbally to their infants (without using the video); and the fourth was the control group, which provided a baseline for natural vocabulary development over a four-week period.

Results showed that the parent-only teaching group was superior to the other three groups in terms of the number of target words learnt over the four weeks. Neither video group differed from the control group.

The simple fact is that babies do not learn well from symbolic media such as DVDs or pictures because they are not yet able to make the connection between the image and reality. It is a shame the suppliers of baby media ignore the evidence base. Or, maybe, as they assemble each year at trade shows and calculate their revenues, they just don't care.

But there are more reasons to be concerned. The tight activity schedules of hot-housed children mean they not only have less quality time with their family, but also limited opportunities for play. This is a real problem since it's long been known that play is critical for children's development. Through play, our children get to initiate their own activities, make up rules, reflect on their feelings, communicate with each other and generally practise the full range of skills they need to have successful adult relationships, all in a low-risk environment. If you've ever watched a young child playing with a toy, you'll notice that she will try many different ways to interact with it. And if she makes a mistake, she won't feel ashamed, but will simply try another way. In true play, there are no mistakes, just different ways of having a go.

In fact, play is so important for child development that the United Nations has included it in Article 31 of the UN Convention on the Rights of the Child: 'Children have the right to relax and play, and to join in a wide range of cultural, artistic and other recreational activities.'

Yet anxious, well-intentioned parents are still vulnerable to the aggressive marketing of the hot-house industry, which claims that 'getting a head start' is more important than play if children are to get the best opportunities in life. Such parents then carefully organise every moment of their children's lives with activities they believe will ensure success. They also inflict their zealousness on educational institutions to an astonishing degree. In one instance, reported in *Time* magazine, parents demanded that nursery schools offer classes in Mandarin, presumably because they believed it's never too soon to prepare for the competition of a global economy. You might chuckle at this, but the impact of such practices is no laughing matter. Ultimately, the hot-housed child misses out on childhood.

THE BEST FRIEND

Best-friend parenting is a form of indulgent parenting that was first described by psychologist Diana Baumrind during the 1960s, and is characterised by a lack of rules and little or no discipline. These parents make relatively few demands upon their kids and have low expectations for their self-control and maturity. For example, they habitually allow their children to stay up late, which results in the kids being exhausted, irritable and unable to cope with school. And when their children inevitably sleep in and are running late, the parents often allow them to skip breakfast, which deprives them of the brain food they need to concentrate on their schoolwork. These poor kids are not only harder to live with, but their self-esteem suffers because they can't manage normal developmental tasks as well as their peers.

While permissive parents are very loving and nurturing, any rules that do exist are rarely or inconsistently enforced and this enforcement usually involves bribery. Without boundaries, the children have no idea how to set limits on their own behaviour, and may be unruly and less academically motivated at school.

The effects of this style of parenting are well documented. In the short term, children raised by permissive parents lack self-discipline, often have poor social skills, can be self-involved and demanding and may be perennially insecure due to the lack of boundaries and guidance. The long-term impact of this type of parenting is a potpourri of delinquency including underage alcohol use, illicit drug use, unsafe sexual practices and other forms of misbehaviour. Baumrind found that teens with permissive parents are three times more likely to engage in heavy drinking. A US study of binge drinking among five thousand 12–19-year-olds revealed that kids from authoritative households were half as likely as teens from authoritarian households to binge drink. Teens from households with permissive parents who were low in discipline and accountability but high on warmth were more than three times as likely to drink as teens from authoritative households.

The key characteristics of best-friend parents are that they:

- are usually very nurturing and loving towards their kids
- rarely use the word 'no'
- have few rules or standards of behaviour
- allow children to stay up late, eat whenever they want, have TVs and electronic gadgets in their bedroom, watch whatever they want
- inconsistently enforce any rules, usually using bribery with toys, gifts or food to do so
- confide in their child and often seem more like the child's equal than his parent.

Of course, the best-friend parent has good intentions, but denying children boundaries does them an enormous disservice. Aside from the negative effects of poor sleep and diet, setting no limits on media exposure means kids are more likely to stumble upon inappropriate screen content, such as real-life violence, drug use and porn, before they are mentally and emotionally ready for it. Interestingly, research shows that the cartoon violence of video games has no long-term emotional or social consequences. Early exposure to pornography, however, can mean children grow up with distorted and unrealistic expectations about relationships and sex. It is also associated with greater risk-taking behaviour. A 2012 study from the University of New South Wales, for example, found that young people who reported having visited sexually explicit websites were more likely to have higher numbers of sexual partners, engage in a wider diversity of sexual practices, and use alcohol or drugs in association with sexual encounters. A US study of 1500 kids aged 10–15 showed that exposure to porn over time predicted an almost six-fold increase in the odds of self-reported sexually aggressive behaviour.

It is often said that children will keep pushing until they find the limits. However, they're not doing this to annoy the adults in their lives, they're doing this for survival reasons – they *need* someone to be in charge. It's overwhelming for a child to feel responsible for their own safety and wellbeing in what can be a frightening world.

Worse, the buddy parent often confides in the child, sharing details of their financial situation, relationship worries (including sexual problems!) and other issues that are way beyond the child's cognitive and emotional competencies. It is *never* appropriate to share details of your adult responsibilities with your child – it creates an enormous burden for them and can contribute to the development of anxiety, depression and other disorders.

All children need to feel a strong connection with their parents, to feel loved, but they also need a regular dose of vitamin 'N' – in other words they need to hear 'no'. If we try to be their 'mate', we will always put our need for them to like us before their need to learn to like themselves. So be a mentor, and help them to learn what is safe and not safe, what is appropriate and inappropriate.

THE TROPHY

Trophy parenting is where parents push their children to achieve the sporting, artistic or academic success that they wished for themselves, creating 'trophy' children they can show off to the world. Such parents see their children as extensions of themselves, and need them to behave in ways that meet their emotional needs. They anticipate that their kids will help them to realise their unfulfilled hopes, dreams, wishes and fantasies. For these narcissistic parents, the child is coached to be a trophy, a living, walking, talking emblem of the parent's success and exceptionality, to be venerated and coveted in the way that the parents would wish for themselves. The child, in this way, serves as a wellspring of narcissistic energy for the parent.

The trophy parent is incapable of perceiving any difference between their own thoughts and feelings and those of their children, and sincerely believes that their attitudes and values are shared. They are unaware that the child's needs are not in concert with their own.

The spawn of this variety of crap parenting learns from the very beginning what is required to capture attention and stay in the good books. They rapidly learn to suppress their own wishes, their genuine selves, and to become the glossy, gorgeous trophy children that will make their parents glow with pride. Their true identity, their real self, disappears entirely.

So what sort of kids does this variety of crap parenting produce? Well, their entire lives become a quest to be parent-pleasers. They struggle to develop self-confidence and are terrified of rejection, requiring continuous reassurance that they *are* pleasing. As adults, they often end up with partners who want them to keep on setting aside their needs, which is very unhealthy for relationships as it leads to resentment and disrespect.

The key characteristics of the trophy parent are that they:

- feel every accomplishment, test score and sporting achievement of their child as a reflection on their own success (i.e. a source of bragging rights or deep shame)
- are overly involved in their child's sport, and feel either personally let down by a loss or elated after a win
- constantly compare their children to others
- feel good when their kids are attractive or smarter than others, and bad when they fail or are in trouble
- have their refrigerators, mantelpieces or walls covered with their child's awards.

THE BUBBLE-WRAPPER

Despite falling crime rates and reductions in preventable disease and injury, a growing number of parents are obsessed with the safety of their children. Their goal seems to be to ensure that their offspring take fewer risks than any other generation in the history of humankind. They spend a disproportionate amount of time and energy reducing potential hazards in their kids' lives.

Driven by the media's never-ending torrent of danger, misery and destruction (fear sells), these parents see impending peril at every turn. They respond by wrapping their children in the modern equivalent of cotton wool (bubble wrap), buying them baby kneepads and hypoallergenic socks and stuffing them with macrobiotic cupcakes in order to save them from the myriad dangers in this complex world. Yet, far from protecting children and helping them to adjust to the world, this trend of hyper-vigilant parenting is actually exposing them to potential harm.

Raising children to be resilient adults means giving them opportunities to manage risk, to endure accidents, and to overcome setbacks. This cannot occur if they are raised in a bubble. How do kids learn to ride a bike? *By falling off!* How do kids learn to deal with pain? By being hurt. How do kids learn to assess risk? By being exposed to danger. How do kids develop immunity? By being exposed to germs.

At some level this must make sense to parents, yet many are hamstrung by their own fear of pain, risk and danger and simply cannot tolerate the idea of their children experiencing them.

The key characteristics of the bubble-wrapper are:

- seeing potential danger at every turn
- infantilising older kids ('10 is the new two').

None of this is conscious, of course. These parents have never wondered why they have such a powerful urge to protect their children. To such a question they might respond, 'It's just natural isn't it?' As a psychologist, part of my job is helping parents understand how their unconscious drives and motivations play out in their relationships with their children.

Like helicopter parents, bubble-wrappers are over-invested in their offspring's lives, deeming it their primary function to level the track, removing all of the hurdles so that their child will never have to withstand any adversities, hardships and other difficulties along their 'path' in life. As we saw above, such an obsession with our children's safety fails to equip them for life in the real world.

On the other hand, when you tear the rotor blades off the helicopter and pop the bubble wrap, amazing things can happen. Take for example what happened at Swanson Primary School in Auckland. Previously, the students were not allowed to engage in playground activities like climbing trees or riding bikes. The principal of the school, Bruce McLachlan, ditched the plethora of playtime rules as part of a successful university experiment. Swanson school signed up to a study by the Auckland University of Technology and Otago University just over two years ago, with the aim of encouraging active play. However, the school took the experiment a step further by abandoning the rules completely, much to the horror of some teachers at the time, McLachlan reported. When the university study concluded at the end of 2013 the school and researchers were amazed by the results. Mudslides, skateboarding, bullrush and tree climbing kept the children so occupied the school no longer needed a time-out area or as many teachers on patrol. Most importantly the school saw a drop in bullying, serious injuries and vandalism, while concentration levels in class increased. Instead of a playground, children used their imagination to play in a 'loose-parts pit', which contained objects such as wood, tyres and an old fire hose. The researchers found that kids were motivated, busy and engaged. This wasn't a playtime revolution, it was just a return to the days before we worshipped at the altar of occupational health and safety policies.

'BUT I JUST WANT THEM TO BE HAPPY!'

Clearly, none of the parents I describe are intrinsically wicked, they want the best for their children but they are simply misguided. They fail to appreciate that the faster we shove obstructions out of the way, the more our children rely on us to continue to do exactly that. They cease thinking for themselves. They don't see themselves as people with the capacity to act. Instead, they feel that life will act on them, or that we will act for them. Neither response to challenge is helpful. Neither response leads to healthy psychological development or resilience.

Young people will feel the most competent when they have to struggle to achieve something – when they need to be persistent, tenacious, and to dig deep as they face a challenge, cope with a set-back or make a mistake along the way. It makes them stronger, more independent and more capable. That is what makes for successful kids – not parents who get all the hard stuff out of the way for them.

Everyone wants their kids to be happy but random events happen and life is not always fair, so inevitably there will be times when things won't go as intended and children will be disappointed. Helping young people realise that they won't be happy all the time is critical. Moreover, they need opportunities to experience feelings of anger, sadness and disappointment so they learn to get over them. Appreciating that all feelings pass and that we can learn from the whole range of emotions is arguably one of the most important aspects of our development as human beings. (I discuss this in more detail in Part 2.)

While we don't want to torment our children, or place them in mortal danger, it is through failure that they learn to be resilient. Parents need to teach their children that anything worthwhile takes time and effort, that everyone fails and that what matters is what you do next. As parents we need to be patient, compassionate and supportive, but we also need to be firm, opinionated and informed.

Informed parents understand why their offspring behave the way they do at various stages, and are able to modify their strategies to best meet the needs of their children as they grow. Taking some time to understand why your kids behave the way they do is a priceless insurance policy, and that's what I want to discuss in the next two chapters.

TANDBERG
I USED TO BE SCARED OF THE DARK

Chapter 3

What Every Parent Needs to Know About Kids Aged 5–12

Trying to get your children to do something before their brain is ready is like asking a dog to recite Shakespeare.

After surviving the nappy years and toddlerhood (Jerry Seinfeld said that having a 2-year-old is like 'having a blender that you don't have the top for'), most parents are probably looking forward to a bit of a rest when their little ones head off to school. Indeed, I get the distinct impression that some parents believe their work is done, and that they now expect the school to take on the task of raising their children. The tendency for some parents to outsource their parenting responsibilities is routinely mentioned to me by educators across Australia, who say they are often asked to discipline children and to talk to them about sex, drugs and cyber safety issues. Once they are at school, kids need your support more than ever, especially as they negotiate the vicissitudes of adolescence. You are going to be better prepared to offer that support if you understand how kids develop – if you can maintain a developmental perspective.

Understanding what to expect of children at different ages will help you to be more tolerant and patient, and to not take their behaviour personally. For example, if you know that most children don't develop empathy until they're about seven or eight, you won't expect a 5-year-old to share his toys. If you know that 9- and 10-year-olds are obsessed with rules and fairness, but at the same time are experimenting with breaking the rules, you'll understand why they can become so upset in team games. And if you understand that the defiance, criticalness and peer focus of teens is developmentally driven and completely normal, you are more likely to handle this frustrating behaviour without damaging your relationship with them.

Although this book is about primary and secondary school-aged children it is important to remember the incredible groundwork that is laid in the first four years of a child's life. The infant brain has been described as the most powerful learning machine on the planet. Babies learn rapidly by observing and copying people, and research shows that they can remember a lot for a surprisingly long time. They can watch an adult do something a few times, for only twenty seconds, and remember how to do it four weeks later. Babies and toddlers are far from empty, passive vessels waiting to be filled – they spend every waking moment using their senses to discover, analyse, respond and file information about how the world works.

Every time your baby learns something new – to focus his eyes, to mimic a movement or a facial expression, to pick something up, form a word, or to sit up – new synaptic connections are being built in the brain. As a new parent I was astonished at the rapidity of this learning. I was amazed and delighted at my son's cleverness and I communicated my delight to him. He responded with smiles and a desire to both achieve and learn even more.

This forming of a powerful attachment between child and parent provides the building blocks for physical, social, language, cognitive and psychomotor development. It is the template for your child's future relationships with friends, partners and ultimately with their own offspring.

Yet it happens so naturally in most families that we don't even notice it and are spectacularly unaware of its importance to human development and by extension to the development of healthy communities. If we can create an environment for our kids where they grow up feeling safe, valued and listened to, they are more likely to become resilient, empathic and considerate young people who will be able to cope with whatever life throws at them. As Jackie Onassis said, 'If you bungle raising your children, I don't think that whatever else you do in life matters very much.'

It is this attachment that leads our children to watch us like hawks and to copy our behaviours, adopt our mannerisms and parrot our expressions. This is the 'modelling' that everyone talks about, and the reason we have to focus more on what we do than on what we say to our kids. This is especially true when it comes to managing conflict, showing affection and even things like our eating and drinking habits – more on that later.

THE CHILD'S BRAIN

When we are born, our brains are less than a third their adult size and contain around one hundred billion brain cells (neurons). Each neuron has a long fibre (axon) for sending information in the form of electrical signals, and a short fibre (dendrite) for receiving signals. The point at which neurons connect and exchange information is called the synapse. At birth, very few synapses have been formed, apart from those that govern our bodily functions such as heart rate, breathing, feeding and sleeping. As babies grow, and more and more sensory information is received in the brain, the dendrites branch out, like little trees, to connect with other neurons. This astonishing synaptic development peaks at about the age of three – by which time a child's brain has shot up to 80 per cent of adult size. Synaptic pathways that are used a lot are strengthened ('brain cells that fire together, wire together'), and those that aren't used begin to drop away ('use it or lose it'). This process of synaptic pruning is a normal part of development, and peaks in the teenage years.

The brain is, above all, a sensory organ that processes the sensations that pour into the body through the skin, the eyes, the nose, the tongue, the joints and the ears. Kids are designed to learn using *all* their senses, so plonking them in front of the TV for hours is akin to synaptic starvation. Here's an analogy that might help. Think of your child's brain as being a little tree. At first there are only a few branches, but if you give this tree plenty of sunlight, water and fertiliser it will thrive and grow lots more branches.

The left side of our brains handles language and reasoning, and the right side handles emotion, movement and the body's perception of space. The two sides are connected by a bundle of nerves called the corpus callosum, which is smaller in boys than girls. This means that boys will approach a problem by favouring one side of their brain, while girls use both sides. Boys' brains also develop more slowly than girls', and the right and left hemispheres are less 'connected'. Parents need to remember these differences and adjust expectations accordingly. Trying to get your children to do something before their brain is ready is like asking a dog to recite Shakespeare – it is just never going to happen. Furthermore, asking a male brain to behave like a female brain is like asking them to pick up mercury with a fork!

THE KEY DEVELOPMENTAL TASKS OF CHILDHOOD

Childhood is a developmental phase between infancy and adolescence with three main tasks:

- learning to feel secure
- learning to explore the world
- learning to be a social being.

As parents, it's our responsibility to provide the right environment for our kids to do the learning that they are designed to do. This means that they need to feel safe, valued and listened to. But they also need to be given opportunities to make mistakes.

Here is a brief summary of the major skills and competencies that children achieve in the primary school years:

- continuing to explore and acquire information about their world and how it works
- planning and undertaking tasks by themselves (initiative)
- learning that behaviours have consequences
- internalising rules (especially socially acceptable behaviour)
- developing a sense of responsibility
- expanding relationships (especially same-sex peer relationships)
- selecting adult role models of the same sex
- becoming increasingly independent
- enhancing their reasoning ability
- developing the capacity to cooperate

STAGES OF DEVELOPMENT

Various psychologists and human development researchers have proposed different theories to describe the stages of child development. Some focus on a particular aspect of development such as cognition (Jean Piaget), psychosocial development (Erik Erikson) or, controversially, psychosexual development (Sigmund Freud, who spent a little too much time talking to sexually frustrated Viennese adults). Others are based on how children learn (Albert Bandura) or on bonding (attachment) with a caregiver in early infancy (John Bowlby).

Interestingly, child development was all but ignored until the early 20th century. Up until that point, children were considered to be 'mini adults', and were treated as such (I'm thinking here of 8-year-olds shoved up chimneys and down coal mines, and 12-year-olds getting married). Little attention was paid to the rapid development of cognition, language and physical growth. When the field of child development finally began to emerge in the 1900s, it first tended to focus on abnormal behaviour (hello, Freud) before it moved on to typical child development and its influences.

Most developmental psychologists combine these approaches in what is called an eclectic approach, where they have taken the best parts of all the theories.

For the purposes of discussion, I have divided what many psychologists call the 'middle years' of childhood (from school to puberty) into early (aged 5–6), middle (aged 7–9) and late or pre-teen (10–12). While the descriptions of physical, emotional and cognitive development will be applicable to most children at a similar age, every child is different and your child's emotional and social development will depend on her temperament, cultural influences and how the adults around her behave. It is also affected by how secure she feels in her relationships with adults and the opportunities she has to socialise with other children.

The following information is just a guide. All children develop at different rates and in different ways. If you are worried about your child's development or if it differs a lot from other children of the same age, have a talk with a teacher or health professional. It will stop you worrying and, if there is a problem, getting in early will help.

Early childhood (5–6 years)

The first years at school are a whirlwind of change for children, where they get to test drive blossoming skills and abilities across a whole spectrum of physical, mental, social and emotional development. They are incredibly creative and enthusiastic problem-solvers, so one of the best things you can do is to give them opportunities to do just that. Other things you can do to help include:

- welcoming their questions and always try to answer them with honesty and developmentally appropriate detail. If you struggle with this, there are some great websites: for questions about sex and reproductive development try The Hormone Factory (thehormonefactory.com); and for drugs there's The Other Talk (theothertalk.org.au).

- providing plenty of opportunities for hands-on creative play (construction, painting, drawing etc.)
- setting limits (5- and 6-year-olds often overestimate their physical abilities).

Social and emotional development

- expands circle of trusted adults (often to include a teacher, coach or instructor)
- initiates more complex and sustained cooperative play (including pretend play and simple games with rules)
- shows an emerging sense of self based on new skills and competencies – 'I can do that!'
- begins to predict and interpret other people's emotions (though empathy does not usually kick in until age eight)
- relies more on language to express feelings
- attempts to resolve the occasional conflict without adult help (but more often needs adult assistance)
- may self-soothe when feeling insecure instead of rushing to parents for comfort (e.g. plays with a toy or uses imagination), though mostly still needs a cuddle

Physical development

- has improved stamina, co-ordination and balance in walking, running, jumping, swimming and dancing (most girls can skip at this age, though some boys lag behind in skipping until as late as eight years)
- has sufficient hand–eye co-ordination for throwing, bouncing, catching and striking a ball
- displays improved fine motor skills (can hit nails with a hammer, use scissors and screwdrivers, dress and undress dolls, use drawing and painting tools efficiently)

- able to get dressed quickly (including zipping, buttoning and tying shoelaces with assistance)
- able to use a computer keyboard and mouse
- shows a clear preference for being right-handed or left-handed

Middle childhood (7–9 years)

Children in the middle years tend to be cooperative and compliant, especially compared to younger or older siblings, and are often the last to get attention in busy families. The most helpful thing you can do for your children at this age is to take an interest in what they are doing, and to take the time to listen to what they have to say. (See chapter 8 for more on the importance of communication.) Other ways you can help your child include:

- reading with them
- having a special time every week where you do something small together
- balancing screen time with other play including physical activity
- encouraging effort as well as achievement
- allowing plenty of down time (not overloading them with after-school activities).

Social and emotional development

- increasingly able to relate to others
- wants to fit in and be accepted by peers
- prefers play with children of the same sex (though not always)
- enjoys sleepovers
- is obsessed with 'the rules'
- enjoys team games, but is not always able to lose gracefully
- understands another person's point of view and shows concern for what others are feeling
- takes care of personal belongings (usually not until nine years)
- 'tests' morality by lying or stealing

Cognitive and language development

- remembers remarkable detail about subjects of personal interest
- speaks clearly and easily in the language you use at home
- is able to describe complicated events
- shows preferences for certain subjects at school
- may have areas of special interest outside of school
- is able to read and write
- understands the concept of money (around six years)
- can tell the time (by around seven or eight)
- knows left from right
- knows the different tenses (past, present and future) and is able to use them appropriately in sentences
- enjoys collecting (e.g. stamps, swap cards, rocks, toys etc.)
- begins to understand the difference between reality and fantasy (e.g. Santa isn't real)
- is able to plan ahead (e.g. getting something ready for the next day)
- is able to overcome emotions to concentrate on a task
- is confident using the telephone (around age eight)
- enjoys telling jokes and riddles

Physical development

- has high energy levels
- values physical skills such as hitting a ball a long way, climbing a tree, riding a bike fast or doing a handstand
- is able to ride a two-wheeler bike without training wheels
- is able to climb and swim
- throws and catches a ball with increasing skill
- writes and draws with greater skill and purpose
- enjoys more organised physical games with more complex rules

Pre-teens or tweens (10–12)

For many children, this pre-teen stage is the beginning of puberty, which signals the transition from childhood to adolescence. As a guide, puberty usually begins at around 10–11 years for girls and around 11–13 years for boys, though it's normal for the start of puberty to range from 8–13 years in girls and 9–14 years in boys. Puberty can be completed in about 18 months, or it can take up to five years. Every child is different, and genetics, nutrition and social factors all play a role in the onset and duration of puberty. For more on the implications for parents, see the following chapter.

Physical development for girls

- breast buds are the first visible sign of puberty (it's normal for the left and right breasts to grow at different speeds and for the breasts to be a bit tender)
- growth spurt (average height increase is 5–20 centimetres; girls usually stop growing at around 16–17 years)
- change in body shape (e.g. wider hips)
- growth of pubic and underarm hair
- menstruation begins (can be irregular at first, and accompanied by headaches and abdominal cramps)

Physical development for boys

- growth of testes (testicles) and penis (it's normal for one testis to grow faster than the other)
- growth of pubic hair, underarm hair, facial and body hair; gradually thickening and darkening
- growth spurt: average height increase is 10–30 centimetres; boys usually stop growing at around 18–20 years; some body parts may grow faster than others leaving some boys looking out of proportion
- has erections (sometimes for no reason at all) and ejaculation (releasing sperm), often during sleep ('wet dream')

- larynx ('Adam's apple' or 'voice box') develops and voice 'breaks' (gradually deepens)

Social and emotional development

- peer relationships can become unsettled for girls, and for boys these relationships can become increasingly competitive
- may experience bouts of unexplained moodiness and irritability (emotional ups and downs can lead to increased conflict within peer group and family)
- prefers to spend time with peers rather than family
- makes choices about appearance and interests based on the approval of friends (parental influence remains important on long-term decisions, such as career choices, values and morals)
- is self-conscious, especially about physical appearance and bodily changes
- is beginning to explore the idea of gender or sexual identity, which may include a 'romance' or special relationship (usually not intimate or sexual)

Cognitive and language development

- begins to think more abstractly
- questions different points of view
- questions parental decisions (can be seen as argumentative, but it shows your child is maturing)
- seeks more independence in decision-making, but is still learning about consequences of actions and needs parents to guide and set limits
- develops a stronger set of values and morals

I'VE COME TO PICK UP MY CHILD FROM THE PARTY
TANDBERG

Chapter 4

What Every Parent Needs to Know About Teenagers

Adolescents are all accelerator and no brake.

Granville Stanley Hall (1844–1924), founder of the American Psychological Association, was the first psychologist to describe adolescence as a discrete developmental phase. It is now accepted that it covers the developmental period between childhood and adulthood – beginning with the changes associated with puberty and culminating in the acquisition of adult roles and responsibilities. Adolescence is a dynamic period of development characterised by rapid change in the following areas:

- physical – onset of puberty (physical growth, development of secondary sexual characteristics and reproductive capability)
- psychological – development of autonomy, independent identity and value system
- cognitive – moving from concrete to abstract thought
- emotional – moodiness; shifting from self-centredness to empathy in relationships

- social – peer group influences, formation of intimate relationships, decisions about future vocation

Adolescence is a biologically universal phenomenon, but the expectations, roles and duration of this phase can vary greatly between different cultures. Cultural norms and life experiences (such as being a refugee) can affect the timing of developmental milestones (e.g. puberty) and expectations of what is considered 'normal' in terms of the adolescent's response to these changes.

The transition from childhood to adolescence is not a continuous, uniform process. While adolescence can be a stressful period, the majority of adolescents cope well with this developmental process and do not have any lasting problems. The key is having an adult mentor, someone they feel they can talk to, and from whom they continue to learn crucial social and emotional competencies, such as anger management, problem-solving, decision-making, and the all-important capacity to name and recognise not only their own thoughts and feelings but those of other people too. So, hug them, enjoy them, play with them and develop family traditions and rituals that will support them all the way into adulthood.

THE EXPERIENCE OF PUBERTY

As we saw in the previous chapter, puberty involves the most rapid and dramatic physical changes that occur to the human body during the entire life span outside the womb. While the average duration is about three years, there is great variability in the time of onset, velocity of change and the age of completion. In general, however, children are reaching puberty much earlier than in the past. The Avon Longitudinal Study of 14,000 children in the UK found 1 in 6 girls began puberty by eight years of age, compared to 1 in 100 a generation ago, and that 1 in 14 8-year-old boys had pubic hair compared to 1 in 150 a generation ago.

One of the consequences of this early physical maturation is that children can feel confused and overwhelmed by how different they are to their peers, making them more sensitive to stress. Others can look a lot older than they are, and may find themselves in situations that they are not ready to handle. As puberty occurs earlier, it's no longer in synchronisation with brain development; so adolescent psychologists are often confronted with a young woman, fully physically developed, complete with hipster jeans, flaunting her rebellion with a pierced navel but with the cognitive capacity of a 13-year-old. A souped-up car with all the extras – but the driver has no licence. These young people haven't spent long enough just hanging out with their buddies – learning how to manage conflict, make moral choices and solve problems – before they suddenly find themselves with a boyfriend or girlfriend.

Combine this with time-poor parents, lack of ritual and tradition, spiritual anorexia, mixed media messages (be sexy, but be good), and higher expectations in terms of material possessions, academic performance and career choices, and it's no wonder that adolescence is a time of such vulnerability.

THE ADOLESCENT BRAIN

Fifteen years ago it was widely assumed that the vast majority of brain development took place in the first few years of life and that it was pretty much done and dusted by the age of 12. Recent research using MRI technology has shown that the brain continues to develop until at least the mid-twenties.

One of the parts of the brain that changes most dramatically is the prefrontal cortex (PFC), which is proportionally much bigger in humans than in any other species. The PFC is involved in a whole range of high-level cognitive functions, including the following:

- decision-making
- planning
- inhibiting inappropriate behaviour
- considering other people's mental states and emotions

As we saw in the previous chapter, grey matter volume increases during childhood due to the sheer number of new connections being made between neurons (each one growing more branchlike dendrites to create pathways for new signals). This development peaks in early adolescence (when girls are about 11 and boys 12½), at which point a serious round of 'synaptic pruning' begins, where neural pathways that are being used are strengthened and those that are not used are pruned away. It's known as neural Darwinism (use it or lose it).

At the same time, the teenage brain develops more myelin (a kind of insulation for neurons that speeds neural processing), but unfortunately, this myelination occurs *last* in the PFC, which, as we have seen, is the area that governs planning, impulse control and reasoning.

The limbic system is the area of the brain that regulates emotion and memory. It influences emotions, our physical responses to those emotions, motivation, mood, and sensations of pain and pleasure. It gives you that buzz when you do fun things – including taking risks. Brain research shows that the limbic system in adolescents is hypersensitive to the rewarding buzz they get from risk-taking. At the very same time, the PFC – the part of our brains that stops us from taking risks – is still under construction, which means that adolescents are all accelerator and no brake.

So while the media and many parents will demonise or parody teenagers as self-obsessed, moody risk-takers, this is largely unfair if we take a developmental perspective and remember that much of their behaviour is a reflection of their cognitive function. This doesn't mean we sit back and accept disrespectful or dangerous behaviour, but that we need to help our teens learn to manage their impulses and make safe choices.

A man is driving home from a long day at work. He is 40-something, runs a flourishing business and has spent his entire day in a very successful board meeting. As he eases his late-model Mercedes through the traffic, he's feeling quietly self-satisfied – a feeling no doubt enhanced by the gin he enjoyed in the boardroom afterwards.

As he walks through the front door of his home he hears the sound of the TV coming from the living room. He pokes his head around the corner and sees his teenage son stretched out on the couch, shoes still on, watching *The Simpsons*. The man is at what some adolescent psychologists refer to as 'the moment of truth'.

What will he do next? He could walk over, tousle his son's hair and fondly say, 'G'day, son. How was your day? What's Homer up to?' But he doesn't. Instead, he strides into the room, glares at his son and says, with a voice fuelled by a strange mixture of gin and a heritage-listed parenting script, 'William! Why aren't you doing your homework?'

William has had a reasonably good day and is in an unusually genial mood. Only mildly irritated at the lack of a warm greeting and the provocative question, he chooses to ignore his father and says nothing. He is hoping his silence will be taken as a non-verbal cue that he does not wish to engage in conversation.

Dad, sadly, doesn't get the hint. He walks a little closer to the fruit of his loins and asks in a louder voice: 'Are you deaf?'

William, more irritated now, sighs and emits a Neanderthal grunt – a further opportunity for his father to back off and take the conversation in a different direction. But now Dad is in the mood for a confrontation, and he walks over to the TV and turns it off. William explodes, gets off the sofa, tells his father to go forth and multiply and in time-honoured tradition storms out of the house slamming the door (for added effect) and yelling to his mother that he's going to his mate's place to watch the rest of the program.

So what went wrong? This man – like tens of thousands of his counterparts across Australia – lacks what is known in psychological circles as a 'developmental perspective'. Back in the good old days, fathers needed only to stare at their errant offspring and most would be rendered mute and motionless. Today's parents, in contrast, can look until their face falls off. It is an obsolete parenting technique. So modern parents must discard the old parenting script and learn a new one. The new script recognises that during adolescence the mind and body undergo tectonic changes. When Dad speaks to William, Dad should remember that William's brain is a work in progress – it will only be fully formed at the age of 23 (or even later). Dad needs to take into account that he is dealing with a unique species – the adolescent – not a miniature version of himself.

THE KEY DEVELOPMENTAL TASKS OF ADOLESCENCE

Adolescence is a developmental period in which the young person must negotiate fundamental psychosocial tasks on their path towards maturity and independence. However, the nature of these tasks, and the importance placed upon their achievement, can vary greatly between western and non-western cultures.

From a western cultural perspective, the major developmental tasks of adolescence are seen as:

- achieving independence from parents and other adults
- developing a realistic, stable, positive identity
- forming a gender identity
- negotiating peer and intimate relationships
- developing a realistic body image
- formulating a moral/value system
- acquiring skills for future economic independence.

STAGES OF ADOLESCENCE

There are three main stages of adolescent development – early, middle and late adolescence. However, age alone does not define maturity and for some adolescents their physical, cognitive and psychological changes may be 'out of sync'. For example, an early developing, mature-looking girl may be physically developed but psychologically immature and emotionally vulnerable. This presents the potential risk of early initiation of risk-taking behaviour such as the abuse of alcohol and other drug use before she has developed the cognitive and psychological capacity to fully understand the potential consequences.

The main developmental concerns, cognitive changes and psychosocial issues for each stage are summarised below, along with some tips for parents on how to help their children.

Early adolescence (10–13 years)

At this age, the biggest question is 'Am I normal?' This is when you'll notice your child beginning to spend a lot more time in front of the mirror, and comparing him or herself to others. Adolescents are very sensitive to teasing about appearance, so *never* tease or criticise them about their body shape or weight. All early adolescents are vulnerable to eating disorders, and sometimes all it takes to put the ball in motion is a seemingly innocuous comment by an adult, so watch what you say. This is also a time when they are prone to blurt out the first thing that comes into their head. Remember, don't take this personally, you are the adult with a 100 billion brain cells all fully wired up. They are still a neurological work in progress.

Social and emotional development

- anxious about body shape and changes
- experiences mood swings
- compares self with peers
- focuses on same-sex friendships more than family
- begins to break childhood bonds that bound them to their carers

Cognitive development

- still has fairly concrete thinking
- still not fully able to understand subtlety
- tends to daydream
- has difficulty identifying how their immediate behaviour impacts on the future

Middle adolescence (14–17 years)

For this age group, the big questions are 'Who am I?' and 'Where do I belong?' Teenagers at this stage are deeply concerned with self-discovery and can appear quite self-obsessed. Couple this with their emerging sexuality and the tendency for risk-taking behaviour and you can see how there's enormous potential for conflict in the home.

While they demand freedom, and fight to attain it, adolescents still need to feel that their parents are capable of taking care of them if life gets overwhelming. This is the classic adolescent paradox. They'll battle to dismantle your authority, but know that they can be undone if they are *too* successful. The more they feel themselves to be truly on their own and without parental support the more vulnerable they are. You need to be a firm but loving mentor, not just a cashed-up housemate.

Social and emotional development

- seeks individualisation by spurning adult control and support
- needs privacy
- concerned with peer group acceptance
- gender identity begins to emerge
- experiences sexual urges
- prone to fads
- identifies with counterculture/youth icons
- experiments and takes risks to test emerging sense of self
- begins to take on greater responsibility within the family as part of cultural identity
- concerned about individual freedom and rights
- able to accept more responsibility for consequences of own behaviour
- needs a mentor or guide who can help nourish their uniqueness

Cognitive development

- able to think more rationally
- able to concentrate for longer periods

Late adolescence (17+ years)

The key question in this phase is 'Where am I going?' To answer this, an adolescent needs to have a strong sense of self that incorporates a realistic body image and an acceptance of gender identity and sexual orientation. With a strong sense of self, they can begin to develop mutually caring and responsible relationships and to form clear educational and vocational goals. The greatest protective factor against kids going off the rails is having a charismatic adult in their lives, someone they can talk to and from whom they can draw strength. For many adolescents this charismatic adult is a parent, but for others it might be a coach, a teacher, an uncle, a grandparent or a spiritual leader.

Social and emotional development

- builds intimate relationships based on mutual respect and affection
- understands sexual preferences
- begins to take responsibility for own life (sets clear objectives and plans strategies to achieve goals)
- explores career/vocation options
- achieves economic independence

Cognitive development

- thinks more abstractly
- able to think into the future and anticipate consequences of their actions

I'D LIKE MY BOY TO FOLLOW IN HIS FATHER'S FOOTSTEPS
TANDBERG

Chapter 5

What Every Parent Needs to Know About Their Own Issues

We can't be perfect parents,
so the best we can do is to
minimise the damage.

It's all very well to understand how our children's development affects their behaviour, but this understanding is a monumental waste of time if we have never reflected on the reasons we behave as we do. Without self-reflection, we risk every interaction with our kids being sabotaged by a tsunami of our own emotional baggage. If your first response to this statement is indignation ('I had a very happy childhood and there's nothing wrong with me'), then I can guarantee you've got some work to do. Psychologists call this 'family of origin work'.

Your family of origin – the family you grew up in, as opposed to the people you live with now – is the place you learnt to be who you are, for better or worse. From your family you learnt how to communicate, how to deal with your emotions and how to get your needs met. You also learnt many of your core values and beliefs. It can be very confronting to examine our upbringing, especially when there is a lot of unresolved grief and pain and we are torn between feelings of loyalty towards our parents and anger at their mistakes and failures. However, such examination is imperative if we are to avoid repeating the same mistakes with our own children.

If you look back, what do you see? Two parents who loved and supported each other most of the time? Or two unhappy people engaged in constant disunity, conflict or even abuse? And what about you? Did you feel loved for who you were, rather than what you did? Were you overindulged and pampered to messianic proportions? Or were you pretty much ignored and left to bring yourself up because your parents were obsessed with their own addictions, career trajectory or artistic expression?

When children do not consistently experience the world as a safe and loving place (and for the first ten years or so, their parents *are* their world), they become overwhelmed by feelings of terror and chaos. Some try to win back the love and protection of their parents by being 'good'. Of course, since the child's behaviour isn't the cause of a parent's failure to love, this unconscious strategy never works. What it does, however, is contribute to later emotional problems (anxiety and depression) and relationship difficulties.

Of course, even the most devoted and caring parent makes mistakes – it's how we learn on the job. The best we can do is to try to identify the maladaptive techniques our own parents used and to try to avoid inflicting the same on our children. Psychologist Donald Winnicott recognised this way back in the 1950s when he talked about being a 'good enough' parent. We can't be perfect parents, so the best we can do is to minimise the damage we do.

IDENTIFYING YOUR EMOTIONAL BAGGAGE

So how do we identify the baggage? It's quite simple. Any time we are interacting with our kids and find ourselves feeling angry (not simply annoyed or irritated, but a red-hot seething rage that is out of proportion to our offspring's behaviour) this is a sign that there's something from our own childhood that hasn't been resolved or healed. Don't get me wrong, emotions are healthy and normal, and we should welcome their expression. It's perfectly understandable to shed a tear when the family Labrador passes on, or to feel furious when your teenager tells you to get f*cked, or vomits on the new rug after raiding the wine cellar. Emotional reactions to loss, accidents and bad behaviour are all fine when they are *only* about these incidents, but psychologists know that people are rarely upset for the reason they think. If we take the time to work out why we are reacting the way we do, we may find that our anger is actually directed towards our partner, who is not pulling their weight, or our boss who is bullying us at work. And sometimes the answer is that we are carrying around anger we don't understand – unconsciously channelling grief and rage from our own childhoods.

Psychologists call this 'ghosts in the nursery', meaning that our children stimulate the intense feelings of our own childhoods. If you experienced critical, harsh or dismissive parenting styles in childhood; if you lived in a chaotic, fear-based environment or you witnessed a volatile, high-conflict relationship between your parents, you can't change that. But you can change how much you allow it to influence your own parenting. The first step is to acknowledge that it happened, and then to ask for help in changing how you think about it. There is no shame in this. Parenting support groups, therapy and counselling can help.

Severe neglect or abuse (physical, sexual or emotional) in one's family of origin can lead to serious, persistent emotional and relationship difficulties. Therapists are trained to help clients overcome the distress associated with such experiences. For example, if you grew up in a home where Dad abused Mum, you learnt that domestic violence was normal – it was something men did and women tolerated. That piece of information was 'stored' in your system of values and beliefs, the bedrock of who you are. You also learnt that Dad didn't have to take responsibility for his violent behaviour because it was Mum's fault he was unhappy in the first place – it must have been, because she always accepted the blame. Later, because of those beliefs, you may have ended up being the victim/abuser in your own marriage.

It takes therapy to work through this stuff. 'Changing your mind' about the rightness or wrongness of what your parents did to each other and to you isn't enough. Changing your mind doesn't alter the basic belief that it's your lot in life to be a victim, or that it's okay to expect everyone else to satisfy your desires even at the expense of their own needs. Therapy is like weeding your emotional garden. 'Changing your mind' or gaining insight is like using a hoe to take the top off a weed; therapy gets the root and all.

Even when we had a secure childhood, there will always be times when we are overwhelmed by anger. The key is to be able to put the safety catch on, take a deep breath and remember that this is about stuff from your own life, not about what your kid is doing. Sure our progeny can be incredibly annoying at times, and quite adept at pressing our buttons, but if we shout or storm off, this is basically an adult tantrum – embarrassing for everyone and a missed opportunity for teaching our kids how to manage their feelings.

In my work with parents over the years, I've found that many are particularly uncomfortable when their children are expressing a strong emotion, whether that emotion is positive (when the kids are shouting and yelling with natural exuberance) or negative (when they're sobbing with frustration and rage). This is because many of us have been brought up to believe that emotion is a sign of weakness and must be avoided at all costs. So when a child is crying or screaming, we start yelling at them to stop and the whole situation escalates until someone lashes out physically (a slammed door, a slap or worse). In these situations, you need some strategies to manage your own anger before you can even begin to help them manage theirs.

ANGER MANAGEMENT

When we really lose it in front of our kids, it can be terrifying, particularly for young children. Try to put yourself in their shoes. First imagine your own partner screaming at you. Now imagine that he or she is double your size and is standing over you while shouting. Imagine that you depend on that person completely for your food, shelter and protection, and that they are the key to your developing sense of self and understanding about the world. Multiply that by a few hundred and you'll have some idea of how scary it is when you get angry at a young child.

Of course, we all get angry at our children, sometimes furious. But we are the parents – our job is to control the expression of our anger and therefore minimise its negative impact. This isn't always easy, especially when we're flooded with fight-or-flight hormones, and our muscles are tense, our pulse is racing, our breath quickened and we're ready to either clobber someone or run a marathon. No matter how hard it is to stay calm at these moments, we know that the last thing we want to do is hurt our kids. We need to walk away, take time out, remove ourselves from the situation so that we don't hit, don't swear, don't use name-calling or sarcasm or even scream at our kids. When your kids watch you deal constructively with your anger, they'll learn how to handle their own rage. You'll become a role model for your child, showing them that anger is part of being human, and that learning to manage anger responsibly is part of becoming mature.

Identify the warning signs

Many parents tell me that they explode into anger without warning, but in fact, there are almost always warning signs in the body. Paying attention to the way anger feels in your body helps you to recognise when your temper is starting to boil and allows you to take steps to manage your anger before it gets out of control. You might feel a knot in your stomach, clench your jaw, feel hot and sweaty, or get a headache. Some people can pace around the house, others literally see red, have trouble concentrating, or their heart may pound or their shoulders become tense. Parents, in my experience, tend to lose it more easily when they are tired or their immune system is low.

Recognise your 'thought triggers'

Sometimes it might seem that situations cause us to feel angry (especially when other people are intentionally cruel, or things go wrong), but anger has less to do with what happens to us and more to do with how we *interpret* what happens – in other words, how we think about a situation. Common thinking patterns that trigger and fuel anger include:

1. Over-generalising

This is where you view a challenging situation as an all-pervasive disaster that exists for all time, not just a problem at one particular moment. For example:

'You ALWAYS interrupt me.'
'You NEVER consider my needs.'
'EVERYONE disrespects me.'
'I NEVER get the credit I deserve.'

2. Rigid thinking

Whenever you use the words 'should' or 'must' it's a clue that you are more likely to get angry when reality doesn't line up with your vision.

'But it's not supposed to be done that way.'
'You must do what I'm asking.'
'I should be there already.'

3. Jumping to conclusions

This is where you assume you know what someone else is thinking or feeling, and assume that he or she has intentionally upset you, ignored your wishes, or disrespected you.

4. Collecting negatives

This is where you collect things to get upset about, usually while overlooking anything positive, and letting these small irritations build and build until you explode, often over something relatively minor.

5. Righteous indignation

This is the tendency to blame others when something bad happens or something goes wrong rather than taking responsibility for your own behaviour.

Take time out

When you feel close to losing it, stop and take a deep breath. Say, as calmly as you can:

'I'm too angry to talk about this now. I'm going to calm down and then we can talk.'

'I can see you are upset. Let's stop now and talk about it later.'

Then move to another part of the house, or another place if you are outside your home. (For young children of five or six, it might be best if you just move to another part of the room as leaving them alone with overwhelming feelings can be even more terrifying for them.)

Some parents are afraid that walking away from an argument is a sign of low emotional intelligence. They are worried that it tells their children that parents are afraid of strong emotions and need to exit. This is not the case at all. By naming the emotion ('I am feeling too angry') and choosing to walk away, you will impress upon your child just how serious the situation is, and you will also model self-control.

When you are away from your child, use this time to *calm down*, not to work yourself into a self-righteous frenzy about how wronged you feel. Get a glass of water, cuddle the dog – whatever dials it down.

Challenge your self-talk

Now tell yourself to get a grip: this is not an emergency – kids need our love most when they seem to deserve it least, and they desperately need our help to learn to manage their big feelings. Recognising that your current way of thinking might be self-defeating (i.e. it doesn't make you feel good or help you to get what you want) can sometimes motivate you to look at things from a different perspective. Following are the four main types of challenging questions to ask yourself:

1. **Test the reality**

   Can I know for certain that what I'm thinking is true?

   Am I jumping to negative conclusions?

2. **Look for alternative explanations**

   Are there any other ways that I could look at this situation?

   If I were being positive, how would I perceive this situation?

3. **Put things in perspective**

   Is there anything good about this situation?

   Will this matter in five years' time?

4. **Use goal-directed thinking**

   Is this way of thinking helping me to achieve my goals?

   Is there something I can do to improve this situation?

Speak calmly

When you have calmed down, go back to your child and discuss what happened. If you've decided that the situation is worth getting angry about and there's something you can do to avoid or improve things, the key is to express your feelings in a healthy way. When communicated respectfully and channelled effectively, anger can be a tremendous source of energy and inspiration for change. Research shows that the more calmly we speak, the calmer we feel, and the more calmly others respond to us. Using profanities and sarcasm might feel satisfying at the time (and we may think this is fine because at least we're not hitting our kids, right?), but this character assassination not only escalates emotions, but also damages the connection we have with our child.

In every interaction with our children, we have the power to calm or exacerbate the situation by what we say and how we say it. Our kids may be spectacularly irritating, but we are not helpless victims. As parents we must learn to manage our own feelings first. Your child may not become a little angel overnight, but his acting out will diminish dramatically once you learn to stay calm.

If, after all your efforts, you still feel angry, look for the underlying feelings. Every time a child pushes your buttons, you can be sure those buttons were installed some time in your own childhood. Anger is always a defence, shielding us from feeling hurt or afraid, and protecting us from feeling vulnerable. Once you get to the underlying feelings, your anger will dissipate. This is where professional help might be a good idea. Seek help if:

- you feel constantly frustrated and angry no matter what you try
- your temper causes problems in your relationships at home or at work
- you have gotten in trouble with the law due to your anger
- your anger has ever led to physical violence.

WHEN PARENTS CRY MORE THAN THEIR KIDS

So far I've been talking about anger, but there is also another emotional scenario that is equally damaging for kids and that's when a parent is depressed. I don't mean having a bad day here and there where you feel a bit unmotivated and flat, but a relentless low mood for weeks on end where nothing you do is enjoyable and you have trouble sleeping and concentrating.

Signs of depression

A person may be depressed if, for more than two weeks, he or she has felt sad, down or miserable most of the time or has lost interest or the ability to find pleasure in usual activities, and has also experienced several of the signs and symptoms across at least three of the categories below.

Behaviour

- not going out anymore
- not getting things done at work/school
- withdrawing from close family and friends
- relying on alcohol and sedatives
- not doing usual enjoyable activities
- unable to concentrate

Feelings

- overwhelmed
- guilty
- irritable
- frustrated
- lacking in confidence
- unhappy
- indecisive
- disappointed
- miserable
- sad

Thoughts

- 'I'm a failure.'
- 'It's my fault.'
- 'Nothing good ever happens to me.'
- 'I'm worthless.'
- 'Life's not worth living.'
- 'People would be better off without me'

Physical

- constant fatigue
- often sick and run down
- headaches and muscle pains
- churning gut
- sleep problems
- loss or change of appetite
- significant weight loss or gain

It's important to note that everyone experiences some of these symptoms from time to time and it may not necessarily mean a person is depressed. Equally, not every person who is experiencing depression will have all of these symptoms.

If you think that you may have depression, there's a quick, easy and confidential checklist you can complete on the beyondblue website (beyondblue.org.au/the-facts/depression/signs-and-symptoms/anxiety-and-depression-checklist-k10). The checklist will not provide a diagnosis – for that you need to see a health professional.

All parents experience stress – it's a normal part of life. Stress is the gap between what we want and what we have, and for some of us, that gap is ever widening due to financial problems, chronic illness or injury, or having children with special needs or a chronic illness. The frustration and anxiety we feel can push us to the limits of our endurance.

No matter how we try to hide our feelings, children pick up on them. Even when you are simply tired or out of sorts, your children will sense a difference and will often hang around you more than usual. This is a survival thing – they depend on you for everything, so they need to make sure you stick around.

More severe parental stress can be confusing and very frightening for children. Parents who are chronically irritable or unresponsive due to depression or anxiety are a danger to their kids. I've seen how children in these situations become withdrawn or begin acting out. Children are often a barometer for how their parents are faring emotionally. Worse, some kids take on the responsibility of trying to look after a distressed parent. This is unacceptable. Children need the adults in their lives to be strong enough to guide, nurture and set limits. Parents with untreated depression and anxiety will compromise their children's quality of life and stall their development. (We know, for instance, that those areas of the brain that regulate stress [the limbic system] are wired very early in life, and that maternal depression can adversely affect healthy brain development in babies under six months.)

It is *never* a child's responsibility to look after a stressed parent. You can help ensure your child never shoulders such an unreasonable load by avoiding comments such as, 'Be extra quiet and gentle with your mum/dad today, as she/he is feeling very sad.' There is nothing wrong with occasionally explaining that you are unwell, tired or sad, but to place the responsibility for your emotional wellbeing on your child is an unbearable burden for them and will result in behaviours that create even more stress for you and long-term emotional problems for your child. Parents who experience prolonged anxiety or feelings of hopelessness and of being unable to cope must get help.

THE KEYS TO RESILIENCE

Psychologists have long known the key factors that contribute to the development of resilience in children and young adults: having the guidance and support of a charismatic adult; being emotionally intelligent; thinking positively; being good at something; and feeling that life has meaning. For most of us, these same factors continue to affect our wellbeing long into adulthood, especially if we are missing some of them. So if we lack resilience as parents, how then can we encourage it in our children? Take an honest look at this list and see if you can improve the factors in your life that increase your capacity to face, overcome and be strengthened or transformed by adversity.

1. Support from a caring partner and friends

The late, great psychologist Dr Chris Peterson summed up decades of positive psychology research with the simple phrase: 'other people matter'. Connections with other people are absolutely fundamental to happiness. We all need someone we can talk to, with whom we feel safe, valued and listened to. For most of us, this need is fulfilled by our partner or a close friend. A longitudinal study from Harvard that followed 268 sophomores over the course of their adult lives showed that the single most important predictor of successful aging (defined by physical and mental health and satisfaction with life at age 75), wasn't cholesterol level, treadmill endurance or intelligence. It was having close relationships. Based on the extensive data collected over seven decades, the author concluded: 'The only things that matter in life are your relations to other people.' Humans are social animals. We have a need for connection, for love and for physical and emotional contact with others. We enhance our own wellbeing by building strong networks of relationships around us, with family, friends, co-workers, neighbours and all the other people in our lives.

2. Social and emotional skills

Merely being part of a family is no guarantee that you will develop the social and emotional skills you need for a positive sense of self. The sad reality is that some families are toxic, and some parents are abusive or neglectful. Our children learn by watching us, not by listening to us drone on about 'acceptable behaviour'. If we are caring and respectful to our partner, children and other people we meet; if we truly listen to our children; if we feel comfortable talking about how we feel and learn to manage our anger, we will be giving our kids skills for life. (See chapter 8 for more on communication, and chapter 10 for more on managing conflict.)

3. Positive self-talk and flexible thinking

Self-talk is the name psychologists give to the endless stream of thoughts that runs through our heads every moment of every day. Resilient people tend to have more positive thoughts about themselves and others, and have more flexible thinking patterns. If they experience a setback, they know they'll be okay. People who have a more negative outlook need help in recognising, challenging and replacing negative thoughts with positive ones. This process forms the core of many 'talk' therapies such as cognitive behavioural therapy (CBT) and acceptance and commitment therapy (ACT), and there is now a raft of evidence to show that these approaches work. According to a 2004 French review of international research, cognitive behavioural therapy is proven to be effective at treating depression, panic disorder, post-traumatic stress, generalised anxiety disorder, bulimia and alcohol dependency.

4. Competence

For most of us, a positive sense of self depends on being paid to do something we are good at. A US review of research into the effects of unemployment paints a bleak picture: losing a job is associated with elevated rates of mental and physical health problems, increases in mortality rates, and detrimental changes in family relationships and in the psychological wellbeing of spouses and children. If we are not working, it is crucial that we find something else we are good at to feel that we are making a positive contribution to the universe. This might be a creative endeavour, or it might be a physical activity or volunteer work. (See chapter 11 for more on the power of giving.)

5. Feeling that life has meaning

Decades of research shows that people who have a sense of meaning and purpose in their lives are happier, feel more in control and get more out of what they do. They also experience less stress, anxiety and depression. But where do we find 'meaning and purpose'? Some people find it through spirituality – the feeling that we are part of something bigger than ourselves (whether that be a church, a trade union, the universe or whatever). The answers vary for each of us but they all involve being connected to something bigger than ourselves.

REWIRING OUR BRAINS

Brain plasticity, also known as neuroplasticity or cortical remapping, is a term that refers to the brain's ability to change and adapt as a result of experience. Up until the 1960s, researchers believed that changes in the brain could only take place during infancy and childhood. By early adulthood, it was believed that the brain's physical structure was permanent. Modern research has demonstrated that the brain continues to create new neural pathways and alter existing ones in order to adapt to new experiences, learn new information and create new memories. The old grey matter doesn't seize up after 30 (or it shouldn't if we keep using it). Thanks to plasticity, we keep on learning for the rest of our lives. Nanna was wrong – old dogs can learn new tricks. This is great news for parents who want to unlearn dysfunctional parenting strategies and replace them with new ones. That's what I want to turn to in the next section.

PART 2

MY TOP PARENTING TIPS OF ALL TIME

In this section I will outline the most important parenting tips I know. These are the ones I use every day in my clinical work and in my own relationships with my kids. I call them my golden rules and they are based on what the science of psychology tells us builds resilience and wellbeing. As Fredrick Douglass once said, 'It is easier to build strong children than to repair broken men.' I suspect that these pieces of wisdom have been passed down through generations but as we have moved to these artificial villages called 'cities' we have destroyed the kinship networks through which much of this understanding and knowledge was traditionally delivered.

Our knowledge about what works in parenting has evolved but the research suggests that the actual practice of parenting hasn't. An example comes from the researchers at Southern Methodist University, in Dallas, who placed voice recorders in the homes of thirty-three different families, which is a very reliable way to get data, as recordings allow researchers to obtain real-time information, which self-reports cannot. During the course of six days, the researchers reported that there were forty-one occasions on which a child was smacked. These occurred in fifteen different families. However, after about 75 per cent of the incidents, the child was misbehaving again within ten minutes. Lead researcher Dr George Holden said the results also showed that 'parents who shout a lot are more likely to hit their children. Parents are hitting their children over trivial misdeeds and some of the mums are doing it a lot more than the self-report data has ever identified. So the message that hitting doesn't work seems not to have penetrated, and that it can result in behavioural problems like aggression, or anxiety and depression.'

Despite the hype, the truth is that the Lucky Country can be a toxic place to raise children. To immunise young people against this requires decent, solid, stable families with adults who look after their own mental health and relationships and then prioritise their children.

DAD
MUM
TANDBERG

Chapter 6

Don't Do Anything for Your Children That They Can Do Themselves

If you really want your children to succeed, learn when to leave them alone.

Way back in 2009, *Time* magazine reported that there was a 'new revolution' underway, one aimed at rolling back the crap parenting – a backlash against what it referred to as the '. . . comical overprotectiveness and overinvestment of moms and dads'. But this insurgency seems to have bypassed Australia.

In the following chapters you will see the recurring messages:

- less is more
- hovering is dangerous
- failure is fruitful.

If you really want your children to succeed then *learn when to leave them alone.* When you lighten up, they'll fly higher.

By 'succeed', and 'fly higher', I don't mean they'll be 'winners' in the way that our mainstream media might suggest (fame, fortune etc.) but that they will have a strong sense of self. This was called 'self-esteem' in the 1980s – a term widely misunderstood to mean a kind of inflated self-regard that depended on children being protected from failure and disappointment.

True self-esteem means we have a subconscious yet enduring knowledge that we are worthy, likeable and okay. Self-esteem doesn't mean we're thinking, 'I am the best, everyone else is not as good as me', or, 'I can do everything perfectly.' A person with a positive sense of self holds a realistic picture of themselves as a worthwhile person. They feel comfortable with who they are and are able to assert their needs confidently without needing to become aggressive. They are also less likely to intimidate or bully others and can question things without feeling guilty or ashamed. But self-esteem doesn't mean we are happy all the time. It's more an underlying hum of wellbeing – the feeling that whatever happens, we'll be okay; that if we do experience some kind of loss or personal tragedy we know we can get through it. Another word for this is resilience.

As we saw in Part 1, children become resilient by being given opportunities to solve problems, to make mistakes, to take risks. Yet overprotective parents are intervening and preventing children from doing this. They are harassing the school if their child does not get straight A's, calling other parents to insist their child be invited to a party, over-scheduling their children in after-school activities and buying them everything they ask for.

When these kids reach their twenties, they are often still living at home, reliant on their parents for financial support and unable to make the smallest decision without consulting their parents. Unfortunately, it's these young adults who most often fit the Gen Y stereotypes that employers complain about: bloated sense of entitlement, constant need for validation, non-self-starters, mediocre work ethic and a general lack of soft skills. A bit of digging usually uncovers that their well-meaning but ultimately destructive parents have done things like write their child's résumé, call in favours to get their child a job, make up a list of 'previous employers' on their CV and even listed themselves as referees.

If you are the kind of parent who has always jumped in to save your child from uncomfortable or challenging situations, learning to stand back is going to be hard for you as well as for your kids. Here are some suggestions for managing the transition from over-parenting back to 'ordinary' parenting.

MAINTAIN REALISTIC EXPECTATIONS

Understanding when to let your child solve a problem, cope with a consequence or try out a new skill comes with a developmental perspective – knowing what your children can realistically (and safely) be expected to cope with at each stage of their development. Some of this is common sense (no one gives the car keys to a 5-year-old), and you have considerable expertise here – you know your children better than anyone – but as we have seen, many parents are denying their children opportunities to learn through their mistakes. By all means, offer your children support as they learn to do things for themselves, but for their sake, resist the urge to take over, or to intervene and protect them from the consequences of their actions. (I talk more about boundaries and consequences in chapter 7, and about helping kids deal with conflict in chapter 10.)

Whenever your children are learning a new skill, and you feel tempted to jump in and play the superhero, it can be helpful to remember the sequence for skill learning:

1. Do it for them (demonstrate the skill).
2. Do it with them.
3. Watch while they do it.
4. Let them do it themselves.

For instance, it's fine to help with homework, but don't take over and do it *for* your child. You might follow the steps above to show them one example, but then leave them to do the rest.

GIVE YOUR KIDS RESPONSIBILITIES

The key to helping kids develop a sense of responsibility is to start early. It's a psychological fact of life that toddlers simply love helping parents around the house. Their brains are wired to imitate, and will flourish when given opportunities to copy what Mum or Dad is doing. Many will regard these activities as a game and they will derive enormous satisfaction from the verbal reinforcement a parent gives them as they do it. The trick is to start them off on little chores around the house and garden – watering the herbs, handing you the pegs as you hang out the washing, taking their plate to the sink. Though many will have the fine motor skills of an elephant on Xanax and will usually create more mess than they clean up, you will have established a routine where everyone helps around the house.

Some people like to post a weekly list of chores (using pictures for young children) on the fridge, with a checkbox for each completed task. After checking the child's work, parents place a star or sticker on the chart. They also list activities that are allowed after work is done – outside play, television time or computer time. When the list is first pinned up, parents explain what's expected and the consequences of not doing what's expected (missing out on the playtime afterwards). The idea is not to remind, nag, scold or complain when children don't do their chores, just to follow through with the consequences. All of this will motivate your child to complete tasks quickly. It also keeps a balance between work and play.

As children get older, parents should work up to more complex (and helpful) jobs such as cooking the occasional meal, raking the leaves or doing the washing. The idea is that children willingly help their parents, not just because of the praise they get for doing the work but because it creates a feeling of belonging and of their being valued members of the family. Child psychologists argue that even basic household chores not only enhance their feelings of competency but offer children multiple opportunities for positive interactions with parents.

Unfortunately, in my experience, many kids rarely help around the house and many more *never* pick up after themselves (putting away their clothes, hanging up their own towel or putting away their own belongings). It may be the complaint of every parenting generation, but slothful child syndrome is a phenomenon that seems to be sweeping the western world. And there is research (at least in America) to prove it. A University of Maryland study showed that in 1985, the average teen (12–17) was doing six hours of housework a week. This dropped to four hours in 1995 and a measly two hours by 2002. In 2013, anthropologist Elinor Ochs studied thirty Los Angeles households and found that children ignored, resisted, or refused to respond to parents' appeals to help in twenty-two of the families, and in the other eight the children were cooperative but did very little. She notes that in other societies, small children are raised to help others (and themselves) as a foundation of cooperation and respect, and that they learn to do this by *watching* others. She says many American parents don't encourage their children to observe people and learn what those around them are doing, focusing instead on naming and classifying objects, with the result that they are less able to care for themselves or help others. These little ones become more dependent on helicopter parents and that continues as they grow up.

Fortunately, the situation is not quite as dire in Australia. Data from the 'Longitudinal Study of Australian Children' shows that while neither girls nor boys are doing large amounts of housework, 10-year-old girls spend thirty-eight minutes per day on chores and other domestic tasks (including making their beds, tidying their rooms, cleaning, cooking and taking care of pets), while boys spend twenty-eight minutes. This sounds a lot to me, given that the vast majority of my teenage clients are asked to do precisely zip! Even though kids have after-school activities and homework, parents must ensure that children pitch in to help.

MODEL FACING CHALLENGES

The best way to teach your kids how to face challenges and manage failure is through demonstration. Think about the last time you did something completely new, for which you had to learn a new skill, and where you felt a bit apprehensive. Did you talk about it with your kids? Did you allow yourself to show your kids how you coped? It doesn't have to be a major event, it can be as simple as cooking something you've never tried before, trying over-arm bowling in backyard cricket, doing an online course, or even playing a video game with them. You can't expect your children to become resilient if you have the spine of a garden snail. As P.J. O'Rourke said, '. . . too many of today's children have straight teeth and crooked morals'.

PRAISE EFFORT AS WELL AS ACHIEVEMENT

Professor Charles Desforges from the University of Exeter in the UK found that the greatest individual characteristic that determined children's success at school was persistence. It was number one by far. In fact, persistence was a staggering seven times more significant than intelligence as a determinant of a child's achievement.

In aiming to be affirming, parents need to be realistic and not give praise for the sake of it. No one can be 'great' or 'fantastic' all the time! Praise includes statements such as 'great work', 'fantastic', 'you are a genius', 'you are the best at that', 'you did so well'. It is right to give praise when your child's achievement is truly noteworthy, but all praise must be genuine and should be only a small part of your dialogue with your children.

Using encouraging comments rather than praise is important because it acknowledges the attempt and the process rather than the end product or finished article. Praising kids for having a go helps them to persist. For example, when a child tries to tie their shoelace but fails, you could say, 'You tried hard, well done' so that their effort is acknowledged, rather than waiting to say 'Great' when they finally tie the lace.

Examples of encouragement rather than praise:

- 'I can see how hard you worked on that.'
- 'I like the way you tried.'
- 'I could see how hard that was and yet you kept on trying.'
- 'I like the way you are working on that.'
- 'I appreciate how you are trying to . . .'
- 'I can see how excited you are.'
- 'You seem happy with what you have achieved.'
- 'I enjoy watching you . . .'
- 'It's fun to work on something and have almost finished it isn't it?'

In other words, you are teaching your children that you don't always have to be a winner to be okay. Life isn't and shouldn't always be about who wins, who gets there first or who is 'the best'. Children are more likely to feel competent and happy if the *process* rather than the end product is emphasised. A sense of personal best is more desirable than constantly trying to be the best in all things. It is vital for children to know that they are valued and loved for who they are, not what they do.

SHANE'S PARENTS LET HIM DO WHATEVER HE LIKES!

TANDBERG

Chapter 7

Give Your Kids a Regular Dose of Vitamin 'N'

I'm tired of hearing adults whining about how hopeless the younger generation is, as if they didn't have anything to do with it!

Just to clarify: vitamin 'N' means 'no'. A straight-out, immovable 'no' that is impervious to consistent badgering, waterworks or other manipulations by angry and disappointed offspring.

However, the tone and delivery of this word is very important. You must be able to look your child in the eye and say it firmly and respectfully – no shouting or hissing it from between clenched teeth. If this is new to you, practise saying it in front of a mirror first, or with your partner.

A firm and respectful 'no' affirms your authority. It tells your child that you are confident in your decision to limit her behaviour, but that you still respect her. If we can show our children how to say 'no' without blame, resentment or nastiness, then our children will be able to do this, too.

Being able to say 'no' is crucial to our children's moral development. It means they can say, 'No. I don't want to. I'm not happy about doing that. It's wrong.' We all want to raise responsible, considerate, cooperative children who do the right thing, but that doesn't imply obedience. Morality is doing what's right, no matter what you're told; obedience is doing what you're told, no matter what's right.

The unfortunate truth is that children who are not regularly and confidently told 'no' never learn to get over disappointment and maintain unrealistic expectations of the world and everyone in it. Swedish psychiatrist Dr David Eberhard recently published a book entitled *How Children Took Power*, which argues that over the past forty years Swedes have adopted an increasingly child-centred approach to parenting. He says children are now key decision-makers in families, and decide when to go to bed, what to eat, where to go on vacation, even what to watch on television. According to Eberhard, the results have been disastrous and include rising rates of truancy, anxiety disorders, self-harm and obesity among children, as well as declining educational performance. Eberhard says that most Swedish kids don't say thank you, don't open doors for people or stand up for elderly people or pregnant women on the subway. If ever there was a cautionary tale for Australia – this is it. Democracy does not work for kids or dogs and the Swedish experience shows it.

However, once you say 'no', you must stick to it. So think carefully about your decision. If kids know that ramping up their whining or complaining means you will occasionally give in, it takes them a lot longer to accept that sometimes they will miss out. It is through *repeatedly* facing and getting over disappointment that a child gradually learns to change their expectations.

When helping a child face disappointment, avoid a harsh, defensive or dismissive approach ('Build a bridge and get over it!' is definitely out). Accept that your child may hate you for a while and be supportive as they come to terms with their loss, because that's what it is: they haven't got what they wanted. Above all, be firm and consistent. This can be quite a challenge as you will see from the example below.

Teen: 'But I *really*, *really* want to go to the party.'

Parent: 'We've already talked about this. There will be no adult at the house.'

Teen: 'But I'll just text you so you know I'm okay.'

Parent: 'That's not the same as adult supervision.'

Teen: 'Even Madeline is allowed to go.'

Parent: 'You still can't go.'

Teen: 'But *everyone* is going.'

Parent: 'That may be so, but you still can't go.'

Teen: 'God, you're so *mean*!'

Parent: [silence]

Teen: 'You don't even care about me! All my friends will think I'm a loser. It's *so* unfair!'

Parent: 'You know our answer.'

Teen: 'I bet *you* went to parties like this when you were my age.'

Parent: 'This is not about me. You can't go to this one.'

Teen: 'So you *did* go to parties like this!'

Parent: 'It doesn't matter what I did. We've decided you can't go to this party.'

Teen: 'I hate you!' [Runs to the bedroom and slams the door.]

WHY KIDS NEED BOUNDARIES

Saying 'no' is the simplest way of setting boundaries for your child's behaviour. A toddler who runs towards the road, pulls another child's hair, or throws a shoe at the cat is firmly told 'no'. Babies and toddlers by nature have little self-control. They want what they want when they want it and if they don't get it, they are unable to manage the frustration they feel (cue the tantrum). Gradually, we show them what they can and can't expect from the world (e.g. they can't have Mum's attention 24/7, they can't eat chocolate for every meal, they can't hit their sister) – these are the boundaries or guidelines for acceptable social behaviour.

If, when they are small, children learn that these boundaries are predictable, consistent and helpful, they will begin to adopt them as their own – they will learn to control themselves rather than needing to be controlled by others. Instead of *us* telling them what to do, they begin to tell themselves what to do.

Most parents have no trouble setting limits on behaviour that is unsafe. But what about teaching our children empathy, respect and responsibility? Empathy is the ability to appreciate another person's feelings and understand their point of view, and it doesn't kick in until children are about seven or eight years old. (Children with an autism spectrum disorder may not develop empathy at all.) However, children need help to develop empathy, and they do that by being around empathic, compassionate adults. For example, if you and your child see someone being victimised or suffering (in real life, on TV or in a book) and you express genuine compassion for that person, your child begins to understand the connection.

THE VALUE OF CONSEQUENCES

It is crucial that our kids learn that their behaviour has consequences, that they *can* hit their brother, draw on the walls, smash the glass, or sneak out of the house at night, but only if they are willing to pay the price. This is how they learn about boundaries – about what behaviour is okay and what is not okay.

Natural consequences are those that most often follow on from a behaviour (you hit your brother and he hits you back); logical consequences are usually set by parents, but can be agreed as a family (if you break something through negligence you pay for it using your own money). Since one of the tasks of childhood is to *test* boundaries, having agreed-on consequences for certain behaviours is an enormous help as it can stop you from losing the emotional plot and screaming yourself hoarse, or making ridiculous threats that you cannot follow through ('You are banned from the computer for a year!').

Natural consequences

Natural consequences involve zero adult interference. Children learn appropriate behaviour from the natural outcomes of unwanted behaviour. For example:

- If you forget to take your coat to the football you will be uncomfortably cold.
- If you leave your battery-powered toy outside it will rust and break.
- If you spend all your pocket money on the first day you'll have nothing for the weekend.
- If you don't turn up to football practice you won't be picked for the team.
- If you punch a wall you will be in pain.
- If you treat your friends badly they will avoid you.
- If you lie to your parents they are less likely to trust you.
- If you are caught stealing from a shop the police will be called.

For teenagers, especially, reality will always make a greater impact than a parent's bad impersonation of Rambo. Having to deal with the outcomes of poor choices is an important learning experience for teens. You can still be on their side and caring even if you don't step in to fix the problem for them. However, parents still need to be vigilant and to ensure that natural consequences are safe. (For example, it's not a great idea to insist that a teenager who loses her train fare should walk home late at night alone.) Parents also need to be ready for anger, blame and disappointment from their teenager: 'It's your fault!' Don't fall for it. Just keep reminding yourself how important it is that they miss out sometimes.

Logical consequences

These require adult intervention and are most often used when a child's behaviour disturbs or hurts other people. For example:

- A child who repeatedly interrupts a conversation in the family room will be asked to leave.
- Children who refuse to clean up their toys will not be allowed to play with them for a certain period.
- Teenagers who come home late from a party will lose the right to go out next time.
- A child who wilfully breaks a sibling's toy or possession will have to help pay for a replacement.

In all of these examples the consequences are related to the children's misdemeanours, and are both reasonable and respectful of their dignity.

Setting effective consequences

The ultimate aim of setting consequences is to help our children learn self-control. Every time we step in and tell a child what to do we may achieve some control over his behaviour, but our child misses out on the valuable experience of choosing how to behave and dealing with the outcome of that choice. Here are five ways to set consequences that help children build self-control:

1. Use immediate consequences

It is important to directly connect the rules to an immediate outcome if possible. If someone is screaming, they go outside until they stop. If someone is arguing in the car, the car immediately pulls over until the argument stops. If siblings are fighting and can't sort it out themselves, they are separated and sent to their rooms. If the consequences are not implemented until the next day, children are less likely to see the connection between their misdemeanour and its consequence.

2. Start small

Start with small things, so that your child has the chance to rein themselves in with a relatively minor consequence (with relatively minor frustration), but knowing that if they don't back down a more significant consequence will be invoked. For example, a child who refuses to turn off their computer will ultimately lose internet access.

3. Avoid consequences that restrict development

Don't set consequences that deny children important developmental experiences, such as missing out on seeing relatives or important attachment figures or attending a sporting event, dance class, school camp or other school excursion. There are many other privileges that might be limited or withdrawn without developmental implications, such as watching TV, listening to music, surfing the internet, making mobile phone calls and having new possessions.

4. Ask 'what' not 'why'

When deciding whether a boundary has been crossed, and whether to implement consequences, never ask 'why' a child performed the unwanted action, as they will then start to list their excuses in an effort to deflect the consequences. Only ask 'what' they did.

5. Don't be a hypocrite

Consequences must apply to parents, too, otherwise boundaries will never work. So take yourself outside if you scream, or put money in the swear jar if you drop the f-bomb, and your kids will internalise the rules even faster.

CONSEQUENCES ARE NOT PUNISHMENT

I've often heard parents use the expression, 'Don't you dare do that or there will be consequences.' This is clearly using the idea of consequences as a threat – a form of punishment. This is not their best use.

Consequences are supposed to give children an opportunity to reflect on their choices without fear so that they learn to internalise the rules.

With punishment (verbal abuse, banishment or smacking), your kids are not learning to behave appropriately because they believe that it's a good idea (internalising a code of behaviour) but because they are terrified of what you will do to them. Indeed, smacking children (corporal punishment) is comprehensively discredited as a strategy for enforcing limits on children's behaviour. Since July 1979, thirty-four countries around the world have outlawed it in the home (twenty-two of them in Europe) and many more in schools. This is because corporal punishment has repeatedly been linked with negative outcomes including increased rates of aggression, delinquency, mental health problems, and problems in relationships with parents. Large, peer-reviewed studies show that the more children are hit, the more likely they are to hit others, including their friends and siblings, and in adulthood, the more likely they are to hit their spouses. Clearly, the more parents smack their children for antisocial behaviour, the more the antisocial behaviour increases.

While we are on the subject of punishment, it's important to note that sending a child to the 'time-out room', 'naughty spot' or 'thinking chair' is nearly always going to be seen by the child as a form of punishment, no matter how you dress it up. On the surface, time-outs seem sensible. They're nonviolent but still get the child's attention. Plus, they give parents and their children a much-needed break from each other while emotions run high. They're also better than yelling, and infinitely better than hitting, but ultimately, they don't help children to behave better. That's because kids see themselves as 'bad' when they are sent into isolation, and people who think they are bad tend to behave badly. Also, when you send an upset child to his room, you are pushing him away just when he needs you the most. Young children (especially under five or six) need our help to calm down.

In volatile family situations where children have behavioural issues, however, time-outs can be very useful.

THE USES OF BOREDOM

Boredom often leads children to pester parents to buy things or do things to assuage their ennui. 'Can I go on the computer?' 'Can you take me to my friend's house?' 'Can I have an ice cream?' We know the slumped, knuckle-dragging posture of the bored child, and often rush to save them from what some people describe as an unpleasant, empty feeling.

But boredom can be a good thing – it gives children opportunities to initiate activities for themselves, which promotes feelings of competence and mastery: 'I can do this!' Cultural expectations that children must be constantly active might even hamper the development of imagination. Neuroscientists have found that the brain is still highly active when disengaged, consuming only about 5 per cent less energy in its resting state than when involved in routine tasks.

So the next time your child complains that they are bored, instead of handing them a clipboard with a list of educational activities, tell them, 'Great! That's awesome. It means you'll think of something really good to do.'

MUM! I NEED SOME HELP
NOT NOW LOVE, I'M GETTING ADVICE ON HOW TO BE A BETTER MUM
TANDBERG

Chapter 8

Listen To Your Children

Poor communication is to a family what the iceberg was to the Titanic.

A family is the place where boys and girls first learn how to limit their wishes, abide by rules, and consider the rights and needs of others. In the process, they also learn myriad social and emotional competencies, such as resilience, problem solving and emotion regulation. As parents, it is our job to ensure that children do this in an environment that is as stable and secure as possible. In my experience, the most important factor in creating such an environment is the ability to talk to each other. With such intricate relationships, poor communication is to a family what the iceberg was to the *Titanic*. Unless there is a continual and respectful exchange of thoughts, feeling and ideas, the ship will take on water, and sink like a stone.

For some people, the talking part of communication comes very easily, but the listening part is like pulling teeth. These people gaze off into the distance, surreptitiously check phone messages under the table, or even slowly back away when it's the other person's turn to speak.

Think about the last time your kids asked a question or came to you with something they wanted to share. Did you glance at them briefly and continue with what you were doing, saying the occasional 'hmm' to indicate that you were *trying* to listen, but felt too busy, distracted or stressed to really offer them your full attention? If this describes your listening style, and your kids are older, I've no doubt that they're no longer that interested in sharing their experiences with you. And no wonder – you're not really listening to them.

HOW TO LISTEN ATTENTIVELY

Attentive listening is the key to connecting with others and building strong relationships. It means taking the time to stop what you are doing and giving someone your full attention. Even if we disagree with what someone is saying, listening first without interrupting gets the conversation off to a positive start.

So how do we listen attentively? When your child is speaking try doing the following:

1. Stand or sit close to them.
2. Make eye contact.
3. Clear your mind and concentrate on what your child is saying, rather than on what you want to say.
4. Let your child finish speaking without interruption.
5. Show your child that you are interested by nodding, smiling or saying things like, 'I see' or 'Really?', 'Oh!' or 'Wow!' (If the subject matter is truly boring to you, focus on how much you love your child, and how important it is to listen to them, and it won't matter whether your brain is interested or not.)
6. Wait until your child is finished before asking a question (and try to ask a question if you can, perhaps to request clarification or further explanation, as it shows that you really *have* been listening).

When we listen attentively to our children, they feel valued and worthwhile. It also strengthens our connection with them, so that our kids feel secure. A child who feels a positive, strong connection to his parents is less likely to act out against their attempts to set limits.

THE POWER OF PARAPHRASING

This is a technique well known to all therapists and counsellors where you paraphrase what your child has said to you. For example:

- 'So what you're saying is . . .'
- 'Oh, so you mean that . . .'

This is especially useful in discussions with teenagers (particularly inarticulate teenage boys) as it gives them the clear message that they are worth listening to, and that their point of view matters. It also gives them the opportunity to clarify what they wanted to say in the first place, which reduces the chance for misunderstanding. Of course, make sure you wait until your child has finished speaking before you begin to paraphrase, otherwise you will defeat the purpose.

REFLECTIVE LISTENING

Reflective listening is a powerful strategy to use when your children are communicating feelings of anger, disappointment, fear or grief. It simply means that you acknowledge your children's emotions without trying to fix them, without forcing the child to feel differently and without distracting them from how they are feeling. You listen to what they are saying and try to understand what is happening for them and then respond without judgement. For example:

- 'I can see that you are really upset about this.'
- 'It must be very frustrating for you.'
- 'I can see that you are very sad about this.'
- 'It seems that you are quite angry about what happened.'

As I mentioned earlier, parents who are uncomfortable with strong, negative emotions may withdraw from, rescue, distract or even reprimand their child in an effort to avoid those feelings. This teaches children that sadness and anger are 'bad' and must be avoided at all costs, which can have all sorts of psychological, physical and social consequences.

Negative emotions are there to help us evaluate experiences, and the harder we push them away, the stronger they become. The key is to accept that they are there, which frees us to find more adaptive solutions to our problems. Being able to put a name to the emotion is also empowering for children. It gives them a frame of reference and helps them understand that emotions are a normal part of life.

However, we still need to set limits on the behavioural expression of emotion. Kids need to know that it's okay to be angry, but it's not okay to be violent or nasty or cruel. For example:

'I can see that you are really upset about this. It's okay to be angry, but it's not okay to hit your brother.'

By acknowledging your child's emotions you are showing your child that it is okay to express feelings, and that we don't need to be ashamed of either having feelings or sharing them, but that there are limits to how we can express them. Physical and verbal abuse and the destruction of property are definitely out.

If your child has a particularly short fuse, it might be helpful to give him or her alternatives for expressing anger in a safe way. Some examples include:

- screaming into a pillow
- punching a cushion
- setting up a punching bag outside.

Always talk to your child afterwards about what triggered his or her rage, and how your child can better manage it when it resurfaces. (See chapter 10 for more on meltdowns.)

TANDBERG
I'M SURE HE'LL BE A GENIUS, I'VE BEEN READING TO HIM SINCE HE WAS AN EMBRYO

Chapter 9

Do Stuff With Your Kids

The family that plays together stays together.

You may be wondering why I would include such a bleedingly obvious parenting tip, but the sad truth is that many kids rarely see one or both of their parents, and when they do, the interactions are all about logistics: getting things done (homework, chores) or getting out of the house to a barrage of appointments. Whenever they do sit down together it's usually in front of a TV, which, of course, discourages conversation. Unless all members of a family are clairvoyants, it is essential for family members to talk to each other. In our screen-dominated culture, where eyes are glued to screens and ears plugged with headphones, this can be a challenge, but I find the best way to achieve this is by doing stuff together.

PLAY TOGETHER

Parents adore playing with their babies and toddlers, and there aren't many doting mums and dads who won't play peek-a-boo with a baby, or get down on the floor to build towers with a 2-year-old. By the time children are at school, however, many parents seem to have had a fun bypass and find it hard to be playful with their kids, yet light-hearted moments of silliness and laughter are like relationship superglue – helping kids feel happy, safe and secure.

Many families have at least one night a week where they do something together such as play board games, have a hit of backyard cricket or play a video game. That's right, I said *video game*! Despite what you may have heard, a plethora of studies now show that video games have a positive impact on young people's wellbeing. This research has been summarised in a 2013 report by the Young and Well Cooperative Research Centre, and shows that video games can positively influence young people's emotional state, optimism, resilience, sense of competence, self-acceptance and social connections. The latest studies are suggesting that *how* young people play, as well as *with whom* they play, are more important in terms of wellbeing than *what* they play. So the bottom line is that playing video games with your kids has a positive impact on adolescent development and long-term family outcomes.

EAT TOGETHER

Simply eating together is a great way to have family time. When the atmosphere is relaxed and talk is easy, you can begin tossing ideas back and forth. Just make sure everyone gets to have their say – for younger children, especially, adults need to model attentive listening.

While sharing a meal has got to be the easiest way to create opportunities for communication, a 2008 survey of 1011 Australian families found that almost a quarter do not eat together regularly. There is a huge amount of evidence that shared mealtimes offer long-term protective effects for children. In 1993, Oprah Winfrey conducted a 'family dinner experiment' where five families volunteered to eat dinner together every night for a month, for half an hour each time. As part of the experiment, all family members kept diaries to record their feelings about the experience. At first, sitting around the table was not highly rated by many families and the time at the table seemed interminable. But by the end of the month the families were happy and planned to continue dining together most evenings if not every night. When the families appeared on the *Oprah Winfrey Show* at the end of the experiment, it was the children who treasured the dependable time with their parents.

If you're not used to eating together, start slowly, with one meal a week, then build up as your family becomes used to the idea.

DO CHORES TOGETHER

Encourage your kids to help you prepare dinner or to wash up afterwards. Standing side by side while you chop veggies, dry up or clear the dishwasher is especially good for shy children or adolescents, who may feel uncomfortable with the eye contact and closeness of talking at the dinner table.

As we saw in chapter 6, giving kids responsibilities from a young age is important if we are to help them develop a sense of self-mastery and resilience. If your child is not already used to helping around the house, it's not too late. Have a family meeting to discuss weekly chores, and allow input and negotiation (depending on their maturity) to ensure that everyone is doing their fair share.

TRAVEL TOGETHER

Some children and adolescents will also open up on a car journey, especially with just one parent present. They find it less intimidating to share thoughts when you are concentrating on driving instead of looking straight at them. So next time you are driving your teen to sport training, turn off the radio or the MP3 player and just see what happens. You could ask them about some aspect of the sport itself, or share something about your own experience.

READ TOGETHER

Some children love one-on-one parent time as part of their bedtime ritual, where the parent sits on the bed quietly and listens to whatever their child feels like chatting about. Subjects may arise as a result of a bedtime story, or sometimes if you just sit with them for a few moments. Let your child take the lead. Don't push them to talk, and listen attentively when they do. It's a great way for both of you to wind down.

TRY FAMILY MEETINGS

If yours is the kind of family where regular meetings are a workable strategy (in other words, the idea does not result in dramatic sighs and eye-rolling) make sure you use them to plan holidays and fun outings, as well as to discuss roles and responsibilities such as pocket money, chores, homework etc. Allowing children some say in family decisions helps them to feel valued and gives them a sense of control over what happens in their lives, which in turn reduces the likelihood of triggering their sensitivity to control.

WE'VE FOUND A TERM TO DESCRIBE HIS BEHAVIOUR
TANDBERG

Chapter 10

Handle Meltdowns With Dignity

Nothing in life is to be stressed over.
It is only to be understood.

Emotions are part of being human. Jealousy, rejection, guilt, anger, frustration, hurt and disappointment are routinely felt by everyone in a family – not only the children. The ability to manage strong feelings without resorting to name-calling, shouting, character assassination or furniture damage is also known as emotional intelligence, and is perhaps the greatest marker of maturity we know. From a developmental perspective, it means we are able to use the thinking parts of our brain (the prefrontal cortex) to soothe the incredibly powerful instinctive and emotional parts (the limbic system). Anger is a normal human emotion and when it is managed properly it is not a problem. Everyone gets angry, and mild anger can help us deal with situations. However, if anger is expressed in harmful ways, or persists over a long period of time, it can lead to problems in relationships at home, school and at work and can affect the overall quality of your own and your children's lives.

BOOST EMOTIONAL INTELLIGENCE

When our children are babies, they need us to help them calm down when they become upset, and we do this instinctively by holding or rocking them. This lays down the neural circuitry that they need for self-soothing later in life. As our children grow, they watch us to see how we handle emotions, and they will do what we do. If we snap at people when we feel stressed, if we slam doors when things go wrong, and if we shout at our kids when they are upset, that's the behaviour they will learn. A recent UK survey of two thousand women by UK feminine hygiene brand Lil-Lets has revealed that on average, a teenage girl will slam a door 164 times a year. On top of that, she'll have 183 arguments with her mother, 257 arguments with her siblings, 127 fall-outs with her friends and will shed tears over boys 123 times a year. That's a truckload of stress for everyone, some of which could be avoided.

If we model emotional intelligence, our children will learn that feelings are okay, that they're manageable (and perhaps the door hinges won't wear out so fast). They'll understand that anger, sadness or jealousy might be a bit uncomfortable or intense, but we'll get over them. There's a great online game called Reach Out Central (ROC) that is designed to help young people improve their communication skills, problem-solving abilities and optimistic thinking. It allows your teen to test drive real-life scenarios and situations and see how their thoughts, feelings and actions can impact on their relationships and moods. The idea is that they take on the role of a character that is new in town. It is up to them to work out how to settle in, make new friends and find their way around the place. What they discover is that the choices they make about friends, partying, work and life can impact on their wellbeing and relationships.

Talk about your feelings

It may be a cliché, but the first step in teaching our kids to manage their emotions is being able to talk about our own feelings. I don't mean a massive D&M, but simply acknowledging them and giving them a label so that they're less frightening or mysterious. If this is a challenge for you, don't worry. You can start small ('I felt so angry when that guy pulled out in front of me on the way home from school'; or 'I feel a bit grumpy today, so I'm going to go for a walk'). Each time you do it, it will get easier.

However, be careful about what you discuss with children and adolescents. It's not appropriate to talk about adult concerns such as money worries, relationship troubles or personal problems that are beyond their experience. As stated earlier, our kids need to see us as strong enough to handle our own issues as well as theirs. I think too many parents are falling into the trap of making their child their confidante. When they walk into my office and say, 'I want to be his friend, and I want him to be my friend,' what they're really telling me is that they don't want to adopt an authoritative role in their child's lives. They are putting their own need to be liked before their child's need to learn to like himself. These parents are not evil, just ill-informed. They sincerely believe it is okay and appropriate to share with a child how they really feel about their mother-in-law, or how they really feel about their boss. What they don't realise is that their child is not morally, emotionally or intellectually prepared to play that role. If you're a 45-year-old and you want a friend, find another 45-year-old, not a 12-year-old.

Welcome feelings, limit behaviour

I sometimes have to remind parents that while the expression of feelings is important for healthy emotional development, they *must* set limits for acceptable behaviour. A burst of anger is almost always accompanied by the immediate disconnection of rational thought, and kids need to know that physically or verbally lashing out is never tolerated. 'It's okay to be angry, but it's not okay to be nasty.'

Psychologists know that anger is a defence against deeper feelings of fear, hurt, loss and disappointment. When those feelings are just too devastating, the brain shifts into attack mode to protect us from feeling so much pain. Sometimes attacking makes sense, but only when there is a physical threat to our survival, which in our society is quite rare.

When we or our children get angry, acknowledging the underlying feelings will help to dissolve the anger. For example, if your son's beloved toy is broken by his younger sister, helping him express his grief means he will be able to let go of his rage. He no longer needs his anger to defend against these feelings, so the anger evaporates. He can then move on to find ways to stop it happening again.

If parents are able to help kids feel safe enough to express their anger and explore the feelings underneath, kids are increasingly able to move past their anger into constructive problem-solving.

Many of the over-involved parenting strategies I discussed in chapter 2 arise when parents unconsciously try to protect their child from experiencing the pain of rejection, the disappointment of failure, and the frustration of missing out. We all want our kids to be happy, but it turns out that protecting children from painful feelings can be very harmful to their healthy development. When well-meaning but overprotective parents intervene to solve a problem (and therefore save the child from feeling anger, frustration etc.), the child is not only denied the opportunity to find a solution (and build resilience), but also to 'feel and deal' with her own emotions. If this happens repeatedly, the child becomes risk averse, avoids new situations and habitually looks to someone else to handle challenges, all of which impede a normal transition into adulthood.

Change your thinking patterns

As we saw in chapter 5, anger is often triggered or exacerbated by rigid, exaggerated or irrational thoughts. The key to anger management is to become aware of these thoughts and to replace them with more rational, realistic ones. Once you can do this for yourself, you will be able to help your children do it, too. For example, if your children say: 'I can't stand this! It's awful! Everything's ruined!' teach them to say instead, 'It's frustrating, and it's understandable that I'm upset about it, but it's not the end of the world.' In this way you are helping them to focus on managing their response to the situation, rather than on blaming the situation. This is also known as 'managing self-talk' and it is such an important skill that I have devoted a whole chapter to it (see chapter 11).

DEALING WITH AN ANGRY CHILD

Because we are all human, and there is no such thing as a perfect child or a perfect parent, most of us will at some stage find ourselves in the red zone with our children or ready to get out the capsicum spray with our teenagers. Here are some tips for managing those Incredible Hulk moments.

Stay calm

When an irate kid emotionally detonates, it's extremely important that you don't lose the plot, too. A child needs his parents most when he is sad or angry or afraid, and you need to model the behaviour you want your children to adopt – not do a commendable imitation of Mount Vesuvius. *You* are the adult in this situation, and it's up to you to step up to the plate of maturity. You cannot control your children, but you can control how you react to their behaviour. So take a deep breath and remember that all kids have 'L' plates when it comes to moderating their emotions and they rely on us to show them how.

Of course, this is way easier said than done. For many of us, when the feeling part of our brains (the limbic system) is activated, it can shut down the thinking brain, and we simply cannot respond rationally, no matter how old we are. If staying calm is hard for you, try taking a few deep breaths, a few steps backwards or even walking away for a few moments first. (See chapter 5 for more on managing your own anger.)

Tag team with your partner

If you need to step back because you don't have the emotional reserves to handle a brewing conflict, tell the child that you're taking time out, but that your partner will be taking over.

Minimise the talking

Until the child has calmed down, there is little point in trying to have a rational discussion about the situation that led to the strong emotion in the first place. A child overwhelmed by feeling is just not going to be up for a 'state of the nation' speech. The most they can handle will be something like, 'I can see you're really upset, so let's talk when you're feeling calmer.' Very young children are often comforted by being held firmly but gently, once again without any talking until they are much calmer.

Try distraction

Distraction is a great way to de-escalate conflict, but is more appropriate with younger children. Anyone over the age of seven or eight is likely to see straight through your ploy and insist on maintaining their stand.

Use reflective listening

When your child is ready to talk, reflective listening is one of the most powerful parenting communication skills going around. It involves carefully listening to what is being said and then restating it in your own words, which not only lets the young person know that they have been listened to, but also gives them the opportunity to clarify their meaning. Parents might begin with statements such as: 'It sounds like you're saying . . .'; 'I can see what you mean . . .'

Reflective listening is also useful to let children know that you empathise with their feelings. For example, if a child is crying, you might say, 'I can see you're really upset about that'; or if they are furious, you could say, 'I completely understand how angry you feel right now – I'd be angry too.' This helps normalise rather than demonise feelings, and for younger children, gives them labels for the strong emotions that can seem so overwhelming.

Separate the child from their behaviour

If a child's strong feelings accompany inappropriate actions (verbal or physical abuse, damage to property etc.) it is important to separate the child from their behaviour. When a child behaves inappropriately she hasn't become 'bad' – she's still the same child you loved before, it's just her behaviour that's 'bad'. This doesn't mean that you must accept or approve of the behaviour, just the child. When parents withhold love and attention from a child who is misbehaving, it can only increase the inappropriate behaviour.

So don't engage in character assassination. Remember: it's okay to be angry, but it's not okay to be nasty – and this goes for everyone in the family. It is always useful to remind an errant child, 'I love you; it's just your behaviour that I don't like.'

Encourage 'I' statements

Allow everyone to say how they feel without blame. This means taking responsibility for our feelings, and not claiming, 'You made me feel so angry', or 'She made me feel like crying.' No one can 'make' someone feel anything. We are all in charge of our own feelings. Model 'I' statements by saying, 'I felt really cross when you did that', or 'I felt really sad when you said you didn't want to come with me.'

Find solutions to the problem

To encourage acceptable behaviour, discuss alternatives ('How could you have handled this better?') or set consequences for that behaviour ('Since you have broken the window, it would be fair if you helped pay for it', or 'If you hit your brother again, your computer time will be cancelled for a week.') If you set consequences, you must always follow through. (See chapter 7 for more on setting boundaries and implementing consequences.)

MINIMISING CONFLICT WITH TEENS

The best strategy for minimising conflict with teens is to have a strong connection with them. This doesn't mean that you control their every move or that they display a fearful, cloying dependence. It simply means that you are able to talk to each other so that you can find a workable solution to whatever led to the conflict in the first place (see chapter 8 for more on communication and connection). Other strategies to minimise conflict are as follows:

Choose your battles

Don't argue over trivial things. No one has ever died from having an untidy room or wearing the same pair of underpants two days in a row, so be sure to choose your battles on the basis of whether the issue will impact on your child's health and safety.

De-escalate the situation

Great solutions to problems don't arise when we're feeling furious and frustrated, but when each party has cooled down and is ready to negotiate. Our IQ actually drops by about 30 per cent when we are angry, so we're working with a lot fewer tools in the toolbox. Your teenager relies on you to take the lead, so here's what to do:

1. State your feelings ('I'm getting upset; let's leave it and talk later.')
2. Listen attentively and get the facts ('I see what you mean . . .')
3. Acknowledge your teen's feelings, experience and point of view ('Let me see if I've understood. I think you're saying you feel . . .')
4. Be supportive ('Don't forget I'm on your side . . .')
5. Make it clear it's not about winning ('Let's finish the argument now, but I want you to have the last word.')

Be a mentor not a mate

Adults who are uncomfortable with the strong emotions of adolescence often go for sarcasm and teasing, which will usually shut down the very communication they are trying to open. If you like to use humour, make sure that it is upbeat and that you are actually funny! So be yourself, while maintaining a professional manner – adolescents expect adults to be an authority, but not authoritarian.

Avoid ultimatums

While it may be tempting to use the 'put-your-foot-down, no-negotiation' approach, or to deliver ultimatums – 'Do this or else!' – teenagers are especially sensitive to control, and will almost always reject an authoritarian approach.

Attack the problem, not the person

Don't accuse, insult or talk down to your teenager, and be conscious of your tone of voice, facial expression, demeanour and body language.

When tempers flare, old resentments are often dragged onto the bonfire. Use reflective listening to keep your teenager focused on the problem at hand, and the need for you both to work together to find a solution.

Be on the same page as your partner

The proper approach, especially with a teenager, is to always give the impression that everyone involved in the conflict is on the same page, whether the parties are in complete and total disagreement or not. Save your parenting debates for pillow talk! A common source of disagreement that parents argue over is at what age their teenage daughter can have someone sleep over. Dads often have the view this will never happen while they have breath in their body, while mothers may have a more liberal view. The child needs to believe everyone is in agreement because if they can find the smallest loophole in any situation, they will by nature exploit it. United you stand. Divided you are cactus.

HANDLING SIBLING RIVALRY

So far we've talked about how to manage anger that flares between parents and children, but what about when the clashes occur between your kids?

Siblings don't choose the family they are born into, and they don't choose each other. They may be of different sexes, are probably of different ages and temperaments, and worst of all, they have to share the one person or the two people they most want for themselves: their parents. Add in any extra members if you have a step-family or live with your extended family and you have a volatile mix.

The two most common faux pas any parent makes in managing conflict between kids are firstly choosing sides and secondly ignoring appropriate behaviour (i.e. forgetting to praise children when they are communicating well, cooperating or 'playing nicely'). It is axiomatic that behaviours that are ignored (go unrewarded) decrease, while behaviours that receive attention (are rewarded) increase.

Remember, as kids cope with disputes, they also learn important skills that will serve them for life, such as how to value another person's perspective, how to compromise and negotiate, and how to control aggressive impulses.

Step back

When possible, let the young people settle their own differences. Allowing children to solve their own problems is great for building resilience, which sounds good in theory, but can be terribly unfair in practice. The adults have to judge when it is time to step in and play UN peacekeeper, which is usually recommended in cases where a contest is unequal in terms of strength or eloquence (hitting below the belt literally or figuratively). Also step in if there's a danger of physical harm.

Encourage time out

Separate the young people until they're calm. Sometimes it's best just to give them space for half an hour or so. If you try to go over the conflict too soon, the fight can spark and intensify again. If you want to make this a learning experience, wait until the emotions have abated.

Avoid blame

It takes two people to fight – anyone who is involved is partly responsible, so don't put too much focus on figuring out which child is to blame.

RECOGNISING WHEN A CHILD NEEDS HELP WITH ANGER

Sometimes, conflict and resentment can go on for so long in a family that its members struggle to say a single civil word to each other. This is often the case if one parent has an untreated mental illness, or if the family is blended and an adolescent's resentment towards a step-parent morphs into murderous rage. Whatever the situation, when children don't feel safe expressing their uncomfortable feelings, they will try hard to repress them, but as we know, repressed feelings have a way of leaping out and surprising everyone, especially the child. Such children may fend off this reservoir of fear, grief or other pain by getting angry and staying angry. When this happens, a child needs professional help. Signs that your child may need professional help include the following:

- has frequent explosive outbursts
- is unable to control aggressive impulses and hits people when aged five or older
- is in constant conflict with others, frequently losing friends and alienating adults
- is preoccupied with revenge and hatred of self or others
- harms self or damages property
- hurts smaller children or animals.

A child with anger management issues is using rage to defend against feeling fear, pain and grief. Therapeutic intervention can help the child work through those feelings and develop the ability to manage all emotions.

TO LOOK LIKE THAT I'LL NEED COSMETIC SURGERY
NO, JUST AN AIRBRUSH AND WHITEOUT
TANDBERG

Chapter 11

See the Glass as Half-full

This strategy is not about what you knowingly provide for your children – what you do for them, how you treat them – it's more fundamental than that. It's the approach you take to the whole box and dice of living, loving and parenting, and has a huge, if imperceptible, influence on your kids. If you are the kind of person who sees the good in a situation, your children will too. If you show empathy for others, your children will too. If you maintain a realistic yet playful approach to your problems, so will they. However, if you're walking around under your own personal thundercloud, it makes it so much harder to implement any of the other strategies I've talked about earlier.

I was at a conference recently where I was fortunate enough to speak with Dr Martin Seligman, widely regarded as the father of positive psychology. He's been researching happiness and optimism for more than four decades and says that if we could help children challenge negative self-talk as soon as they first learn to string sentences together, we could halve the rates of depression.

Self-talk is the endless stream of thinking that goes on in our heads, mostly without us even being aware of it. Studies show that virtually *none* of it is useful or creative and, unfortunately, for an increasing number of people, it is relentlessly negative. You know the kind of thinking I mean: 'That's too hard', 'I'll never be able to do that', 'I'll stuff it up', 'Bad things always happen to me.'

Psychologists have long known that an optimistic point of view is a distinct advantage when it comes to happiness and wellbeing. Optimism is also correlated with excellent mental and physical health and success in personal relationships, business and education. When optimists experience a challenge or setback, they think of it as a temporary situation which is unlikely to happen again and about which they can do something. A pessimistic person, on the other hand, tends to view a setback as a situation that's likely to continue, is going to have a terrible roll-on effect into other areas of their life and that there's nothing they can do about it.

Seligman says that human beings have tended to dwell on the possibility of negative events for survival reasons – how would we have avoided dangerous situations or predators if we were busy smiling at the beauty of the clouds or the colour of the sky? Other research has focused on how our early experiences (attachment problems, abuse) may hardwire our brains to become acutely sensitive to stress so that we are prone to think negatively and develop anxiety, depression and other emotional disturbances.

Whatever the cause, if you or your child are prone to seeing the glass as half-empty, the great news is that you can learn how to develop a more positive outlook by changing your self-talk – that endless inner chatterbox who comments on the minutiae of daily life. Helping people change their self-talk is part of what I do but there are also great websites such as MoodGym, ReachOut and eCouch and fabulous smart-phone apps like MoodKit and iCBT that can help as well.

Here's what I recommend for developing a more positive outlook for yourself and your children.

FOCUS ON THE GOOD STUFF

When you are yakking around the dinner table, instead of taking this opportunity to whinge about the seven types of crap that happened to you today, talk about the good things. By default, the human brain tends to ignore what goes well and focuses instead on what might go wrong. Given the media adage 'if it bleeds, it leads', we are daily bombarded by local and international reports of death, suffering and mayhem. Even our movies and TV shows have grim themes (violence, incest, rape, murder and serial killing). Terrible things do happen, and while our survival depends on our awareness of such things, our *sanity* depends on being able to focus our attention on the myriad small, joyful things that together make a happy life.

To help us focus on these we can use an old technique that used to be called 'counting your blessings'. It simply means we share three things that went well or felt good that day. They don't have to be earth shattering: patting a dog on the way home from school; finishing a difficult test; serving well in a game of tennis (even if we lost the match). This redirects our attention towards the positive.

I'm a big fan of the Happy Rambles website, where children keep an online journal of things they are grateful for. This becomes a virtual record of the many life situations that make them happy, and research shows that revisiting them from time to time creates an 'upward spiral', helping to build a more positive outlook.

DO ONE KIND THING A DAY

Henry James once said, 'Three things in human life are important. The first is to be kind. The second is to be kind. The third is to be kind.' Human beings are hardwired to be kind and helpful as this helps to create deep connections with others and ensures the survival of our species. Countless studies show that giving connects us to others, increases life satisfaction, provides a sense of meaning, increases feelings of competence, improves mood and reduces stress. Kindness creates stronger communities and helps build a happier society for everyone. And it's not all about money – we love giving time, ideas and energy, too.

People used to talk about the 'helper's high' and scientific studies show that helping others activates the areas of the brain associated with pleasure, social connection and trust. In his book *Why Kindness is Good for You*, David Hamilton details the scientific evidence that proves that kindness changes the brain, impacts the heart and immune system, and may even be an antidote to depression. When we're kind, our bodies are healthiest. Kindness and caring also seem to be contagious. When we see someone do something kind or thoughtful, or we are on the receiving end of kindness, it inspires us to be kinder. In this way, kindness spreads from one person to the next, influencing the behaviour of people who never saw the original act. So do one kind thing a day, and encourage your children to do this, too. Kindness appears to be contagious, according to a study done by researchers at the University of California, Los Angeles, the University of Cambridge and the University of Plymouth in the United Kingdom. The study found that when we see someone else help another person it gives us a good feeling, which in turn causes us to go out and do something altruistic ourselves. This study was the first of its kind to systematically document this tendency in human nature. Researchers performed two experiments in which they showed viewers a nature documentary, a funny TV clip or an uplifting segment from the *Oprah Winfrey Show*, and then asked them to voluntarily help with another task. In both cases, participants who watched the *Oprah Winfrey Show*, and subsequently experienced the elevated feeling, were more likely to help.

Like all positive parenting strategies, kids will learn more by watching you be kind. Acts of kindness don't need to be massive to make a difference, they can be as simple as opening a door for someone, making your partner a cup of tea, or offering to help out at your local school.

HANG OUT WITH HAPPY PEOPLE

Positive psychology research shows that people who have close, positive relationships with their family and friends are not only happier but also healthier. Not having close personal ties poses the same level of health risk as smoking or obesity. A network of social connections or high levels of social support increases our immunity to infection, lowers our risk of heart disease and reduces mental decline as we get older. The late Professor Chris Peterson, one of the founders of positive psychology puts it simply: 'Other people matter.'

However, the research also shows that to be truly transformative, the *quality* of our relationships is very important. We need to experience lots of positive emotions together, to be able to talk openly and feel understood, to take turns giving and receiving support, and to share activities and experiences. We all know people who have completely toxic and destructive relationships fuelled by anger, resentment and fear. That's not the kind of connection I'm talking about here. If you feel trapped in a relationship like that (whether it is with your partner, family or friends), it is important to seek help.

One of the greatest gifts we can give our children is to show them how to connect with others and maintain friendships. We can tell them that a friendship is a bit like a garden: sometimes it needs to be watered, sometimes it needs fertiliser and sometimes it needs to be left to lie fallow for a while.

Close friendships provide a sense of belonging, which is closely related to resilience, that capacity we all long for in our children, to be able to face, overcome and be transformed by adversity.

Having a strong network of friends is a great way to inoculate our kids from loneliness later in life. A large meta study carried out by researchers at Brigham Young University, which reviewed 148 studies involving a staggering 308,849 people, found that loneliness is just as detrimental to health as not exercising, smoking fifteen cigarettes a day, and alcoholism, and more than twice as bad as being obese.

Still more astonishing is a *Journal of Clinical Oncology* study from 2010 that examined 2230 cancer patients in China. Social wellbeing, including friendship, turned out to be the number one predictor of survival. There is no doubt that some of this derives from the fact that socially isolated people tend to exercise less, eat crap and imbibe of the grape way too much, but some researchers believe that loneliness has a negative health impact all of its own.

LISTEN FOR SUBTEXT

The idea that thoughts influence emotions (and that positive thoughts can create happiness) is as old as Socrates, but I'm always surprised when people don't make the connection between what goes on in their heads and how they are feeling.

To help our kids become more aware of the relationship between negative thoughts and negative feelings, we first have to help them pay attention to the subtext in their conversations. For example, when a child is distressed (tearful, angry, flat, unmotivated, frustrated), they might say any of the following:

'Why does this always happen to me?'
'I won't make any friends at this new school.'
'No one is going to like me.'
'Everyone thinks I'm stupid.'
'I always mess things up.'
'I always make mistakes.'
'Everybody hates me.'
'I'm never going to get a girlfriend.'

Each of these comments is an example of the pessimistic (or catastrophic) thinking that underlies the feelings – the expectation that bad things will always happen, no matter where we are or what we do, and there is nothing we can do about it.

Martin Seligman, the trailblazing researcher on optimism, says we can teach children how to be optimistic. The trick is to remember that we can perceive a setback any way we choose. As William Shakespeare said: 'There is nothing either good or bad but thinking makes it so.'

The first step, then, is to help them to become aware of the thinking patterns that trigger distress and to challenge them. For example:

- 'Are you thinking this way because you are feeling bad right now?'
- 'Could you be feeling this way because of the way you are looking at the situation?'

- 'What are some of the good things about this situation?'
- 'What other explanations might there be for what happened?'
- 'What evidence have you got that these people are thinking badly of you?'
- 'Can you really know that this is true?'
- 'What could you do next time this happens?'

The key is for children to see that they are not powerless in the face of setbacks – *they get to choose how to think about them*, and this changes how they feel. However, when children are overwhelmed by negative feelings, it can be quite difficult to think rationally. In these situations, they need to first accept that they are having these feelings. The harder we fight something, the stronger it gets (what we resist, persists). That's when mindfulness can help.

PRACTISE MINDFULNESS

You may have heard of mindfulness in the context of meditation, where we learn to sit with our thoughts and feelings, not judging or getting caught up in them, but just allowing them to come and go. The goal is to draw our attention *away* from thinking. This may sound counterintuitive, but studies show that quietening the mind actually helps people to learn more effectively, think more clearly and perform better. It also helps us feel calmer, less anxious and less depressed.

Some people practise mindfulness by drawing their attention into their bodies – becoming aware of their breathing or other sensations in the body while they do everyday things like walking and eating. Others expand their attention to the world outside their bodies, listening to a bird, watching a leaf fall, noticing shapes, colours and textures around them. Some people like to set aside a time to do this every day (like a meditation) and others do it to particular cues, such as when hanging out the washing, while waiting at traffic lights or when they first sit down at their computer.

Like meditation, mindfulness can have profound effects and more and more doctors and psychologists are referring clients to mindfulness courses to reduce stress and help prevent depression. It is now recommended by the UK National Institute of Health and Care Excellence and is increasingly used in business to improve staff health and satisfaction; in sports training to improve performance; and with children and young people in schools to enhance wellbeing.

Make sure you practise it yourself first before you talk about it with your kids. Download the free Smiling Mind app at smilingmind.com.au.

TANDBERG
MY CHILD HAS SO MUCH IN COMMON WITH PICASSO AND EINSTEIN

Chapter 12

Stick To Routines

If your household is completely out of control, how can you expect your children's behaviour to be anything but out of control?

I know it sounds obvious and even a bit dull, but there's a mountain of research to show that kids who have a stable home life with predictable routines around sleeping, eating and bathing are far more likely to become happy, healthy adults. While kids may whinge about these routines, they nevertheless find them comforting. Life is always going to throw curve balls, so having that consistency helps them to feel secure enough to cope. If your household is completely out of control, how can you expect your children's behaviour to be anything *but* out of control?

A 2013 study of more than ten thousand children in London found that kids with erratic bedtimes were more likely to have behavioural, social and emotional problems. Children aged 5–7 whose bedtimes were irregular or who went to bed after 9 p.m. were likely to come from more socially disadvantaged backgrounds. They were also more likely to have poor routines such as skipping breakfast, not being read to daily, having a television in their bedroom and spending longer in front of a TV than children with earlier bedtimes.

Another study in the US found that small changes in household routines, such as limiting TV time and increasing sleep time, helped to minimise excess weight gain in young children at high risk of obesity.

If you've had routines in place since your kids were small, they will still no doubt complain about having to go to bed, having a shower or turning off the computer, but they will not have the major meltdowns typical of kids who are not used to routines. Even adolescents need to feel secure at home before they can take steps into the wider world.

But having routines doesn't mean boot camp. Over-controlling parents who run a tight ship will create just as many problems for children as those who abandon ship and let the kids mutiny. Over-controlled children may become withdrawn and anxious, constantly fearful that they might do something wrong. Or they may become defiant and oppositional because they feel so angry and resentful towards the parent. However, any conflict is the *adult's* responsibility. It is our job to avoid battles. We do this by setting expectations and guiding, nurturing and prompting children to meet them – not bullying our kids into 'obedience' and 'total compliance'. Another way to look at this is that expectations, routines and rules are there for *mutual* benefit.

SLEEP

Sleep is a biological necessity, as important as food and water. Deprived of it, adults are not only accident-prone but have, among other things, high cholesterol, obesity, poor immune function and depression. Yet many of us treat it as an optional extra – going to bed late, taking our digital devices into our bedrooms and drinking alcohol or coffee before bed. These are all habits that interfere with healthy sleep, and while we might try to set good sleep routines for our kids, we mustn't forget that they are also learning by watching what we do.

Like adults, sleep-deprived children are more accident-prone and more likely to get sick, but they are also irritable, fidgety and have trouble concentrating or remembering information, which has obvious implications for learning.

So how much sleep do children need? Sleep requirements vary from one child to another, depending on physical activity levels, general health and individual metabolic factors. However, the following is a rough guide:

- Toddlers (1–3 years) 12–14 hours
- Pre-schoolers (4–5 years) 10–12 hours
- School children (6–12 years) 9–10 hours
- Teenagers (13–19 years) 8–10 hours

Teen sleep

It's 8.30 a.m. and we are standing outside a typical school in a typical suburb in an Australian city. As students emerge from cars, buses, trains or trams we see many pale, sleepy faces – much eye-rubbing, yawning and thousand-yard stares. Within half an hour some of these young people will be completely zonked out, heads on desks, fast asleep, while others will be zoned out, oblivious to the learning going on around them.

Why is this happening? In all of us, 'sleep pressure' (the internal feeling of 'sleepiness') builds with each passing hour of wakefulness, and dissipates when we go to sleep. This sleep pressure is regulated by our 'sleep/wake homeostat' (a bunch of chemicals in our brains), and researchers suspect that during puberty, hormonal changes cause a shift in a teenager's sleep-wake cycle. The build-up of 'sleep pressure' takes longer so bedtimes (and waking times) get later, a trend that continues until 19.5 years in women and 21 in men before it slowly reverses. Unfortunately, early school start times mean our teenagers are constantly sleep-deprived (a 7 a.m. wakeup call for a teenager is like a 5 a.m. wakeup call for a 55-year-old adult!), impacting on their physical health, mood and cognitive ability. Some teens are using caffeinated energy drinks to compensate for sleep loss, which is only adding to the problem, as the half-life of caffeine is 5–9 hours.

Bedtime routines

Studies show that increasing your child's sleep by as little as half an hour each night can dramatically improve school performance. So make sleep a priority: set limits and boundaries around bedtime from an early age, and encourage your children to develop good sleep habits.

Winding-down routines for kids aged 6–12

- Try turning off the TV just before dinner and leaving it off. This creates space for some family time or for children to have a quiet play before bed.
- Have a set time for washing/bathing and getting into pyjamas.
- Read with your child, or for older children, encourage them to read in bed.
- Make sure there are no TVs, computers, electronic games or phones in your children's bedrooms.
- Bedrooms should not be too warm, and need to be dark. If your children need a night-light, make sure it has a very low wattage, and regularly check with them if they still need it on.

Winding-down routines for teens

- One hour before bed, encourage your teen to stop homework, computer games or any other activity that gets their mind racing.
- Suggest your teen have a shower and a hot milky drink (or herbal tea) to help them relax.
- Get them to charge laptops, phones and other devices in the living room (so their rooms are free of electronic distraction).
- Turn on a lamp in their room for them to read for a while.
- Make sure their room is dark and not too warm.
- In the morning, open blinds and curtains and flood the room with daylight as it helps wake up the brain and reset the circadian clock.

To improve your child's sleep, the sleep boffins suggest that we follow the same bedtime routine every night for at least four weeks. After that, we should begin the routine 10 minutes earlier for one week at a time, until they are getting enough sleep (i.e. they are waking up refreshed).

HYGIENE

For younger children (and especially babies and toddlers) bath time can be a soothing and relaxing way to wind down at the end of the day. By the time children are in primary school, they should be starting to manage their personal hygiene without having to be reminded every day. This means remembering to clean their teeth after breakfast and dinner, washing their hands after the loo and before meals etc.

As for bathing, routines depend on the age of your kids, your cultural practices and whether your house has a bath or a shower – every family is different. If a daily bath has been the norm, children often see it as a rite of passage to start having showers like Mum or Dad.

As teenagers enter adulthood, it is important to teach them about proper hygiene, which, if practised, can help maintain teen health and help them to develop positive habits they will follow for the rest of their lives.

As most parents will tell you, teenage boys tend to emit a very strong smell – due in part to the hormones they secrete in their sweat. They also develop more sweat glands, particularly apocrine sweat glands that are located under the arms and in the genital area. Bacteria feast on apocrine sweat and the decaying bacteria cause this rather unique pong. Using an antibacterial body wash might help, along with daily (at least) showers.

Parents often make the assumption that their adolescents will somehow magically learn what they need to know about hygiene, but unfortunately this is not the case – someone has to put their arm up (no pun intended). If parents squib this responsibility, their teenager may not only be more prone to developing rashes and infections, but also (and more importantly) their son or daughter may face serious social consequences. It is social death to become known at school for being smelly.

Showering

Most primary school kids don't wash or shower every day, unless they play sport, but once the puberty fairy visits, daily showering is as essential as cleaning their teeth. Advocate that they use a mild soap and concentrate on the face, hands, feet, underarms, groin and bottom. Scrubbing under the fingernails is important, too.

Washing hair

Some teens may prefer to shower daily, but wash their hair on alternate days (especially if they have long, thick or dry hair). Others may want to wash their hair daily, particularly if they have oily hair, which otherwise can look greasy and aggravate acne.

Using deodorant

At puberty, glands become more active and the chemical composition of the sweat changes, causing it to smell stronger. When you first notice it, take them to buy their own deodorant (they're much more likely to use it if they have chosen a scent they like). Encourage them to use it daily.

Changing clothes

Before puberty, your child may well have been able to wear the same shirt (or even the same underwear and socks) for several days (!) without anyone noticing. After puberty, that won't wash (ha ha). Encourage your teen to understand that along with showering, wearing clean clothes each day is an important part of their hygiene routine.

Preventing acne

At around the age of 10, encourage your children to wash their face morning and night. Although they may not have any acne at that age, daily face washing is an important habit for kids to have in their teens.

Shaving and hair removal

When you notice hair on your son's upper lip, you can offer a brief course on razor use. Whether or not he wants to shave yet, at least you've provided the information. As for young women shaving their legs and underarms, that's a personal decision. If your daughter has fine, fair hair on her legs, try to discourage her from shaving – tell her she'll be able to afford an overseas holiday in her forties using the money she saves on razors, waxing and other hair-removal hoo-hah.

Maintaining good oral health

Start good habits early, with twice-daily brushing and regular flossing. Make sure you take your children for dental checkups every six months (or twelve months if money is tight). Teens can get pretty lax about their oral hygiene (though that may change when they start kissing!), so keep encouraging them to brush and floss daily.

FOOD

The most important routine around food is to eat regularly as a family. Research in the US has found that sharing meals is correlated with a stack of positive outcomes for kids, including doing well in school, delaying intercourse until after the age of consent, eating vegetables, learning big words and knowing which fork to use. The same research found that children in families who rarely ate together were more likely to smoke cigarettes, drink alcohol, do drugs, get depressed, develop eating disorders and contemplate suicide. Of course, this isn't a cause-and-effect relationship, it's just that parents who eat with their kids give them the opportunity to develop a raft of social and emotional skills. Children learn how to listen and how to express themselves. Even arguments about who isn't eating or who wants to talk first allow children to practise waiting their turn and dealing with frustration, anger and conflict in a safe environment.

Healthy eating habits

For many parents, battles over food – especially eating vegetables, fruits and other healthy foods – are a major headache. Here are some effective way to avoid stress and arguments over food:

- Have regular mealtimes.
- From the time they are toddlers, always serve children a portion of everything others are eating.
- Ensure that healthy food is always on the menu. Children whose palates have been compromised by salty/sugary processed food (e.g. smothering everything in tomato sauce) are more likely to develop weight problems.
- Never use threats, guilt or bribery to get children to eat healthy foods. Emotional battles over food almost always exacerbate eating issues, and can prolong them for months or years.
- Make sure 'treats' are available at other times of the day rather than as a reward for eating dinner. (That's right. Say goodbye to dessert as a reward for eating veggies. Your children will have fewer issues with eating, and better health.)
- Involve children in the preparation and/or serving of a meal – it is a great way to encourage their commitment to eating it!

Allergies

Food allergies are a fact of life for many families and can be stressful for both parents and children. Allergies to peanuts, eggs, gluten, food additives and lactose are common, with some children experiencing severe reactions including rashes, breathing problems and anaphylactic shock. Other children have milder reactions that nevertheless affect behaviour, such as irritability, anxiety, fatigue or hyperactivity.

Food allergies are a common cause of unexplained, consistent misbehaviour. If you suspect that your child is reacting to certain foods, follow this up with your doctor as soon as possible.

Preparing meals

Encouraging kids to prepare their own meals has enormous benefits for their developing sense of competence and independence. Young children can start by helping to make their own breakfast (pouring the cereal, spreading the toast), packing their own lunchbox and helping set the table for dinner. Serving evening meals that the children can assemble themselves (such as tacos, wraps or burgers) is also a great idea. As they get older they can graduate to pouring liquids, cutting and peeling fruit and vegetables, measuring and so on. If they show an interest in preparing a meal by themselves and you know they have the skills, let them do it, but stay nearby to offer help if they need it. Cooking is very educational as children need to use their maths and language skills to follow recipes, measure accurately, understand cooking terms and learn about different foods. Preparing food for family and friends also gives them a sense of accomplishment. But best of all, cooking promotes smart food choices, as the research says that children and teens who help prepare food are more likely to taste the food.

Teenagers must learn how to cook for themselves using wholefoods – fresh meat, vegetables, spices and herbs – not just pre-packed foods in boxes or jars. Schools are doing what they can to educate kids to make better food choices, but they are pushing poo uphill if our kids get home to Maccas three nights a week. It's our job as parents to help our kids develop healthy eating habits. And we desperately need to do something to reverse our national weight gain and its rampant side effects, which show up in the form of mostly preventable, but ultimately debilitating, diseases. In the last twenty minutes, four Aussies have died because of what they eat. On the basis of present trends we can predict that by the time our kids are 21, they'll have a shorter life expectancy than earlier generations simply because of obesity.

Teaching your teen to cook does not mean they have to be master chefs, but they do need to know how to shop astutely, how to prepare wholefoods and how to reuse leftovers without poisoning their flatmates. Plus, they'll need a collection of favourite recipes. It's a good idea for teenagers to be in charge of cooking at least one meal a week.

AFTER-SCHOOL ACTIVITIES

In planning what children do after school, parents need to distinguish their own needs from those of their children. Some confuse the two, and that is the single most common cause of over-scheduling (rushing children from one lesson to the next so they are constantly knackered and never get a moment to muck about and just be kids).

Sometimes children will ask to do things after school because they have a genuine interest in the activity, while others want to be with friends. That's fine. But if *you* suggest an activity, and your child decides to try it, keep an eye on her. If she gives it a red-hot go but is not enjoying herself and is resistant, back off. She may decide to try it again later, or may need to try something else. This is not about you, it is about your child finding joy and flow in something outside of school, whether that be playing soccer, squad swimming, learning the didgeridoo or taking origami lessons.

Generally speaking, most children aged 5–6 should only be doing one activity a week (school is enough of a shock to the system without needing to load them up with extra commitments). As they get older they can add another activity, though that depends, of course, on the individual child and the family's resources.

In the last few years, some have argued that childhood has moved indoors, and this may be one reason parents are keen to encourage their children to do a regular sporting or outdoor activity after school. Children need help to regulate time spent on computers, smart phones, tablets etc., which means parents must set limits. We also need to encourage a balance between screen time and other activities that use more of our senses: sport, art, music, drama or just generally being socially engaged with parents and other children.

For children in the early primary years, transitions between school and other activities can be a challenge, and they may need a warning or a reminder. For example, parents can use the five- or ten-minute signal for leaving a venue: 'We're going in five minutes.' Always allow more time than you expect for transitions, especially for 5- to 7-year-olds. Even getting dressed or getting in and out of a car can take a bit longer than you might think. Children have a very different sense of time and it's important not to expect them always to be able to move smoothly from one activity or situation to the next.

FAMILY RITUALS

Some families I work with spend most of their free time either rushing from place to place or preparing for the *next* day of rushing (school sport, swimming, after-school tutoring, dance classes or music lessons). In these families, there is no such thing as 'family time', and that may be one reason they end up needing family therapy.

The busier our lives, the more important it is to make sure we schedule time to get together as a family unit, to debrief and regroup. Such traditions help communicate 'this is who we are' and bestow upon families an all-important sense of belonging. The traditional Sunday roast (or barbecue), the Friday night football, the Saturday night movie are all ways to reconnect as a family. Religious and cultural rituals are important for some families and for others simply gathering around to eat a meal together is enough of a daily ritual to strengthen family bonds. Others might be:

- playing a ball game or backyard cricket together
- showing home movies from when the kids were babies
- having a meal at a pub, cafe or restaurant together
- getting out old photo albums and encouraging the kids to ask about the rellies
- taking a family holiday together.

YOU'LL BE LUCKY IF YOUR FATHER GIVES YOU ANY QUALITY TIME
BECAUSE HE NEVER GAVE ME ANY!
TANDBERG

Chapter 13

Get a Life

Parenting is not meant
to be an exercise in martyrdom.

In the first weeks and months of parenthood we can become so completely overwhelmed by the needs of the new baby that everything else in our lives (work, marriage, friendships, hobbies) comes a distant second. And this is all fine, and sometimes even necessary, as we learn to get in tune with our baby's needs – to understand when she's hungry, when she's tired or when she just needs to be held. Recent research, however, suggests that in the first six months or so, new mums and dads need to get out and about with their babies as much as they can – taking the baby along with them to the gym, to the movies, to sports practice or wherever, and offering feeds whenever the baby seems hungry or stressed. If we think of our babies as needing to fit in to our lives rather than the other way around, life becomes easier for everyone.

LOOK AFTER YOUR RELATIONSHIP

Half of all new parents say that they have less time to talk with their partner after the baby is born, and many experience conflict. For some, relationship issues predate their decision to have children, and the arrival of offspring becomes the straw that breaks the camel's back. Indeed, ABS statistics from 2009 report that the median duration of marriage in Australia is 8.7 years.

Putting effort into your relationship is crucial for many reasons. It shows your kids what a healthy relationship looks like, which means they are more likely to have a healthy relationship themselves when they reach adulthood. It also means that you and your partner are going to be on the same page when it comes to setting boundaries, which is actually easier for everyone. It may sound counterintuitive, but when parents present a united front, it gives children a sense of security, and helps them to 'know their place' (i.e. that you are the parents and they are the kids). Of course, you and your spouse aren't going to agree on every minute detail, so when you do have to discuss an issue, it's good for the kids to see you do it in a way that is respectful, or if you lose your tempers, that you can apologise to each other, get over it and reach a compromise.

Playing good cop, bad cop (where one parent stands firm but the other caves in) is toxic. Kids will always sniff out inconsistencies between parents and hone in on them like a missile to exploit loopholes and play you off against each other. Smart parenting is about never giving them the opening. For instance, if your beloved makes a snap decision about setting a limit with the kids, you must support that decision no matter how ludicrous it sounds. Later, when you are alone, you should discuss the decision with your partner, explaining your thoughts and feelings, and come to some agreement about handling the same situation in the future. As much as possible, avoid having one person make independent decisions. If, for example, you think that your kids shouldn't play video games on school nights but your partner feels that it's okay after homework is done, you should discuss this first, and come to a compromise of, say, two nights a week.

If it makes you feel any better, I have never met two parents who have taken an identical approach to running a household, hanging with the kids, resolving conflict or granting privileges. However, when it comes to setting limits on their children's behaviour, particularly those that relate to safety and wellbeing, I always encourage them to reach a compromise and maintain consistency.

Reaching a compromise is easier when you have a strong connection with your partner, but maintaining that connection takes effort. Research shows that your family's wellbeing is contingent on the strength of the marital bond. Here are some ideas for keeping your relationship strong:

1. Spend at least twenty minutes a day in dialogue with your partner. For some couples, their only down time is after the kids are in bed. Try to turn the TV off so you can talk (and one of you doesn't fall asleep). Even if you have to do chores together (cooking or washing up), it doesn't matter – as long as you are connecting with each other.
2. Focus on your partner's positive qualities; reflect on what first attracted you to each other. Take time to remember positive experiences you shared; tell the kids how you met; show them photos of your lives before their arrival.
3. For every negative comment or behaviour towards your partner, make sure that there are at least *five* positive ones. This is the magic ratio that Robert Gottman found in his studies of happy couples. Simple things like making your partner a cuppa, stroking their shoulder as you walk by, thanking them for something they've done.
4. Ask each other out for a date *at least* once a month, and it has to be just the two of you. An old-fashioned movie night, or a dinner, or meeting for lunch near your workplace – whatever floats your mutual boat. Put it on your phone calendar, put it in digital stone, and unless the world is ending don't change it for any other event.

LOOK AFTER YOURSELF

For many parents, finding time for themselves after they have kids is way down their list of priorities. Not only do they rarely get to see each other as a couple, but their own interests can take a back seat to the needs of their children. This is ultimately unhealthy for the whole family. Parenting is not meant to be an exercise in martyrdom. The more we allow ourselves time to recharge our batteries, the more emotional and physical energy we'll have for our children. A great way to think about this is the 'eggs in the basket' test. Imagine you have thirty eggs and each one represents a unit of your life. Imagine then that you have three baskets in front of you. One is your 'Self' basket; one is for 'Family' and the other is for 'Work'. How are you currently distributing your eggs? Most parents say that the ratio is five for Self, ten for Family and fifteen for Work (or for those who don't work and take care of the kids, it would be five for Self and twenty-five for Family).

Either combination is unhealthy for you psychologically. Believe it or not, the optimal distribution is for you to put fifteen eggs in the Self basket, ten into Family and five into Work. The rationale for this is that if you invest in your own wellbeing, the ten eggs that you place in the Family basket will be double-yolkers and the five that you invest in Work will be solid gold.

So how do you invest fifteen eggs in your own basket? Meet your needs for sleep, exercise, nutrition and companionship.

Get enough rest

In chapter 12, I talked about the importance of creating routines around bedtime so that your children develop healthy sleep habits. The same applies to you. You may think you can survive on five hours a night, but it will be at great expense not only to your emotional and cognitive functioning, but your physical health. When you're sleep-deprived, your metabolism slows down to try to conserve energy so that you can get through the much longer day, and that slow-down in turn triggers cortisol which, among other things, boosts your appetite. Lack of sleep also leads to lower levels of leptin (the hormone that tells your body you're full) in the brain, leaving you susceptible to overeating. This is the sleep–weight gain connection.

The following tips give you the best chance of having a restful night's sleep:

- Go to bed at around the same time every night.
- Avoid nicotine, caffeine and alcohol for several hours before sleep (or, better still, altogether).
- Follow a relaxing bedtime ritual an hour before you sleep (which might include bathing, reading, herbal tea or hot milk etc.).
- Ensure your room is dark and cool (not too cold).
- Get up at the same time every morning and let in lots of light to help reset your body clock.
- If your partner snores and refuses to get help, use earplugs or move into another room.

Eat real food

This is one of the kindest things you can do for yourself. Healthy eating, along with exercising and sleeping well, is one of the biggest antidepressants going around (especially if you do all three with other people). You have more energy, more patience, sharper thinking and will be at your best for raising happy, healthy kids.

By 'real' food I mean fresh wholefoods such as vegetables, fruit, unprocessed grains, nuts, seeds, eggs, milk and meat. The more you keep away from processed stuff in boxes, packets or tins the better. This means you have to cook – a lot – because even the best restaurants load everything with fats, salt and sugar to keep the customers happy. Your plate needs to be 50 per cent vegetable (you heard me!), 25 per cent protein and 25 per cent grains. There's nothing wrong with the occasional takeaway or restaurant meal, but keep your snacks (and your children's) as healthy as you can (fruit, nuts, yoghurt).

Stay connected with others

After you've had children, friendships wax and wane and this is normal. If you aren't working, it's really important to regularly catch up with friends and family. Even better, join a committee at your child's kindergarten or childcare centre, work in the school canteen, or help out with the annual fete or school concert. Or you could join a gym or sports club, or enrol in some yoga, music, dance or art classes. All of these activities get you out of the house and keep you connected with your wider community, reminding you that you are not only a parent, but also an individual who has interests, ideas and talents to contribute.

Accept help

Don't play the martyr – take up offers of babysitting from friends or family so that you can go out with your partner. And if you are overwhelmed by household chores, and it's stressing you out, pay a cleaner or a gardener. Anything that makes you a more relaxed parent is good for your kids. However, if you are finding parenting unbearably stressful, and either you or your child are not coping, see your doctor. (See chapter 5 for more about signs of depression.)

Ditch the idea of perfection

Despite what you may have read in magazines, there is no such thing as a perfect parent. I know that sounds depressing, but the truth will set you free. Many of us have elaborate fantasies about parenthood, which combine the finest aspects of *The Addams Family*, *The Brady Bunch* and *My Three Sons* with a dash of *Nanny McPhee*. Anyone who pictures parenting as a rom-com full of sparklingly clean, obedient children who accompany you on photogenic family trips to the beach while you write the next great Australian novel on your laptop needs to wake up and smell the coffee. Hang on, there isn't any freshly brewed coffee because you haven't got time to make it in between two loads of washing, feeding the dog, making three lots of school lunches and driving your kids to childcare, kinder and primary school in three different places. I'm not saying parenting isn't filled with wonder, joy and transcendent love, but there's plenty of hard work and heartbreak in between. So give yourself the same support and encouragement that you give to your kids. Tell yourself you've made a big effort, or done a good job, because you have – you are raising human beings, and they will be okay.

IT'S NICE TO FEEL SECURE IN YOUR OWN HOME
TANDBERG

PART 3

AN A TO Z OF PARENTING STUFF

In this section, I want to tackle an A to Z of common issues facing parents and young people today. Each topic is introduced with a 'dear doctor' letter that I have composed from my own experience as a parent; my thirty years in clinical practice; the research I have undertaken in my role as Channel 7's *Sunrise* parenting expert; and the questions I have answered as agony uncle for *New Idea* and *Girlfriend* magazines.

When I first accepted the offer to write the advice column for *Girlfriend* way back in 2003, I copped quite a bit of flack from some of my colleagues. Yet I regarded this – and still do – as an exceptional opportunity to keep myself anchored in the real world, hearing from young women each month as they struggle with the vicissitudes of teenage life. On a personal level, some may consider it a disadvantage to have an encyclopaedic knowledge of Justin Bieber, 5 Seconds of Summer and One Direction, but on a professional level, I am constantly challenged by the psychological, moral, ethical and legal dilemmas that our readers sometimes present. After all, what do you say to a 14-year-old who comes home early and finds her mother in bed with a neighbour? Not to mention the 15-year-old who finds her father watching teen porn?

Of course, the list of parenting concerns in this section is by no means complete – no publisher would take on such a gargantuan tome – but if you don't find a topic of interest in the contents list, check the index, as it may be that I've called it something else (for example, if you're looking for advice about smacking, it will be in the 'Discipline' section).

ADHD

I have three children and my middle son (he's five) is incredibly naughty compared to the others. He also seems to have a huge amount of energy compared to most boys his age, and cannot sit still for more than a minute at a time. He can be quite disrespectful to adults, but my main concern is that he is very rough with other children to the point where he often hurts them. 'Accidents' (broken things, someone hurting themselves) usually turn out to be his fault. I'm worried that he may have ADHD, but when I mention this to friends, they tell me I am overreacting and that he's just a normal boy. What should I do?

For most young children, distraction, praising good behaviour and using a time-out system as a consequence for unacceptable behaviour all work well. It's crucial, however, that the time-out is not seen as a punishment. The parent calmly directs the child to sit in a boring place for several minutes. Consistency in using the time-out procedure is also important. This means that all other adults (grandparents, childcare workers and friends) who care for the child should utilise the same technique. But if this does not work and it is clear that your son's behaviour is well-established, then you need to get him assessed by a behavioural paediatrician or child psychologist. The signs and symptoms of attention deficit hyperactivity disorder (ADHD) typically appear before the age of 12, and like most things, early diagnosis and prompt treatment are associated with a better outcome.

ADHD is one of the most commonly diagnosed chronic psychiatric conditions in today's school-aged children. Symptoms of the disorder include being easily distracted, forgetful, fidgety, unable to complete tasks and easily bored. However, to receive a diagnosis of ADHD by a child psychologist or psychiatrist, a child must have at least six of nine symptoms of either hyperactivity or inattention; the child's behaviour must be causing problems in his or her life; and the symptoms must not be explainable by any medical condition or any other mental disorder. (Children can be inattentive, impulsive and hyperactive if they are abused, malnourished, depressed or have impaired vision.)

If your boy does happen to have ADHD, just remember that it doesn't detract from his natural talents. In my experience, young people with ADHD are some of the brightest, most creative, intuitive, imaginative, passionate and sympathetic people you could ever meet. (Don't forget that Albert Einstein, Orville and Wilbur Wright, Thomas Edison, Pablo Picasso, Lewis Carroll, Eleanor Roosevelt and Louis Pasteur were all thought to have ADHD – and they transformed the world!)

And if medication is discussed, just remember it should always form part of a comprehensive treatment plan that includes psychological, behavioural and educational interventions. This means regularly seeing a psychologist (or other mental health professional); finding out everything you can about ADHD; and getting his teacher/school to help. Unfortunately, new research shows that teachers know very little about ADHD and other developmental disorders, such as ASD, so you may need to become his advocate at school.

Adoption

My husband and I have a 5-year-old ('biological') daughter and are just about to adopt a 6-month-old baby daughter. (I was unable to conceive again after complications during the birth.) How should we tell Millie about her new baby sister? And when should we tell our new daughter that she is adopted?

Millie is obviously old enough to understand that her new sister didn't arrive the usual way (unless, of course, you've told her that babies are 'found under cabbage leaves' or brought by Mr Stork) and there are some brilliant children's books to start the conversation with her. Read *Maggie Can't Wait* by Frieda Wishinsky, and answer her questions as honestly as you can. As for when to tell your new daughter, some psychologists would argue that the earlier you tell her the better, because this affords her plenty of time to come to terms with the news and to assimilate the notion of being adopted. (And with her having an older sibling, you might have to get in quick before Millie blurts it out when they're in the middle of a fight!)

Others maintain that children should not be told too early because they lack the cognitive or emotional maturity to process this and might become distressed or confused. I think your decision should be based on your assessment of her temperament and personality and how bright and secure she is. One thing the experts do agree upon is that irrespective of whether you tell her now or wait a little, she should definitely hear the news from you, not someone else. I recommend reading her one of the many children's books on adoption, such as *I Love You Like Crazy Cakes* by Rose A. Lewis. Hearing the news from you sends a message that adoption is a good and noble thing and that she can trust you. Learning the news accidentally can engender resentment and distrust and may lead her to view the adoption as disgraceful because it was kept hushed up. Some adopted children develop a deep-seated belief that they were relinquished because they were naughty, but honest, positive, open discussions reduce the likelihood of such beliefs forming.

Alcohol

My son is in Year 8 and has been invited to a couple of parties where there was alcohol present. At one party the parents hosting the event served the alcohol and at another party it was smuggled in by one of the kids. He told me he hadn't imbibed, but I hate the idea that he's hanging around kids who are drunk and making stupid decisions. Part of me wants to stop him from going to the parties, but I'd feel so guilty. I'm really confused. What's your advice on this?

Quite frankly, parents who think it's okay to let 14-year-olds have a couple of beers need their heads examined! The National Health and

Medical Research Council's *2009 Australian Guidelines to Reduce Health Risks from Drinking Alcohol* advises young people not to drink *at all* until they're 18. That's because the research is clear: alcohol has devastating consequences for the developing brain, damaging the parts responsible for memory and learning.

US research shows that 47 per cent of kids who drink alcohol before the age of 14 will go on to become alcohol dependent, compared to 9 per cent of those who start drinking after the age of 21. You don't need to be a brain surgeon to understand the dire consequences of alcohol dependence for young people (or older ones for that matter).

Alcohol is a depressant, meaning it depresses the central nervous system, slowing down the messages coming to and from the brain. But it also triggers endorphins, which leads to feelings of wellbeing, unself-consciousness and disinhibition. Young people, by virtue of their brain development, are not very good at assessing risk or making judgements, so when alcohol is added to the mix, what little voice of reason they possess goes out the window and they find themselves doing impulsive, stupid and often dangerous things. Kids who drink are more likely to become sexually active, engage in risky, unprotected sex, and become victims of sexual abuse or date rape compared with those who don't drink. Alcohol use can lead to accidental injury, assault and property damage, and is a major cause of death through car accidents, drowning, suicides and homicides.

From my point of view, this is no longer a moral issue. This is a health issue. And there is a huge discrepancy between what parents are actually doing and what they should be doing. This is where crap parenting really comes to the fore, when 'best friend' parents buy alcohol for their kids, and relinquish all moral responsibility for their child's mental and physical wellbeing. Kids need boundaries because they provide a sense of security. Most teenagers really do want to know what is right and what is wrong. They want some guidance in navigating life. Teenagers will still test the limits from time to time, but clear boundaries provide the stability and security that will allow them to thrive.

A recent Deakin University study of 14-year-olds in Melbourne schools found that rates of teen binge drinking were reduced by 25 per cent when parents set rules against adolescent alcohol use. The research team, led by Professor John Toumbourou, conducted a two-year Resilient Families parent education program in twelve schools through the early secondary school years, providing education on the harmful impact of adolescent alcohol use and encouraging parents not to supply or allow adolescent alcohol use.

Some of this information must be getting through. In 2002, national school surveys showed 29 per cent of 12–15-year-old students used alcohol each week; by 2011 this figure had dropped to 11 per cent. But while it's great that more parents and young people are aware of the potential damage that alcohol can cause to the teenage brain, the young person's brain is still vulnerable until the early to mid-twenties. When the US introduced legislation in 1986 to increase the legal drinking age to 21, road fatalities for young drivers fell by 16 per cent, and in Australia, there is some support for similar legislation. According to a survey by the Australian Institute of Health and Welfare, household support for raising the legal drinking age to 21 rose from 40.7 per cent in 2004 to 50.2 per cent in 2010. It remains to be seen whether our political leaders have the intestinal fortitude to take on the alcohol industry.

Anxiety

My 12-year-old daughter is a complete perfectionist when it comes to projects and assignments. She worries about her marks constantly, and unless she gets 100 per cent for everything, she becomes quite distraught. We don't put pressure on her at all to succeed academically, and I often tell her that she only needs to do her best, but somehow she is always anxious about her marks. How can I help her reduce the amount of pressure she is putting on herself?

Children who have perfectionist tendencies exhibit a range of behaviours. Some take pleasure from completing difficult tasks and though they set high standards for themselves, the tasks are basically achievable. Others may be children similar to your daughter who are unable to glean satisfaction from their efforts either because, in their own eyes, nothing they do is ever good enough, or because their goals are completely unrealistic. There are some great books for your daughter that deal with the topic of perfectionism. My favourite for school-age children is *Be a Perfect Person in Just Three Days* by Stephen Manes. The stories can help her get a better perspective on her feelings. There is great power in storytelling, so also talk to her about some of your fears and failures, both as an adult and as a child. Remember that young children tend to idealise their parents. Some may even assume that you've never made a mistake. One of the disadvantages of this naive belief is that your child may assume that she's not allowed to be imperfect. By talking about the time you failed a spelling test, lost a job or came last in a race, you'll help her gain the realisation that she, too, can make mistakes and survive them.

Given the enormous pressure that perfectionists put themselves under, it should come as no surprise that perfectionism is associated with psychological symptoms including disordered eating, anxiety and depression. This doesn't mean your daughter is in danger of developing any of these problems, though it is worth being aware of the connection.

Anxiety is very functional. Human beings actually need a certain amount of stress or arousal to motivate us to give our best performance. If approached in the street by a mugger, for example, the anxiety we feel (the fight-or-flight response) enables us to react quickly to protect ourselves. A manageable level of anxiety about end-of-year exams, or an upcoming race or sporting competition, has been shown to be useful in enhancing performance. Anxiety is a normal response to something which is terrifying or complicated. Adrenalinee flows into the bloodstream, priming muscles, focusing attention, flooding the body with oxygen and releasing chemicals that transform the sugar in the bloodstream into energy. This fight-or-flight response happens to everyone if they are faced with a difficult situation. However, for some people this anxiety is all-consuming and is triggered by experiences that some might consider quite ordinary or manageable. When anxiety begins to interfere with your daily life, it becomes an anxiety disorder, such as a specific phobia, panic disorder, generalised anxiety disorder, agoraphobia or post-traumatic stress disorder.

The most recent figures from the Australian Bureau of Statistics (2007) show that anxiety disorders are the most common form of mental illness for young people aged 16–24 years (15 per cent), yet only about a quarter of sufferers get help. Common psychological symptoms include intense fear and apprehension, unbearable tension, uncontrollable worry and catastrophic thinking. Such thoughts ratchet up the fight-or-flight response described earlier, resulting in a range of physical symptoms, including nausea, racing heart, chest pain, involuntary shaking, increased sweating and difficulty breathing.

The most common form of treatment is cognitive behavioural therapy (CBT), sometimes along with a short course of anti-anxiety medication, but more often with lifestyle changes such as practising relaxation techniques, undertaking regular aerobic exercise and monitoring moods.

My daughter is eight years old and terrified of the dark. If we are in the house and still up and about she will be able to stay in her own bed, falling in and out of sleep, but once we go to bed and the house becomes silent and dark, she will wake and run to our bed. As soon as she's in bed with us, she will fall asleep. What is going on and what can we do to help?

It is most likely that your daughter is suffering from anxiety, affecting her independence, and your general quality of life. Anxiety is thought to affect around one in ten children, which makes it a very common, if not the most common, childhood wellbeing issue. You are not alone in being confused. Many parents of children with anxiety are often confused. It seems that anxiety is part of your child's personality, so how do you change it? The best way of knowing whether your child has an anxiety issue that needs attention is by looking at whether 'it affects the way the children are leading their lives'. And the main criterion is avoidance – avoidance and hesitance. Your daughter avoids sleeping on her own. The place to start is with her fears. While your child's worry may seem general, the research shows that often those fears are specific. She may, for instance, fear that when you guys go to bed, burglars will enter. Sit down with her and talk about these fears. Write them down and, if you like, get your daughter to give these fears a rating out of ten. When you have a list, discuss with her about how she might like to be free of those fears and how you are going to be working together to achieve this. And, most importantly, that you are going to work in small steps, and that there will be rewards along the way. Rewards are an extremely important part of the process. They are reinforcing and you need to use a combination of material things (treats) and non-material things such as parental praise and quality time spent together. Never resort to punishment, it's counterproductive. Your list lets you in on what your child is thinking; now you need to work on that thinking. You need to get your child used to what they're afraid of, working step by step on the problem. It's important here to have the right size steps and to gauge your child's readiness for each step. A child who always sleeps in her mother's bed can start with a cot next to the bed, then move the cot to the other side of the room, then to the doorway, then the hall, until finally the cot is in the child's room. This exposure in degrees actually works as further evidence (of safety) for the child. The burglar doesn't come. We like to reassure our children when they're frightened, we kiss and hug and hold them. But in the situation of long-term anxiety, it actually signals to her that there really is something to be scared of and in fact rewards the anxiety with lots of affection and attention. Instead, you have to train yourselves to reward your daughter's bravery in facing her fears. Professor Ron Rapee, Australia's foremost expert in child anxiety has a great five-point plan: 1. Show love and care always. But within that, ask yourself, truthfully, can my child do this on her/his own? 2. Identify what your child is afraid of. Get your child to express their fears. Then, logically, perform a reality check. This is concrete and holds vague, imaginary fears up against the reality. 3. Always use small steps. 4. Rewards must be given as soon as possible after the child has performed the step. These rewards need to be practical, realistic and meaningful to the child. And don't forget the impact of praise! Plenty of it, it's important. 5. Be consistent. It takes dedication and practice and patience for the best results.

Asperger's syndrome

My sister suspects my 6-year-old son may have Asperger's as he's not interested in playing much with other kids and gets extremely stressed out in crowds. I think she's probably overreacting, but I would still like to find out if there is any truth to her suspicion. What should I do?

The first thing to point out is that as of May 2013, Asperger's syndrome was no longer listed in the Diagnostic and Statistical Manual of Mental Disorders (DSM-V). Instead, people are diagnosed as having an autism spectrum disorder (ASD) along with specific descriptions of severity and any intellectual or language impairment. This doesn't mean people won't still be using the term Asperger's, it's just that when it comes to paperwork, health professionals can choose whether or not they comply with the DSM-V guidelines.

ASD is a neurological developmental disorder that affects communication, social interaction and behaviour to varying degrees. At the more severe end of the spectrum, children have delayed language development, intellectual impairment and unusual repetitive behaviours, and can often receive a diagnosis before the age of three. At the other end of the spectrum, children with Asperger's have an average (or higher than average) vocabulary and IQ, so it can be harder to make a diagnosis until the age of seven or eight. Children with Asperger's are sometimes described as 'little professors' because they are often extremely knowledgeable about their favourite topics and also have advanced language skills for their age. They have trouble reading social cues and find it difficult to adjust their behaviour to suit different contexts.

The most recent ABS data suggests that 1 in 60 Australian children has ASD. It is not known what causes the disorder, though there is some evidence of a genetic link. Here are some of the more common behaviours that can indicate that a person has ASD:

- They can initiate interactions with others if they need something or want to talk about their own interests, but once finished, they're not able to sustain the interaction.
- They interact in an awkward or stilted manner (for example, avoiding eye contact or using a flat or monotone voice).
- They seem to have trouble empathising with others.
- They have restricted or obsessive interests that make them seem like 'walking encyclopaedias' about particular topics.
- They become stressed and anxious when routines change.

If you feel that these symptoms may be present in your child, first speak to your GP. They can guide you through the steps you need to take to obtain a detailed assessment, which usually involves a multidisciplinary team comprising a paediatrician, psychologist or psychiatrist and speech pathologist. Research consistently shows that early intervention greatly improves outcomes for young people with an autism spectrum disorder.

Bathing, showering and hygiene

My 11-year-old daughter hates having showers. She says she'd rather have a bath, but I hate the waste of water, and anyway, isn't she too old for baths? She hasn't hit puberty yet, but she still has greasy hair after three days without a shower. How should I deal with this?

It's hard for parents to know when to ditch the nightly bath-with-toys routine. Some children prefer showers from an early age (some have no choice if their home is tub-less), while others like the routine and relaxation of bathing in a tub. Every family will have their own preferences, but it's important to get your kids to take responsibility for their hygiene from an early age. If children don't bathe daily, make sure they wash their hands before dinner, and that after dinner they wash their face and hands thoroughly with warm, soapy water and a facecloth. Some children also find a footbath relaxing (a nice way to save water and to clean dirty summer feet). In your daughter's case, you could phase in showers gradually, allowing her to have a bath once a week as long as she has at least two showers as well. It won't be long before you can't get her out of the bathroom, so don't stress!

My 15-year-old son will not brush his teeth. Until about a year ago, I would have to remind him to do it every day. It was a constant battle. So I decided to back off and not make it a struggle that dominated our relationship. But he still doesn't do it. His gums are swollen and his teeth are yucky. I'm worried that this will lead to dental problems in his twenties! What do I do?

When kids hit puberty, the research suggests that it is not unusual for teenagers to go through a period of months, maybe years, when their tooth-brushing habits slip or, as in your son's case, may be non-existent. However, you are right to worry, as recalcitrant teenagers who give brushing the brush-off could be establishing a lifetime pattern of dental neglect. If your child is susceptible to cavities (and this is more likely if you live in an area without fluoridated drinking water), or there is gum disease in your family, your teen is asking for trouble. Unfortunately, nagging doesn't work (as you point out). It just triggers defensiveness, which shuts down communication. Make six-monthly appointments with your dentist (or a hygienist) and get them to talk to your son about cleaning and flossing. An authoritative but neutral outsider can win your son's respect and may have better luck encouraging him to brush and floss. Once that conversation has taken place, leave him alone. Try using positive forms of reinforcement ('Your fangs look great when you smile – they're so white!') but avoid full-scale bribery (e.g. don't pay him to brush his teeth; he needs to do it because he values having fresh breath and a bright smile). It's important to understand that bribery can become an ongoing pattern that ultimately teaches your child to act out to get what they want.

An electric toothbrush works for some kids. And don't forget to practise what you preach. Most importantly never, *ever* use a visit to the dentist as a threat of punishment, as this can create phobias and have dire consequences for his future dental health.

Beauty pageants

My 9-year-old daughter adores dressing up her Barbie dolls and having a pretend beauty contest. She also loves putting on make-up and dressing up in high heels and pretty dresses. Should I enter her in a real beauty contest? I know there are a few in Australia now, but I've heard good and bad things and I'm finding it really hard to decide.

There is nothing wrong with your daughter putting on Mummy's make-up, lipstick or playing with dolls. But your daughter needs to be in a pageant like a fish needs a bicycle! The child beauty pageant movement, with its over-the-top grooming, suggestive dance routines and expensive glitzy costumes is psychologically *toxic*. Do you really want your daughter to believe that her physical appearance is the most important part of her being female? These pageants don't just reinforce stereotypical norms about female beauty, they also sexualise young children and increase the risk of child sexual abuse by undermining the important social norm that children are sexually unavailable. And as far as Barbie is concerned, you might like to choose a doll with a more lifelike female figure. Barbie's legs are 50 per cent longer than her arms, whereas the average woman's legs are only 20 per cent longer.

This means that if Barbie were real, the length of her legs in proportion to her torso would make her unable to walk. Also, a 'real-life' Barbie would weigh about 45.8 kilograms and be about 213 centimetres in height, giving her a body mass index of 10, which means she would lack the 17–22 per cent body fat required for menstruation (let alone pregnancy). Also, poor Barbie's body would have room for only half a liver and only a few centimetres of intestines, as opposed to the usual 7.9 metres, so she would suffer from chronic diarrhoea and would eventually die from nutrient malabsorption and malnutrition. Apart from that she'd be fine.

If you decide not to enter your daughter in a beauty pageant, your decision will be in line with organisations such as Collective Shout, the Royal Australian and New Zealand College of Psychiatrists and the Australian Childhood Foundation, all of which have called for the banning or restriction of such events. In 2013, the French Senate voted to ban beauty pageants for children under 16 – and to impose up to two years in prison and steep fines for adults who try to enter children into such a contest. *Vive la France!*

Bedtime

My 15-year-old and I are constantly battling over the issue of sleep. She does not see why she should sacrifice a glorious entertainment binge (TV, social media etc.) for a few boring hours of shut-eye. She insists all of her friends stay up quite late, often until midnight, but I try to encourage her to hit the pillow by 10 p.m. Is this one of those teenage issues (like messy bedrooms and purple hair) where I should just pull back a bit and let her go?

Sleep is a biological necessity, not a luxury or an indulgence, and research has shown that adolescents need 9–10 hours a day. However, teenagers are officially the most sleep-deprived segment of the Australian population. The problem is that during adolescence, the natural circadian rhythm of childhood changes, and there is a delay in the onset of sleep due to hormonal changes and the later release of melatonin. So when a teenager says that they are not tired at 11 p.m., they are telling the truth. This trend for later bedtimes (and waking up later) continues until 19.5 years in women and 21 in men. Then it reverses, so that by the time we're in our mid-fifties we wake at about the same time we woke before puberty – usually about two hours earlier. This means that a 7 a.m. alarm call for a teenager is the equivalent of a 5 a.m. start for a 55-year-old. No wonder teenagers are falling asleep at their school desks!

'Sleep on it' is an old saying that's now validated by research. In 2003, Wagner and his colleagues proved that our brains keep working away at problems while we're asleep. When we're snoozing our minds perform a kind of Tetris with our thoughts; they all get stacked up as neatly as possible so things make more sense in the morning. The same study found that teenagers who'd had 8.25 to 9.25 hours sleep were three times more likely to be able to work out a tough maths problem than their sleep-deprived buddies.

But sleep deprivation has far more serious consequences than reduced academic performance. Sleep plays a major role in neuro-endocrine function and glucose metabolism, and there is now a stack of evidence that chronic sleep loss increases the risk of obesity, diabetes and weight gain. One study found that young men who slept four hours a night on six consecutive nights had insulin levels comparable to the early stages of diabetes. Similar studies have shown higher levels of the hormone ghrelin, which signals hunger, and lower levels of leptin, which signals that we are full. Inadequate or disturbed sleep is also linked with mood disorders, although scientists are not sure how the connection works (whether sleep influences mood and anxiety levels, or vice versa). We do know that lack of sleep has adverse effects on mood and behaviour, including irritability, insensitivity, low mood, loss of sense of humour, and impulsive behaviour. If kept awake long enough, animals die from a lack of sleep – and scientists say this happens because the immune system collapses and infection overwhelms the animal. Chronic sleep deprivation, rather than a short-term interruption, is most damaging to the immune system, so it seems there's some truth to the expression 'sick and tired'!

If you can't convince your daughter of the importance of sleep for academic achievement, physical and mental health or longevity, you could try appealing to her vanity. Sleep serves a range of beauty functions. Tissue repair happens while you're asleep, which can help heal pimples, minimise UV damage, brighten the whites of your eyes, reduce under-eye bags and boost nutrients to the skin – making you generally healthier inside and out.

All in all, if your daughter is dependent upon an alarm clock (or you) to get her out of bed, if she takes a long time to properly wake up or if she feels sleepy and irritable during the day, it means she is probably not getting enough sleep. Even just an extra thirty minutes a night can make a big difference.

To help her sleep:

- Remove *all* screens from her bedroom (TV, computer and mobile phone) – these are distractions that keep her hyped up.
- Avoid caffeinated drinks (especially after midday). The half-life of caffeine is 5–9 hours, so it stays in her system keeping her revved up for ages.
- Make sure her bed's juuust right, Goldilocks-style – too hot or too cold will disrupt her snoozin'.
- Avoid arguments before bedtime – fighting raises adrenaline levels, which will make her want to run away or punch someone, not nap.
- Encourage her to have at least twenty minutes of exercise every day.
- Get her to set aside thirty minutes of chill-out time before she goes to sleep, during which she performs the same routine, e.g. turns off the screens, does her ablutions, dims the lights, sprinkles some lavender oil on a hankie near her pillow and reads a book.

Bed-wetting

I have a 10-year-old stepson who has lived with us full-time for four years and as well as the usual challenges that come with raising a stepchild there is one particular problem that I struggle with. The issue is that he is wetting his pants during the day but only at times when he is far too focused on playing games and does not listen to what his body is telling him. The most frustrating part is that we have four toilets in our house so I see that there is absolutely no excuse for this. He has also wet his pants during lunch breaks at school when he has been playing and not wanting to be left out of the game. Further, I have concerns that he doesn't even get changed when he does it. Instead he stays in the wet clothes all day until it is discovered. I am particularly strict about hygiene and I have taught him well regarding all aspects of being clean so this issue is very distressing for me when he just doesn't understand or care about how dirty it is. When we are out of the house often he will approach me about something and I can clearly see he needs a bathroom but he won't say anything until I ask if he needs to go. He always leaves it until the last minute and at 10 years of age I find this unacceptable when even my 2-year-old nephew and niece know better. I have raised the issue with his father, but he is unable to offer any assistance. Background information is that he has also seen a counsellor for about twelves months for issues around his mother's behaviour, who is living in another state. The counsellor seems to think that the toileting is not directly related to anxiety or emotional problems. Any help or advice would be so much appreciated. I'm at my wit's end.

Your stepson could be suffering from enuresis, a medical condition where people are unable to control urination even after they are considered old enough to be able to. Daytime enuresis is a common childhood problem and Australian research suggests that weekly daytime wetting occurs in 5 per cent of Australian children, most of whom (80 per cent) also wet the bed. (US statistics are comparable, with an estimated 7 per cent of 5-year-old boys and 3 per cent of 5-year-old girls having the condition. This drops to around 3 per cent and 2 per cent for boys and girls respectively by the age of 10.) Most children outgrow this problem by the time they become teens.

Enuresis is a very frustrating condition for parents and many become angry at the repeated need to clean or throw out soiled underwear and clothing. Punishing or shaming a child for wetting themselves will frequently make the situation worse. Doctors describe a downward cycle where a child punished for wetting feels shame and a loss of self-confidence. You have made the assumption that his enuresis is the result of being lazy and/or distracted, when it could actually be the result of some longstanding physical problem. You now have two steps to take. The first one is to consult a paediatric urologist, which is a surgical subspecialty of medicine dealing with the disorders of children's genitourinary systems. The most common problems they deal with are those involving disorders of urination. They will be able to rule out any physical issue. You will need a GP's referral. Once the doctors have excluded a physical cause, I would seek a second psychological opinion, as after twelve months of counselling his behaviour should have improved.

My 6-year-old daughter still wets the bed every week. We do all the right things with her: avoiding big drinks before bed and we've put a plastic mattress protector on the bed so when she has an accident, it's not a big deal, but I think she is starting to get self-conscious about it and is really worried about school camp. My partner says he used to do the same when he was a boy and he says he just grew out of it. But I'm wondering if she has a physical problem. Should we take her to the doctor?

There are lots of reasons why children wet the bed at night when they are already toilet-trained during the day. It could be that they simply haven't developed the necessary bladder control, or that they sleep so heavily that they can't wake up when their bladders are full. Some children produce more urine at night than others, and others have bladders that just can't hold a lot.

Bed-wetting is a common childhood problem, and you are right to avoid making a big deal out of it. It is estimated that around 20 per cent of 5-year-olds wet the bed, but by the age of 10 the proportion has dropped to around 5 per cent, and by 15 to less than 1 per cent. Reassure your daughter that bedwetting is normal, that there is nothing to be ashamed about, and that she will grow out of it. Have you told her about her dad? It might help her to know that someone else in the family used to wet the bed. By all means take her to the doctor, as it will put your mind at rest, and it might also make your daughter feel more confident.

Besties

My daughter is 11, yet does not seem to have a close friend like most of the girls in her class. She has a broad mix of friends at school, socialising with a couple of younger children and a handful of boys her own age with whom she shares a passion for Minecraft *(she affectionately calls them her 'nerds') but does not seem interested in having friends over to play or for sleepovers. She is not yet showing signs of entering puberty like many of the girls in her year. I've asked her about whether she wants to have friends over and she insists that she doesn't – that she's happy to play with them at school. Do you think I should be worried?*

In the upper primary years, boys and girls tend to go about building peer group relationships in different ways, with boys maintaining a more fluid arrangement (swapping and changing based on interests) and girls attaching themselves to one or two 'besties'. Of course this is by no means the gold standard, and it certainly doesn't mean your daughter is abnormal if she hasn't ensconced herself in a particular peer group. Psychologists refer to these girls as 'floaters' – girls who have friends in different groups and can move freely among them. These girls are not competitive, they don't want to exclude people, tend to avoid conflicts and are more likely to have higher self-esteem, as their sense of self isn't based on one person or one group. A 'floater' has influence over other girls but doesn't use it to make them feel bad. If your daughter insists that she is okay about this, trust her. We know that through friendship children learn a huge amount about themselves and the world, but in childhood those friendships need not necessarily be with peers: they can be with teachers, coaches, younger children and relatives. It is only in adolescence that peer friendships become an important source of security as young people emancipate themselves from adult carers. Having close relationships with friends provides love, meaning and support as they find their way in the world.

I have a 13-year-old daughter who thinks my wife and I are ridiculously overprotective because we don't let her catch public transport to go shopping with her friends. We're quite happy to take her to her friends' homes and to netball, but we don't want her walking the streets.

I completely understand your hesitancy, but it is very important that you allow your daughter to grow up. Her desire to be with friends her own age is incredibly powerful at this time, and it is crucial that she be allowed to do so, as it helps her develop a sense of self and enables her to begin the journey towards independence. Of course, every adolescent is different, and you are in the unique position of being able to judge how much rope to give her. You need to ask yourself some key questions. Does she have a history of making safe and sensible choices? (The greatest predictor of future choices is past choices.) What are her friends like? What is her temperament? Does she consider the risks of a situation or is she a sensation-seeker? If she makes sensible choices, hangs out with peers who tend to do the same, and prefers to avoid risks then you can have more confidence in allowing her to catch public transport with a phone (in case of trouble) and a few friends.

Of course, avoid going overboard like Lenore Skenazy – the infamous mum who, in 2008, made the controversial decision to allow her 9-year-old son to take the New York City Subway home alone and wrote about it in a column in the *New York Sun*. Skenazy received a flood of reactions, ranging from accusations of child abuse to fond memories of first-time subway trips and childhood freedom. Life for your 13-year-old is not the same as when you were growing up and there are more social toxins around than ever so perhaps start cautiously with a few short trips and when she has shown herself to be responsible, she can graduate to more adventurous ones. It is essential you keep the lines of communication open, make clear your expectations, values and beliefs, and monitor and supervise via mobile phones and text messages.

Bikes, scooters, skateboards and other wheels

I am nervous about letting my 11-year-old daughter ride her bike to her friend's house alone. It's a twenty-minute ride, and although there is a bike path on the bigger roads and she can take a few back streets, I feel awful about letting her go. I am a recreational cyclist, and my husband is a very regular cyclist (he commutes on his bike), so we are a pretty bike-aware family, but I'm still anxious. I make her text me when she gets there and I even consider driving behind to check she's okay. Is this normal?

I'm guessing you are more nervous about her safety as a cyclist than about stranger danger, and unfortunately you are right to be wary. A 2012 report by the Australian Institute of Health and Welfare found that in the eight years between July 1999 and June 2007, pedal cycles were the most common mode of transport involved in childhood injuries requiring hospitalisation. In the 5–14 age group, roughly 45 per cent of the 58,692 cases of transport-related injuries involved a bicycle. But before you throw the Malvern Star on the tip, remember that during the same period, almost half a million children were hospitalised as a result of an injury, with falls being the most common cause (three times more common than bikes). So your daughter has a much greater chance of hurting herself falling down the stairs. The report also found that boys outnumbered girls by a factor of 2 to 1, so your daughter is already ahead of the eight-ball by having no Y chromosome.

As a cyclist yourself, you'll already know that it is a brilliant way to exercise, blow out the cobwebs and help save the planet. Ultimately, deciding when to let your daughter travel solo on a bike depends on a range of factors, including her experience as a cyclist, her maturity and her awareness of road safety issues. If she has been riding regularly (a couple of times a week) since she first learnt to ride (most children learn at around age five), chances are that she will have a good level of skill. Many schools run bicycle safety programs, where children actually learn to use bike lanes and bike paths safely. I'm sure she would already be aware of the following top tips for bicycle safety:

- wear a properly fitted helmet
- make sure your bike is the right size for you
- check tyres and brakes
- wear bright or reflective clothing
- use hand signals
- always keep at least one hand (preferably two) on the handlebars
- watch out for driveways and parked cars.

If your daughter has the necessary maturity, road sense and physical skill to ride to her friend's house, it's your job to let her do it. I know it can be hard for parents to let their children take risks, but it's the only way that children build resilience and confidence. Keeping her wrapped in cotton wool robs her of the chance to develop into a responsible, independent young woman.

My 10-year-old son wants to ride his skateboard to school. He's been learning for the past year and his skill level seems okay (he doesn't fall off) and although he doesn't mind wearing his helmet at the skate park, he says he doesn't want to wear his helmet out in the street as it's not cool. He doesn't play any sport so I'm keen for him to exercise and I don't want to put him off skateboarding by insisting that he wear his helmet. What should I do?

It's great that your son has found a physical activity that he loves to do, but if he's skating on a footpath or bike path, and is still learning, he is at greater risk of colliding with pedestrians, cyclists or stationary objects such as walls or telephone poles (which, incidentally, cause the most serious injuries). Small-wheeled contraptions such as skateboards, scooters and inline skates might look inviting because they are so compact and low to the ground, but they are notorious for tipping their riders on a slick surface or when tiny wheels hit a speck of gravel. Unless your son is approaching the skill level of Tony Hawk, I would recommend you pull rank on this one and tell him that for his own safety (and that of others) he either wears the helmet or walks to school. He can keep skateboarding for the skatepark.

Birthday parties

My 9-year-old daughter talks about her birthday for eleven months of the year (I'm not kidding). It's a huge deal to her, and she is obsessed. Her friends have had some over-the-top celebrations, including group tickets to a pop concert, a party catered by a professional catering company and a trip to the cinema in a limousine. I feel under enormous pressure to give her a really special birthday, but cannot compete with her peers. How do I handle this?

When I was growing up, birthday parties used to mean a cake from the local supermarket, a handful of balloons and a game of pin the tail on the donkey. Not any more. Celebrities have upped the ante with their children and many compete to outdo one another. There's Tori Spelling, who provided her child with a six-tiered cake and 170 different kinds of snacks, and Tom Cruise and Katie Holmes, who reportedly shelled out $100,000 for Suri's second birthday party, $45,000 of which went to Austrian chef extraordinaire Wolfgang Puck for the catering. As a result, many ordinary families feel they must provide expensive, over-the-top entertainment from professional entertainers, snow machines or solar-powered bouncy castles.

First of all, you need to decide what you are prepared to pay for and organise, and to come up with a list of three or four options for the party theme. Then you can sit down with her and ask her to decide on one of the options. This way she is still getting a choice. Home parties are far less expensive than hired venues and you are free to hold the party at whatever time suits your family and guests, plus you can choose the food. It's also important that you don't feel pressured to invite everyone in the class. Many parents think it unfair for their child to have to choose whom to invite from among their peers, and worry that their child (or they) might not be liked if they don't invite everyone. But this keeps alive the myth that life is fair and just, and denies children the opportunity to experience missing out. In the 1990s, one school principal offered parents the sensible advice that the maximum number of guests should equal the age of the birthday girl or boy: six for a 6-year-old, nine for a 9-year-old, and so on.

Body image

My daughter is 14 and has become incredibly obsessed with her body. She used to be a bit of a chubby child, but ever since she started high school, she's become more body conscious. Her school books are covered with scarily thin models and I am worried she's striving to be that way too and may develop an eating disorder to get there. How can I bring this up without offending her, and what do I say?

Many girls today are obsessed with their looks, endlessly comparing themselves to peers and judging each other by their weight, shape and appearance. The National Eating Disorders Collaboration survey in 2010 revealed that of Australians aged 11–24, approximately 28 per cent of males are dissatisfied with their appearance compared to 35 per cent of females. The Australian National Survey revealed that body image was identified as the number one concern of 29,000 males and females. The Longitudinal Study on Women's Health found that only 22 per cent of women within a normal healthy weight range reported being happy with their weight. Almost three-quarters (74 per cent) desired to weigh less, including 68 per cent of healthy weight and 25 per cent of underweight women. With that type of role modelling, it is hardly a surprise that a 2011 UK survey of 810 people aged 11–16 revealed that over half of the girls and more than a third of the boys said they compared their bodies to those of people on TV, with about a quarter of both gender willing to undergo cosmetic surgery to create the look they wanted.

Body image is more than the way your daughter *sees* her physical self; it's also the thoughts and feelings that accompany her perception. It is important to understand that these feelings can be positive, negative or an amalgamation of both and that they are influenced by both genetic and environmental factors. Your concern is legitimate, as many paediatricians are worried about a spate of eating disorders affecting young people at the upper end of the healthy weight range. Doctors have hospitalised children who have lost up to a third of their body weight over a few months. Some worry that zealous anti-obesity campaigns could be encouraging healthy kids – like your daughter – to obsess over their weight and being thin. The fear is that some moderately overweight girls, who are still maturing height-wise, might be susceptible to the media hype surrounding various diets such as low-carb, low-fat, sugar-free or, God help us, regular fasting. Reality TV shows and celebrity gossip magazines don't help either. Dieting is anathema to healthy development. Most high school curricula are onto this, and teach kids about healthy eating. However, you can help by doing the following:

1. Tell your daughter that a little bit of weight gain is normal around the time of adolescence as it helps to sustain her growth spurt.
2. Never make negative statements about people's food choices, body size or weight.
3. Always compliment your daughter on her efforts, talents and accomplishments (so that the focus moves away from her appearance).

4. Watch a makeover/weight loss reality TV show with her and do some healthy deconstructing. In other words, help her understand the 'message' in the show and to whom the advertisers are hoping to market their products during the show. Discuss the values of the show's creators, and uncover any hidden meanings – intended or unintended. If we can help kids spot the techniques being used to persuade them to adopt an attitude or behaviour, they are more likely to question them and to think for themselves.
5. Get her a copy of *Real Gorgeous* by Kaz Cooke, which affirms that there are many different body shapes out there and may help her to learn to love the one she has.
6. Download Body Beautiful, the first app designed to promote positive body image among women and girls. It features inspirational quotes, media articles, videos and tools to help its users develop a positive self-image. Celebrities quoted include Tyra Banks, Demi Moore, Ralph Waldo Emerson and even Ben Stiller's character in *Zoolander*.
7. The SeeMe website is also a great tool to promote positive body image. It tackles the impact of young people's internalisation of idealised media portrayals of beauty and gender stereotypes.

My 17-year-old daughter is a beautiful young woman, but all she ever talks about is how ugly she feels. She's even talking about cosmetic surgery, now. I feel so powerless to help her. Is there anything I can do?

Sadly, your daughter is not alone. The 2013 Mission Australia Youth Survey found that 42.1 per cent of teenage girls still consider the issue of body image a major worry compared to only 14.4 per cent of young males. This is despite the implementation of the Voluntary Industry Code of Conduct on Positive Body Image to guide the media, fashion and advertising industries to adopt more body-image friendly practices, and the best efforts of the Butterfly Foundation's 'Free to BE' campaign.

Disturbing research being undertaken by Dr Meredith Jones at the Sydney University of Technology is also looking at the large numbers of Australian women in their twenties who are going overseas for cosmetic surgery. More than twenty tourism outfits are offering 'surgery getaways' to Thailand and Malaysia, where cosmetic surgery is far cheaper than in Australia. They are neglecting to consider that if there are complications with surgery and revisions are needed, that initial cost can increase significantly.

The fact that your daughter is considering cosmetic surgery suggests that, like many teenage girls, she is having negative (and completely irrational) thoughts about her body that are causing her to feel distressed and anxious. She needs help challenging this negative self-talk so encourage her to think about her friends, talents and achievements. Talk to her about the inner attributes that make her special. Encourage her interests, whatever they are. Help her to find what my friend Steve Biddulph calls her 'spark'. If she doesn't want to talk to you, surround her with other adults (aunts, uncles, friends) to whom she can confide. *Change Your Thinking* is a great book by psychologist Sarah Edelman to help her find more positive ways of dealing with negative thoughts and emotions. There is also MoodGym (moodgym.anu.edu.au), a free, interactive online program, which provides cognitive behavioural therapy interventions.

If none of these approaches work and her behaviour persists, consult a specialist adolescent psychologist. Try the Australian Psychological Society's 'Find a Psychologist' service on 1800 333 497.

My 8-year-old is often teased about being fat, and has experienced this since prep. She is perhaps slightly on the more 'solid' side of normal, but I would never call her fat. I am so worried about how self-conscious she is becoming. She's even started depriving herself of treats when eating in public. What can I do?

First, you need to determine if this teasing constitutes bullying. Ask your daughter how often this occurs, when and who the perpetrators are. If it is always the same children teasing her, and the taunting is ongoing and frequent, then it sounds like bullying. You need to tell her that this is not her fault, she is not alone, she doesn't deserve it, and that there is something she can do about it.

1. Tell her not to react to the taunting by fighting back. Explain to her that bullies want to get a reaction out of her. If she stays calm, ignores them and walks away, it will (for most) become boring for them and they will be more likely to leave her alone in the future.
2. Work with her on building her confident body language. Make sure she understands that if she appears insecure and hesitant the bullies are much more likely to pick on her. Teach her to hold her head up high, put her shoulders back and to stand tall.
3. Explain that she should not go anywhere where a bully can find her alone. She will always be safer when her friends or other people are around.
4. If she is cornered by the bully, tell her to find an adult she trusts – if it is at school that person should be a teacher. This is not 'dobbing'. Bullying needs to be taken seriously, and sometimes the best solution is getting help from adults.
5. If the person teasing her or making comments about her weight is a 'friend', tell her to let them know that their comments about her weight make her feel bad ('I feel sad when you tell me that').

There is another, more subtle issue at play here, too – the pressure of repeated and overpowering messages in our advertising, retail, publishing and broadcasting industries that women (and girls) must be thin, pretty and sexy to be worthwhile. The 2008 Senate Inquiry into the Sexualisation of Children in the Contemporary Media Environment seems to have had very little effect (don't get me started!). Indeed, a 2013 study found that one-third of 7-year-old Australian girls surveyed wanted to be thinner, despite the fact that they were all within a normal, healthy weight range. The pressure to have a 'perfect' appearance places children at greater risk of developing eating disorders at an age when nutrition is crucial – while they are still growing. This means parents and teachers are left with the lion's share of the work to help children develop a realistic body image. As parents, it's up to us to be good role models. In your case, be aware of your own eating habits, and your beliefs and prejudices about weight, as research shows that mums have a big influence on how their daughters see their own bodies. Even 4-year-olds pick up on it when their mums make negative comments about their own weight or body shape, and notice if they use body language (stooping, folding arms) to 'hide' parts of their bodies. The last thing I want to do is to make parents feel guilty about helping to create body image problems for their children, but it is very important to understand the connection. There are fewer books about positive body image for children than for teens, but you could try *Beautiful Girl* by Christiane Northrup and Kristina Tracy.

Body piercing

My 6-year-old daughter is desperate to have her ears pierced and insists that she will be able to look after her ears during the healing process. I'm not so sure about that given how I have to remind her daily to clean her teeth (!) but I'm also concerned that she might suffer an injury if another child accidentally pulls out her sleeper or stud. And is it just me, or do pierced ears in young children look cheap? I was 12 before I was allowed to have pierced ears. Should I adopt the same guidelines for my daughter?

This is a real and common dilemma faced by many parents. Some of your friends will tell you that it was no problem in *their* (paragon of virtue) daughter and while it is true that some girls can manage their own hygiene and safety with piercings before the age of 12 (as well as cook, clean and calculate pi to a trillion decimal places), your daughter might not be one of them. The answer depends, as you have already seen if you have ploughed through this book, on the individual psychology of your child. Even if she does seem responsible enough to manage the twice-daily cleaning for two months, don't fall for the current trend of multiple ear piercings. Start with just one piercing in each earlobe, and then wait and observe how she cares for them before allowing any more. Children are still growing and their lobes have not reached the final size and shape. Also, piercings through the cartilage in the upper part of the ear that become infected are very difficult to treat because cartilage doesn't have its own blood supply and oral antibiotics can't reach the infection. This can result in serious illness and cartilage deformation. In the final analysis, allowing your daughter to have her ears pierced is a very individual decision. It depends upon your personal beliefs, your observations of your child and the degree to which you feel pierced ears are important.

My 15-year-old son came home with a bandaid on his ear yesterday. He says it was an injury he got in a basketball game, but I have a feeling that he has pierced his ear, despite my warning that he could not do so until he was older. How should I deal with this?

To be honest with you, getting a piercing is pretty low down on my list of priorities for taking on a 15-year-old boy. My advice for parents of teenagers has always been to choose your battles. Middle adolescents are trying to answer the question 'Who am I?' and they need some space to experiment with aspects of identity. You obviously don't want him to experiment with drugs and alcohol, so giving him the freedom to make safer choices such as colouring his hair like an exotic Peruvian butterfly or getting a piercing can give him enough leeway so that you're not constantly at war. By respecting his independence on less-important things, he may be more willing to listen when it really counts. And he will have more practice at making decisions. It's natural for 15-year-olds to push boundaries, so make the ones you set count, and be the rock your teen needs.

Bullying – when your child is the victim

At school pick-up the other day, my 8-year-old son's teacher pulled me aside and told me she'd noticed a change in his behaviour. She said he'd become even more withdrawn in class and was sitting alone to eat his lunch and she wondered if everything was all right at home. I was surprised at this, as I hadn't noticed anything unusual, except perhaps that he was a bit quieter than normal. (He is a shy child anyway, so it is hard to tell.) I thought he must be tired, but being busy with work and whatnot, I hadn't followed up on it. That night, after some gentle questioning, it all tumbled out. Another boy was constantly calling him derogatory names, but sneakily, when no one else was watching. He was very upset about it, but begged me not to mention it to anyone as he didn't want to be seen as a snitch (or dibby-dobber or whatever they call tattle-tales now). I'm so worried. What can I do?

In Australia, depending on who collects the stats, at least 1 in 4 students will have been bullied at school, on the way home, or via social networking sites or mobile phones – making it the most common form of violence young people in this country experience. So if your child comes home and says s/he has been bullied the first step is to stay calm, listen carefully and determine whether or not what has happened is actually bullying.

Bullying is defined by the National Centre Against Bullying (NCAB) as the intention by one person or group of people to repeatedly cause hurt or harm to another person or group of people who feel helpless to respond. Bullying tends to be ongoing, is often hidden from adults and will probably continue if no action is taken. In schools, a lot of bullying seems to be the product of thoughtlessness, where young people's developing brains can't switch off their low tolerance to difference. Since your son is shy, it is entirely possible that this 'difference' might cause him to be victimised. Yet whatever the cause, your son is being bullied, so what now?

All schools have a legal obligation to provide your child with a safe environment in which to learn, so if you believe that that they have failed in this duty of care your first task is to write down the 'who', 'what' and 'where' of the incident and then send these details in an email to your child's teacher. Sending an email is important, as it creates a paper trail. I suspect you will have a very supportive response from your son's teacher, but if you don't, remember that you have the right to request an appointment and if possible take someone with you for moral support. Once you have outlined the problem and the school has indicated that it will respond, don't leave without making a follow-up appointment as you have a right to know what actions the school has taken to ensure your child's safety. If you feel your concerns are not being taken seriously then you also have the right to take this to the deputy principal, principal, regional office and, if necessary, the minister for education in your state or territory. And in more serious cases, if you believe that a law has been broken, you can also make a complaint to the police. Never *ever* contact the parents of the alleged bully as you may end up being assaulted or abused yourself – leave it to the authorities.

All Australian schools should have strategies for dealing with bullying built into their code of practice, and you will almost certainly have seen this document when you enrolled your son. Professor Ken Rigby from the University of South Australia says schools have six main ways of handling bullying (though there are seven if you count doing nothing):

1. The traditional disciplinary approach
2. Strengthening the victim
3. Mediation
4. Restorative practice
5. The support group method
6. The method of shared concern.

It's beyond the scope of this book to go into detail about each of these methods, but the important thing is that the school *follows up your complaint*. However, that doesn't mean you sit back and do nothing. The fact that your son has experienced bullying is a call to action – a sign that you both have some work to do – and there is much you can do to help him develop his anti-bullying skills. Here are some of the best tips:

1. Build strong relationships at home. Do you and your partner have a strong connection with your son, built up over the years by spending lots of time together doing different things? Lonely children are more likely to be bullied, and to allow themselves to be bullied. That connection, however, needs to be positive – built on love and respect, not fear. Parents who hit or shout at their children teach them that physical and emotional violence are the best ways to respond to interpersonal problems. If your discipline methods use power over your child, he will learn to use power over others, or to let others use power over him.

2. Model respectful assertiveness. Do you back down when someone pushes you around, but later feel resentful? Or do you assert your own needs or rights without being aggressive or disrespectful to the other person? Whatever you do, your son is learning from you. Give him phrases that he can use to stick up for himself:

'It's my turn now.'
'I want you to stop that.'
'It's not okay to hurt someone.'
'I don't like being called that. I want you to call me by my name.'

3. Use role-play to coach your child in handling teasing and bullying. Explain how bullies want to provoke a response that makes them feel powerful – they want him to get emotional and fight back. Tell him that he can't control the bully, but that he can always control how he responds to the bully. The idea is to withdraw from the situation in a way that everyone saves face. For starters, teach your child to count to five, to stay calm and to do one of the following:

- Ignore the bully: Pretend they're invisible; look at something else and laugh; pretend you are bored or walk away without looking at them.
- Use bland replies: 'Really?', 'So?', 'Oka-a-ay' ,'And your point is?' or 'Thanks for that.'
- Use a non-defensive question: 'Why would you say that?' or 'Why would you want to tell me I am dumb (or fat) and hurt my feelings?'
- State firmly what you want: 'I want you to leave me alone,' or 'I want you to stop teasing me.'
- Name the bullying behaviour and say no: Teach your child to face the bully by standing tall and using a strong voice, but without getting emotional. Your child should name the bullying behaviour and tell the aggressor to stop: 'That's teasing. Stop it.' or 'Stop making fun of me. It's mean.'

4. **Teach your son that it's okay to ask for help.** Your son also needs to know that it is completely okay to be frightened, and that there is no shame in walking away, or in asking an adult for help.

Bullying – when your child is a bystander

I recently learnt from another parent that one of my 9-year-old daughter's friends has been bullied at school by another child in their group. When I asked my daughter about it, she said she had seen the bully pick on her friend, but hadn't felt she could do anything about it. I was bullied at school myself, so I hate the idea that my daughter watches this kind of behaviour and doesn't feel compelled to do anything to help. Should I encourage her to intervene?

Bystanders play a central role in the bullying process. Onlookers give bullies more incentive to embarrass and threaten their victims because the bully has an audience. Research by Professor Donna Cross and others shows that peers are present for around 85 per cent of bullying interactions, and can have various roles in the bullying process, from facilitating to inhibiting bullying. It appears that 20–30 per cent reinforce the bullying, 26–30 per cent remain passive onlookers and less than 20 per cent act to stop the bullying and defend the student being bullied.

Unfortunately, many people (both adult and younger) believe that being a bystander is the best choice to make. There are many reasons for this. Some may believe that the bullying scenario is 'none of their business', and choose not to take sides because it seems too invasive or interfering. Others feel that stepping in will make them the new focus for the bully, making the whole scenario even worse. Many children also fear that intervening in a bullying situation by telling a teacher will earn them the label of dobber or snitch. Some also believe that intervening won't have much effect, especially if they've approached teachers before regarding bullying and no action was taken.

Thanks to just about every Hollywood movie ever produced, most of us would like to think we would do something to stop a bully, but the truth is we rarely do because we're terrified we'll become the next target. We need to change our focus from the perpetrator to the victim, and work out a way to support the victim by removing them from the bullying situation. Explain to your daughter that she doesn't need to confront the bully. She can simply go and stand next to her friend, turn her away from the bully and walk her off in the other direction – towards adult help – saying *'You look upset'* or *'I've been looking for you'* or *'The teacher wants to see you.'*

Bullying – when your child is the perpetrator

Our 7-year-old son is well behaved at home but we've had reports that he's quite naughty at school and that he teases other children. What should we do?

First you need to verify these reports with the school. Talk to his teacher (or the principal) and find out exactly what he has done, to whom and how often. Once you have this information, talk to him about what you have learnt in a calm, non-judgemental manner. Listen to his side of the story and try to understand what's behind the bullying behaviour. Is he being teased by other children and is simply retaliating? Is there something happening at home that might account for him feeling insecure? Sometimes big changes such as a new baby or a divorce can result in kids acting out.

Studies show that there are several risk factors that can contribute to bullying behaviour:

- lack of parental warmth and involvement
- overly permissive parenting with poor supervision and few limits on children's behaviour
- an authoritarian parenting style using punishment (physical or emotional)
- having an older sibling (especially brother) who bullies
- having friends who bully.

Of course, it might also be the case that your son has not yet developed empathy (it usually kicks in by about the age of seven, but it can also take a bit longer). Here are some short-term tips for encouraging him to understand how his behaviour is affecting others:

- Ask him how he would feel if someone teased him a lot. By encouraging him to put words to his own feelings, you are helping him to identify the feelings of others. Now ask him how the other children might feel to be teased.
- Do some role-play with him, where he first plays the bully and you play the victim, and then reverse the roles. Tell him how you felt when he teased you, and then ask him to tell you how he felt when you teased him. Practise apologising to each other, with the aim of him apologising to the children he has bullied.

Make your expectations of his behaviour crystal clear. Tell him that the bullying has to stop. Call the school regularly to check how your child is behaving. Meanwhile, listed below are some other long-term strategies for encouraging empathy:

- **Use reflective listening:** This means acknowledging (reflecting back) his feelings (e.g. 'I can see you're feeling angry') without trying to rescue him from them (by distracting him or solving the problem that led to them). This not only shows him that it's okay to share feelings, but also allows him to put a name to them. While it sounds simple, stopping for a moment to hear how he feels is very powerful and plays a huge role in the development of empathy. When children believe that their feelings are important, they are more likely to consider the feelings of others.
- **Be empathic:** Show your son what empathy looks like by being an empathic, caring person. That means being able to say things like, 'I'm sorry you are feeling so sad' or 'It must have been hard to lose the race' or to your partner, 'I wanted to watch that show, but I know you prefer this one.' This will show your son that people make decisions by taking the needs of others into consideration.
- **Be consistent and attentive:** Children who feel safe and secure tend to develop empathy for others more quickly.

Finally, if the behaviour does not stop, seek mental health counselling for your child.

I've just heard that my 13-year-old daughter is bullying another girl at her school. I'm really shocked by this, as she's always been a popular, confident child. I just can't understand why she would do it. I'm really upset and have no idea how to handle this. Please help.

First off, don't shout at her or put her in stocks. Start by talking to the school and finding out what has been happening. Once you have that information, ask your daughter for her side of the story. Stay calm and non-judgemental – resist the urge to comment, question or react (no one elected you Senator Graham Richardson) – just listen. Ask her if she knows why she might be doing it. Some children bully because they themselves have been bullied, so listen carefully for clues that she might have been a victim of bullying (you will need to pass on this information to the school). Sometimes children join in with a group that uses bullying behaviour to avoid being bullied themselves. If your child is bullying so she can fit in, talk to the school about strategies she can learn to resist joining in with the bullies.

Most people believe that bullying is the purview of those with low self-esteem, but Australian researcher Dr Helen McGrath has conducted an extensive review of international studies and found that many children who are bullying actually have quite inflated views of themselves and are low in empathy and high in narcissism. She suggests that this may be the result of the 'self-esteem movement' that began in the eighties where, with the best of intentions, parents told their children that everything they did was wonderful and shielded them from having to deal with challenging situations. McGrath says parents need to shift the focus away from self-esteem, which builds on personal achievement and constant comparison with others, and over to self-respect, which is about behaving with morality and dignity. It's being able to say: 'I'm a good person, I treat other people well; I'm pleased when I succeed at things, but I'm humble about it, not superior, and I accept myself with all my limitations and I can deal with life.'

Studies at UCLA have also found that bullying (in the form of physical aggression or spreading rumours) can actually boost the social status and popularity of middle school students. Researcher Jaana Juvonen suggests that anti-bullying strategies need to be much more subtle than a 'no tolerance' approach and recommends schools put more effort into educating bystanders. Most Australian state schools distribute documents that outline the school's anti-bullying strategies at the beginning of each school year, and you can usually access these via the school's website. Check yours to see how they handle bullying and discuss any concerns you have with the school principal.

Whatever is behind your daughter's bullying, you need to tell her that her behaviour is unacceptable and that you want it to change. Talk to her about empathy, and ask her to consider how her bullying is hurting the other child. Most kids who bully are good kids who have learnt some bad behaviour. As long as you keep the lines of communication open with your daughter and she understands what you expect of her, there is no reason to assume that she will be a bully for life.

Choosing schools

I'd always thought it would be fine to send my children to the local public high school, but am disappointed to learn that most of the mothers I met at the primary school are determined to send their sons and daughters to the nearest independent school (private or Catholic). I feel under enormous pressure to send my children to a private school, too, so they can be with their friends, but it just doesn't sit right with me. I am so worried that I might be making the wrong decision by going public. I'd never expected to experience such peer-group pressure at my age! Do you have any advice?

Your confusion is understandable given the allure of a private school's safe, privileged environment and the fear you may have that your child will 'miss out' in a public school that is constantly struggling to make ends meet. But the truth is, research consistently shows that class size, school size, composite classes, manicured gardens and spacious buildings don't make a scrap of difference to your child's academic achievements. My friend the late Professor Ken Rowe crunched all the numbers back in 2003, and found that the quality of teaching is the single most important influence on students' academic performance. Great teachers are mentors – they teach children, not subjects, and they help children find their spark. And great teachers are, in turn, mentored by their principal, who engages with his or her teachers and the community, and creates a culture of continuous learning and development. The fact that you pay thousands of dollars a year to send your child to a private school is no guarantee that they will have wonderful teachers. Also, the financial burden of school fees can mean some parents become angry and resentful when their children do not perform well, causing all sorts of issues for the family. Read David Gillespie's book *Free Schools: How To Get a Great Education for Your Kids without Spending a Fortune.*

Chores

My son, who is in Year 9, is downright rude when I ask him to help around the house. He refuses to keep his room in any kind of order (his uniform is always dirty and crumpled as a result of spending the past year on the floor) and he will only agree to help out with washing up and other chores if it is in exchange for extra time on his computer. He and his younger sister have always had little 'jobs' to do since they were preschoolers (taking their plates to the sink, putting their clothes in the wash, etc.), so it's not as if the idea of helping out is completely alien. How do I get him to help?

You've done the right thing starting early with chores. Having your kids do small jobs around the house (especially those based around responsibility for their own stuff) helps them to develop a sense of competence and to understand that they are part of something larger than themselves – their family group. You want them to learn that doing household jobs is just part of life, and that we all have to do them to keep the household running. The fact that he is resisting sounds like a simple case of boundary testing. He's a teenager, and part of his mission in life is to see what he can get away with (and in the process trying to press as many of your buttons as is humanly possible). He's not five years old any more, and your authority no longer carries the weight it once did so you need to change your approach. For a start, you may need to back off from insisting he keep a clean room. He sees it as his space – his territory – and a way of asserting his independence. You can, however, discuss with him what is reasonable in terms of health and hygiene – rubbish goes into the bin, dirty clothes in the laundry hamper (unless he wants to share his room with mutant rats and cockroaches), but the rest is up to him. As for household chores, you may need to discuss a list of jobs he is expected to do in exchange for more of the adult freedoms he desires. So if he wants today's wi-fi network password, or some money for the cinema, explain that he will need to walk the dog, mow the lawn or empty the dishwasher. If he doesn't fulfil his responsibility, express disappointment and ask when in the next thirty minutes he'll do it. If he still doesn't do it, then whatever privilege the chore was tied to vanishes. There's no point screaming at him or threatening to ban him from the computer for life – this will only send your blood pressure into the stratosphere, trigger defensiveness and shut down communication channels.

My 13-year-old daughter is unbelievably messy. She cares nothing about her clothes and possessions, often loses and breaks things and I'm constantly reminding her to take out her dirty washing. I'm a very tidy person, so every time I walk past her bedroom, I'm sorely tempted to rush in and clean it up, even though I know I shouldn't. I'm so sick of asking her to clean her room, and sometimes I've really lost my temper with her. What should I do?

If your daughter helps around the house in other ways, if she is generally kind and respectful, then I have to say that this may be one of those issues where you need to choose your battles. Whether or not her room is tidy is *breathtakingly* insignificant in the scheme of things. We could light a city with the amount of energy parents expend yelling at their kids about whether their rooms are tidy or not. And I've been through the peer review literature – there is not a single case of a child dying from an untidy room, yet you would think it was the next zombie apocalypse. Parents have got to learn to choose their battles, and the battles are alcohol, drugs, sex and curfews. These are the issues relating to their safety, yet they are very rarely topics of conversation because parents are too busy whining about their rooms.

Of course, there is some substance to the argument that a modicum of order will make life easier. Who hasn't lost their keys/wallet/important document/favourite shirt in the maelstrom of an untidy room? Perhaps you could explain to her that when she's a little older, a bit of room organisation might help her to get out of the house to see her friends more quickly, so it's a good habit to get into now. Or you could point out that white-tailed spiders like to nest in clothing left on the floor. Whatever you do, don't tidy her room (or worse, clean it and then attack her for not doing it). This sends her the clear message that if she ignores a problem for long enough someone else will come and fix it. It also tells her that you don't trust her to do it well enough.

And don't play the fascist card, either. Threatening her with the withdrawal of privileges in the absence of a negotiated deal more often leads to anger and resentment than a clean room. Kids learn best when the consequences of making bad choices have been clearly discussed and will not come as a surprise, not when random consequences are imposed by a controlling parent. The Attila the Hun approach ('Do it because I said so') will always lead a family to the Dark Side. If you value tidiness and she doesn't, you cannot force her to adopt your values. It's only when she can't find something important, or her friends express disgust at the state of her room, that she might consider adopting tidiness as a value of her own.

As parents our aim is to guide, nurture and prompt – not to bully children into obedience and total compliance with our wishes. Any expectations, routines and rules in a family should be there for *mutual* benefit but it is our responsibility as adults to avoid battles.

Computer obsession

I cannot tear my 12-year-old son away from the computer. He even hates leaving it for fifteen minutes to eat his dinner! I'm worried he might be addicted. What can I do?

My philosophy of parenting is that we should only argue over things that matter; namely, things that relate to the wellbeing of our children. This generation was born with a mouse in its hand, so an hour or so of computer time is no big deal. But hours on end is *not* okay, especially if it interferes with schoolwork and family time.

Over the past decade there's been a tonne of media interest in the idea of addiction in the cyber world. Variously labelled 'problematic computer use', 'internet addiction disorder', 'pathological computer use', 'internet overuse' and 'compulsive internet use', its sufferers are basically spending so much time in front of a screen that it interferes with their daily lives (sleeping, eating, showering, working, socialising, etc.). Clinics are opening up all over the world to treat this condition, with some psychologists claiming to have diagnosed children as young as four. However, medical opinion is still very much divided on whether or not it can be considered a genuine clinical disorder. Part of the difficulty is that people with problematic internet use often present with other underlying issues, such as depression, anxiety or obsessive compulsive disorder (OCD), and it can be hard to determine the direction of any causal relationship. Also, people can certainly develop pathological connections to pornography, shopping or online games via a computer, but does this mean the medium itself is addictive?

Indeed, the most recent edition of the Diagnostic and Statistical Manual of Mental Disorders (the DSM-V) has not seen fit to include internet addiction in its list. I mean really – when Mummy takes the tablet away does a temper tantrum or a flood of tears mean your child is an addict?

A more useful way of looking at internet use is to consider not simply how much time someone is on a computer screen, but what they are actually doing. Is your son playing a game that he loves? Is he social networking with friends? Is he doing his homework? From your description I'm guessing he is playing a game, which means he will be hooked right into the reward system that ensures kids keep playing (levelling up, being able to buy stuff using game tokens, etc.). I'm sure that if you let him, he would play it until he bled from the eyeballs! As parents, it is our job to help our children learn to manage their impulsivity. This means we need to set boundaries.

We set boundaries in the real world, so the online world should be no different. How you do this will depend on your parenting style, but in my experience, an autocratic approach (my house, my rules) just creates conflict, as does screaming at your child 'That's it! You are banned from the internet for a week!' especially when you inevitably fail to follow through with those consequences.

The best way to set boundaries is to 'externalise' the rules, agreeing on them as a family rather than making them up as you go, and to base those rules on values – what the family wants (rather than what they don't want). Here are the most important ones:

Use the internet in a family space: Make sure that the computer and any other devices that your children use are in a public space such as a lounge room or living area. This is especially important for young children as it means you can see the sites they are using and be ready to answer any questions they might have. And as seductive as it is to allow older children to take laptops off to their bedrooms so they can 'do their homework' and give you some peace and quiet, they must always use the internet in a public space, not in private. This is something that is in line with the family values of health and safety, and also helps to make computer time more of a family activity. Even though kids will be glued to their own screen, they are more likely to share experiences with parents and siblings ('Come and look at this!') and to troubleshoot technical problems together. Even older teenagers should not be allowed to keep a laptop (or a smart phone) in their rooms, as it promotes poor sleep habits. You can simply say that until they can pay for their own wi-fi, the internet needs to be accessed in a public space.

Set time limits: Limit the time they are allowed on the devices. Understandably, this won't be so easy on their mobile phone, but at night, the computer shouldn't be a portal to constant interaction. It should be used first and foremost to complete their homework. Then, sure, an hour should be allowed and allocated for social interaction. If this isn't stipulated and controlled, believe me, your teenager will be on there until you physically pull the plug around midnight.

Teach the Seven-Second Rule: The Seven-Second Rule is a good one to share with kids when it comes to social media. If your child is feeling irritated or angry about something that someone has posted, and is itching to make a knee-jerk response, get them to have a good look at what they are about to post or send on SMS, Twitter or Facebook, and if anything seems even *slightly* risky, tell them not to hit the send button. Instead, tell them to look away for seven seconds, take a breath, and then look at the message or post again. If they are still feeling irritated or angry, get them to step back for another seven seconds until they are calmer and can more accurately judge whether what they are about to send is going to cause more problems.

Learn how to set parental controls: Nowadays, it's not only computers, laptops and mobile phones that connect to the internet, but game consoles and TVs. Make sure you know which devices can connect to the internet and that you understand how to set parental controls. These are tools to help you set time limits (locking) and to filter or block inappropriate material. They are not the answer to your child's online safety, but they are a good start and they're not as difficult to install as you might think. Service providers are working hard to make them simple, effective and user friendly.

Here are some handy links for the main games consoles:

- Xbox: support.xbox.com/en-US/billing-and-subscriptions/parental-controls/xbox-live-parental-control
- Playstation: manuals.playstation.net/document/en/ps3/current/basicoperations/parentallock.html
- Wii: http://www.nintendo.com.au/parental-controls-wii

Curfews

My 15-year-old daughter is going out with her 16-year-old boyfriend next Saturday night on their first real date (they are going to the cinema in the city). When I suggested she should be home by 10 p.m. (as she lacks experience on public transport), she stormed off in a fury, claiming that I treated her like a child. If I am so concerned about her safety, should I drive to pick her up?

Making the transition from childhood to adolescence is always tricky because your relationship with her is changing. She is seeking greater independence, which is a natural and normal part of her development. You are caught up in the time-honoured struggle to find a balance between giving her greater freedom and setting necessary boundaries. Since she is changing rapidly, it is normal for you to feel a lack of control and for conflict to increase. Clear communication and negotiated boundaries can help to ease some of the tension.

Most teens respond well to parents who have high expectations but who also grant them a certain amount of autonomy. So, rather than just setting a 10 p.m. curfew, negotiate a time you can both live with. Allowing her to have a say will increase her feelings of independence and encourage ownership of the time. Also agree on a consequence if she breaks this rule. It is important that she feels that the consequences are fair and make sense. Remind her about the curfew you have agreed upon before she heads out. This helps reinforce the agreed-upon rule. It is reasonable and respectful to allow a buffer of a few minutes, particularly if they are using public transport or taxis. If she is delayed, send a text to show your concern. Enforce consequences for broken rules, but avoid constantly reminding her of her mistake.

Cyber-bullying

My daughter has suddenly stopped using her smart phone and it's freaking me out. She's 14, and usually spends half of her life on it (you should hear the battles we have about keeping it out of her bedroom at night) so for her to suddenly leave it in the kitchen for two days is very weird. When I asked her about whether it was broken or if she was out of credit, she snapped at me and almost shouted, 'I don't want to talk about it!' Should I be worried or is this just a teenage moment?

A sudden change in phone or internet usage is a classic sign that your daughter may be the victim of bullying. Once it was fists, elbows, sticks and stones – now bullies have new weapons: mobile phones, tablets, YouTube, social networking sites and microblogs. Today's bullies are just as likely to waylay their victims from a mobile phone as they are to come out and fight in the real world. That's not to say that real-life bullying in the form of schoolyard brawls or being excluded, ostracised and humiliated by the mean girls at recess has vanished, simply that the opportunities for brutality are now augmented by 24/7 availability. The bully not only follows your child home but, by virtue of the technology, settles into your house.

The privacy afforded by mobile and internet technology can make it very difficult to know when your child is being bullied. (It's not like the old days when kids came home with black eyes, torn clothing or missing books.) But apart from changes in usage, there are other signs to look for:

- receiving more frequent text messages or ones at odd hours of the day or night
- having trouble sleeping or having nightmares
- becoming withdrawn and not socialising with friends
- feeling unwell and not wanting to go to school.

To my mind, cyber-bullying is the deliberate and repeated harassment of someone using technology (online or via mobile phone) and includes behaviours such as posting hurtful messages or images, sending repeated unwanted messages, excluding someone from an online group, creating false social-networking profiles to impersonate and ruin someone's reputation, and encouraging others to bully the victim.

According to Professor Donna Cross, the most common vehicle for cyber-bullying among Australian teenagers is SMS.

While many young people are able to shrug off the odd nasty text message, for those who are cruelly or repeatedly targeted, the mental health effects can be severe. This is partly because a text once shared, cannot be deleted – the gossip, lies, doctored photos and unwanted videos on social media stay around long after any bruises would have faded. Like any abuse, cyber-bullying can have various effects on young people including poor performance at school, feelings of sadness, physical illness and low self-esteem. For some young people, cyber-bullying can be the straw that breaks the camel's back and, when combined with other factors in their lives, can sometimes lead to serious mental health issues such as anxiety disorders and depression, and may even lead to self-harm and suicide.

It's really important to open a dialogue with your daughter. I know you have already tried to do this, but don't give up. Speak to her while you are in the car together, or doing some chore side by side.

- Let her know that you are there for her if someone is bothering her, that you don't judge her and that she doesn't have to deal with it alone.
- Remind her that it's not her fault that she is being cyber-bullied and that she has options.
- Ask her how she has been handling the perpetrator (victims should ignore the bully and never respond to their messages or taunts. Bullies and trolls thrive on the feedback they receive from their victims – retaliation may further inflame the situation and can work against your daughter, as other people might think she is part of the problem).
- Ask her if she knows how to block contacts on her phone (or ask her to show you how to do it on yours as a way of introducing the topic). Kids need to know how to filter email messages and block posts or contacts on social media.

- Ask her to keep a record of the harassing messages and any replies as this may help the authorities learn the identity of the perpetrator (this becomes necessary in cases where the bullying or harassment breaks the law, i.e. when the bully threatens physical harm, expresses interest in activities of a sexual nature or suggests any kind of potentially illegal behaviour).
- If it is clear that she is deeply uncomfortable talking to you, refer her to the school counsellor, GP or other trained counsellors, such as those available at Lifeline (13 11 14) and Kids Helpline (1800 551 800).
- If you think she would prefer online help rather than face-to-face, point her to some of the great fact sheets written for young people:

  Youth beyondblue

  youthbeyondblue.com/factsheets-and-info/fact-sheet-20-bullying/

  Headspace

  headspace.org.au/is-it-just-me/find-information/bullying

  ReachOut

  au.reachout.com/Cyber-bullying

  Cybersmart

  cybersmart.gov.au/Teens/How%20do%20I%20deal%20with/Cyber-bullying.aspx

  Bullying No Way

  http://bullyingnoway.gov.au/

I have a shy sixth-grader who recently started at a new school (we moved from interstate). One day he was browsing a social media site and came across an unauthorised web page about his new school with pictures of students, including one of him tagged 'The Fat Ugly F@#k'. Upset, he posted a reply expressing his feelings and outrage. Since then, the postings have become much nastier. My son endured many weeks of humiliation and hurt before he could bring himself to tell us what was going on. We didn't know because he was too embarrassed to tell us. I have banned the computer, but what else should we do?

Victims of cyber-bullying are very often in a vulnerable psychological situation, so your response to him, and how you proceed with the school is critically important. Your first task is to acknowledge how hard this must have been for him. Recognising your child's pain and affirming that what happened wasn't fair or right is important validation. Listen to him without judgement, blame or attempting to leap in and 'solve' it. Instead, quietly ask questions to find how long the cyber-bullying has been going on, the names of those involved (if known), and any other information that might help (such as text messages, posts, websites, etc.).

Being cyber-bullied is bad enough, so don't do anything that makes your child feel even more isolated. Banning him from the internet will make him feel even more like a social pariah – accessing instant messaging, email and social networking sites is how children connect with each other. Record everything that has happened in an email. Formally tell the school what has transpired and arrange an immediate meeting with the principal. Save the evidence and bring it with you. Hopefully, they have trained their teachers and have a zero-tolerance policy on cyber-bullying. Expect them to respond quickly. They should be able to identify the ringleaders and, with the help of the perpetrator's parents, have the creator of the unauthorised school page remove it from the social media site.

Dating and relationships

Our 13-year-old daughter wants to go to the pictures with a boy she likes. Is it just me, or does 13 seem too young for a serious boyfriend?

There isn't a 'right age' to start having intimate relationships – every child is different, and every family will handle this life stage differently. By 'intimate', I don't necessarily mean sexual, although those feelings may be part of an intimate relationship; I mean a very close, emotional connection with one particular person. Most teens of this age have got their hands full starting high school and managing their peer friendships – learning how to listen, how to talk to each other, how to manage conflict, make compromises and solve problems. It may be that your daughter is simply 'trying out' what it might feel like to go out with one particular boy. The only way you can be sure is to talk to her. Ask her why she wants to go out with him separately, rather than in a group. (Does she want to get to know him better?) Also ask her if any of her friends have boyfriends or girlfriends (which may mean she feels under pressure to conform). More importantly, you need to find out the age of the boy. If he is 16 (or older) he may be sexually more experienced and this can have legal implications. Whether or not you allow her to go out with him will depend on how well you know your daughter. Ask yourself the important questions:

1. Does she have a track record of making good decisions or is she easily led into unsafe situations?
2. Does she hang out with sensible kids or is she susceptible to dodgy peer pressure?
3. Is she a sensation-seeker by temperament or more risk averse?

If you've kept the lines of communication open with your daughter you can also broach other important topics such as curfews, breaking up kindly, respecting other people's boundaries and the big one – sex. You should also agree on some strategies for what she should do if she feels unsafe or threatened. It's a good idea to develop an emergency 'come and get me' plan. For example, if she sends you a text message with a sad face emoticon it could be the signal for you to ring her and arrange to collect her immediately.

Depression in young people

My 15-year-old daughter has been extremely moody for the past few weeks. She is very negative about the future and extremely self-critical. She doesn't want to go anywhere with her friends, and just hides in her room every night until I call her for dinner. When I ask her if everything is okay, she snaps at me. I think she's having trouble sleeping, which might explain her behaviour. How can I help her when she won't talk to me?

Anyone who has lived with teenagers for even a nanosecond knows that from time to time they can be down in the dumps, cranky and irritable, and that this is to be expected given the hormonal maelstrom that is changing their brains and bodies. Noticeable changes in mood also happen after a stressful life event, such as a recent death, family separation, physical trauma, or being bullied at school. In most young people, these feelings may last for a few moments, a few hours or at the most a day or two. However, if a teenager or a child has a pervasive sense of despair that lasts longer than two weeks and interferes with their daily lives, they may be suffering from depression.

Depression is an illness that is much more than sadness – it is a relentless hopelessness that leads people to lose interest in everything that once brought them joy or pleasure. Normal stresses can seem unbearable, and the strain of soldiering on and trying to pretend that 'nothing is wrong' can exacerbate the illness.

The following list shows the kinds of behaviours and symptoms typically associated with depression:

- avoidance of friends and other usual pursuits
- decline in academic performance
- increased irritability, anger or hostility
- indecisiveness
- absence of energy and motivation
- feelings of numbness and emptiness
- changes in appetite (loss of appetite or overeating)
- disturbed sleep (insomnia or hypersomnia)

- increased sensitivity to failure or rejection
- complaints about headaches, stomach aches, tiredness, 'growing pains'
- persistent sadness and bouts of crying
- feelings of worthlessness, pessimism and gloom
- restlessness, agitation
- disruptive and antisocial behaviour (e.g. uncharacteristic bullying)
- risk-taking (e.g. inappropriate sexual contacts, reckless driving)
- drug and alcohol abuse

This list is not meant to alarm you, but to help you understand when you really need to worry. Depression is nobody's fault, and is caused by the complex interplay of many different factors, both genetic and environmental. According to the most recent figures from the Australian Bureau of Statistics, 6 per cent of young Australians aged 16–24 years were diagnosed with depression in 2007. However, depression has high rates of comorbidity with anxiety and substance abuse disorders, so when you factor in that 15 per cent of young people have an anxiety disorder, and 13 per cent a substance abuse disorder, the number of young people suffering from depression is likely to be much higher.

The important thing is to try to open up a dialogue with your daughter so that you can arrange to take her to see a GP. Be patient with her. She needs your support, not your criticism. Try talking while you are doing something together (making dinner, driving somewhere). If she doesn't like the idea of seeing the 'family' doctor, find her one she does like – she might prefer someone younger, or a female doctor.

If the doctor suspects that your daughter is depressed, psychological therapies such as cognitive behavioural therapy (CBT) and interpersonal therapy (IPT) are still considered the first line of treatment for diagnosed depression and anxiety in children and teenagers. These therapies help young people change negative thoughts and feelings, encourage them to get involved in activities, and help them identify ways to manage the illness and stay well. In severe cases, antidepressant medication may be recommended along with psychological therapies. Don't be afraid if this happens – the short-term use of antidepressants (specifically the SSRI sertraline) has been found to be very effective in treating anxiety and depression in teenagers. There are also some excellent websites that can help both of you, including Youth beyondblue (youthbeyondblue.com), ReachOut (au.reachout.com) and Headspace (headspace.org.au), which have fact sheets on depression and young people as well as online chat and telephone support services. Orygen Youth Health (oyh.org.au) and the Black Dog Institute (blackdoginstitute.org.au) are also great for parents.

Whatever you do, do *something*. Depression won't 'go away' by itself, so it is crucial that you follow up the doctor's recommendations. Above all, be patient, kind and loving.

Digital devices (iPod touches, iPads, tablets and other portable screens)

My 5-year-old came home from school the other day and asked if I would buy him an iPad for his birthday, claiming that several of his classmates had them. I've only just got a smart phone myself, so it's a bit of a shock. I like the idea that he could play games on a larger screen and that it might help him with his reading, but I'm not so keen on him being able to access the internet. My instinct is to say no, but am I being a troglodyte? How should I handle this?

I don't think you are being a digital dinosaur, I think you are simply being cautious. The reality is that this is a generation born with a tablet in their hand. Many time-poor parents download age-appropriate apps for their youngsters, convincing themselves of their educational benefits. They may even secretly harbour the belief that by exposing their 5-year-old to an iPad that they are raising the next Steve Jobs or Bill Gates. The truth is that no one really knows. Studies on the developmental impact of tablet use in preschoolers are still years away. That is not to say that there aren't plenty of child development experts who are already concerned. UK psychologist Dr Aric Sigman argues that the amount of screen time children are allowed is already too high. He says that by the time they're seven years old the average child born today will have spent the equivalent of two years (twelve hours a day) watching screen media. And he believes this overexposure is leading to a generation of children who are developing a lifelong dependency on small screens.

Dr Michael Rich, director of Boston's Center on Media and Child Health, says that playing games activates the brain's dopamine pathways – its pleasure centre. Many apps are designed to encourage children to keep playing by offering rewards or exciting visuals at unpredictable times – which, Dr Rich says, gives a dopamine squirt. That dopamine rush is the same effect triggered by playing the pokies, which we all know can lead to serious addiction. However, I have plenty of colleagues, especially at the Young and Well Cooperative Research Centre, who cogently argue against such fear-mongering. Personally, I wonder if there is even all that much difference between a 6-year-old's obsession with *Minecraft* and my own childhood obsession with Lego – after all, they both involve building and creating. Stay tuned: in a couple of years we'll have some more answers. In the meantime, strive for balance. The Michael Carr-Gregg Digital Equation for kids is that every hour of screen time should be balanced by one hour of real-world activity.

Discipline

I've got two gorgeous kids aged four and six but they are a bit of a handful. They fight a lot and are very headstrong. It's hard to get them to sit at the table to have dinner (they're constantly getting up and down, and helping themselves to things in the fridge etc.). And getting them to stay in bed and go to sleep is the bane of my life. My husband doesn't come home until after

7 p.m., so I'm pretty much exhausted by then and all he sees is chaos and misbehaviour. He thinks I'm too lenient and that the kids basically rule the roost. I know it's important for us to be on the same page, so what can I do?

The first rule of parenting young children is to provide lots of engaging indoor and outdoor activities – kids aged four to six tend to misbehave when they are bored. Do you have a 'craft' area, where they can help themselves to paper, pencils etc.? And do you have play equipment outside for them (a sandpit, swing or trampoline)? If you do have all of this, they still might need your help to get started. For example, draw with them for a few moments, perhaps setting them a drawing task, and then leave them to it. Play is the business of childhood, allowing your children free rein to experiment with the world around them and the emotional world inside them. The research is clear about how play builds their imagination, promotes social skills, advances physical development, and helps kids work through the emotions. Time spent with children playing is never wasted.

Second, and this is crucial, you must create daily routines for eating, bathing, sleeping and playing and stick to them. Young children love routines – they help them feel secure – but it can take a bit of persistence on your part to set them up. Just keep acknowledging their feelings while you maintain your expectations: 'I know you feel angry with me because you want to keep playing and don't want to have a bath right now, but we always have a bath after dinner.' Routines help children understand that there are limits on their behaviour; in other words, that they can't do whatever they want whenever they want. Your job as a parent is to extend the idea of these limits to their social behaviour, letting them know what the consequences will be if they break the rules. Consequences must always be negotiated beforehand, be reasonable, related to the misdemeanour and respectful of the child's dignity. For example, when they are playing, the rules might be that they take turns; that it's okay to be angry but it's not okay to be nasty; and if they do hurt someone they won't be able to play with the toy/do the activity any more.

Third, when they do break the rules, you need to stay calm and give them clear instructions to stop what they are doing, and remind them what they should be doing instead. Praise your child if they stop.

Finally, if they do not stop what they are doing, follow through with the agreed consequence. 'You know the rules and you chose not to stop, so I am taking away the toy now. You can have it back after dinner.'

Our 10-year-old daughter is incredibly stubborn and defiant. She refuses to do things we ask (when she doesn't see the point) and can be quite cruel to her younger brother. Yesterday she told me she hated me and stormed out of the kitchen. We are at our wit's end. We've sent her to her room and tried withdrawing privileges (computer time) but nothing works. We've also talked to her about the impact of her behaviour on other people (i.e. us) but this just makes her even angrier. We have a stable, loving family and have set clear boundaries for our children's behaviour, so I have no idea where this is coming from. She's never like this at school or around other people, and when she's in a good mood, she's great fun. Is there something wrong with the way we are disciplining her?

The word discipline (like disciple) comes from the Latin word *disciplina*, which means instruction/knowledge. Discipline, then, is really another word for teaching, and when we're talking about kids, it's about teaching them acceptable behaviour – how to follow the rules that help them fit in to their family and into society.

However, discipline is not punishment, and should never be seen as punishment. There's an Olympic stadium of research to show that punishment (whether it be a smack, banishment to another room or withdrawal of privileges) does not help kids behave better. In fact corporal punishment (hitting a child) is linked to increased rates of aggression, delinquency, depression, anxiety, drug use and relationship problems in later life, and is now a criminal offence in some countries. Punishment might stop a particular behaviour in the short term, but it denies children the opportunity to set their own moral compass. They are following the rules not because they want to do the right thing but because they want to avoid punishment (and they often don't do the right thing when parents aren't watching).

As parents we must set reasonable expectations for behaviour, but that does not mean punishing children when they don't comply. This just creates resentment and encourages defiance and conflict, which you discovered the hard way when you sent your daughter to her room and took away her privileges. Trying to talk to her about her behaviour when she's angry won't work either. When the adrenalinee is pumping the thinking part of her brain shuts off. Always wait until you and your daughter are calm before discussing a particular incident.

When your daughter behaves in a way that you want to discourage, wait until you are both calm, then ask a question beginning with 'what'.

What were you thinking when you pushed your brother?
What were you feeling before you slammed the door?
What will you do next time when you feel like acting that way?
What will you do now to make it up to your brother?

These types of questions will get her to reflect on her feelings, thoughts and behaviour, and open up conversations that lead to learning. When she expresses her frustration, hurt or disappointment, listen to her. Don't interrupt. She has to follow the rules, but she's allowed to have her own opinions and feelings about them. If you offer her empathy and respect, she'll be much more willing to listen to you when you remind her of the rules. This is called setting limits with empathy, otherwise known as authoritative parenting.

If she still chooses not to follow the rules, it will be a sign that your relationship needs strengthening and that you need to build up trust and respect. Even when she pushes your buttons, don't react. It takes two to have a fight, and you don't have to attend every argument to which you've been invited. If you feel that you're about to lose your temper, withdraw yourself from the situation: 'I feel really unhappy about what just happened and I need to think about it for a while.

We'll talk about it later. I don't want to talk about it right now.' Make sure you do follow up, and use 'what' questions as described above.

Divorce and separation

My husband and I are going through a trial separation and will likely divorce. When he moved out last weekend we told the kids (they're 11 and 14) that we were going to try living apart for a while to see if we got along better. They were really upset, and for the past week have been asking when their father is coming back. We are both really worried about the kids and how this will affect them in the long term. How can we help them through this?

Divorce can be one of the most traumatic events in a child's life (and in an adult's life, let's be honest) but it doesn't have to be a disaster. The fact that both of you discussed the separation with your children, and that both of you are worried about its impact on them, means you are on the right track. As long as you can keep things cordial between you, there is no reason to assume that your divorce will create long-term emotional problems for your kids. I'll grant that some of the research does look scary at first, with the kids of divorced parents having higher rates of dropping out of school, substance abuse and serious mental illness than the children of non-divorced families, but this says less about the experience of divorce itself and more about the family members' psychological and socioeconomic situation. Other research has found that for girls in particular, the experience of divorce makes them more resilient, competent and responsible.

Australian statistics show that children fare the worst when a divorce is acrimonious, conflict-ridden, and the children are used as pawns by warring parents. Despite the emotional strain this separation is bound to cause for you and your husband, it's vital that each of you stays attuned to the feelings and concerns of your children and that you work together to give them clear and consistent information about what's happening. Given that you are united in your desire to help your kids, you are well ahead of the game.

One way to make it easier on the kids is to sort out the practicalities well before you break the news of the divorce to them. Children need to know the 'who, what, where, when and how' of the divorce because it helps them to feel more secure. Who is moving out? What house will we live in? Where will we go to school? How often will we get to see Mum/Dad? Who gets the family pet? The news should be delivered by both of you, preferably on a weekend and in the morning, so they have time to absorb the information and ask questions.

It's also important to allow your children to express their feelings about the divorce. Let them know it's okay to feel sad or angry, and that you are both there to help them if they need you. (This is always a tough one for parents out of touch with their own emotions – if you feel uncomfortable when they are crying or angry and find yourself saying 'Calm down' or 'That's enough now', it's clear you've got some work to do.) Of course, they also need to know that there are limits, for example, 'It's okay to be frustrated but it's not okay to hurt someone or smash something.'

Explain that the divorce is not their fault. This is important, as children who believe that they are somehow at fault may harbour fantasies about their parents getting back together and divert a lot of emotional energy into trying to make that happen.

Emphasise that both of you still love the children, and that they don't have to 'choose' between you – both of you will still be involved in their lives (hopefully equally in terms of time).

Tell them that the divorce is about change, not blame. Divorce can be a scary concept, but all it really means is that your family will be experiencing some changes, and change is okay.

My husband and I separated a few months ago and I am a bit nervous about my children (aged seven and 11) having Christmas lunch with my ex and his new girlfriend. I understand that they need to see their father, but I feel really anxious about them spending most of Christmas Day with a stranger, and I think they are worried, too. How do I handle this?

Your anxiety is understandable, but research shows that children whose parents' divorce is recent and reasonably amicable will always benefit from seeing both parents. Visiting their father will not only help reinforce the idea that both parents are still there if they need them, but also lessen their insecurities about having had no control over the divorce and new relationships. Basically, your children's needs should be paramount, and in this case, your children will take their emotional lead from you. If you are feeling nervous, they will feel nervous. You can't change what has happened, but you can change the way you think about it, and in doing so, shift your emotional response. First, reinforce the message that you are really happy for Daddy to have a new friend. (Think about it: if he's happy, he's going to be a better father.) Second, explain that even though he's not living at home any more, he will always love them and want them to be part of his life. Third, tell them that it's normal to feel a bit worried about meeting someone for the first time, but that Daddy's girlfriend will probably be even more nervous than they are. Finally, don't forget that the person under the most stress on that day might well be you, so make sure you take care of yourself by spending time with your extended family as well. Family Relationships Online (familyrelationships.gov.au) is a website with some excellent information about relationship issues for all families (whether together or separated).

Driving a car

My 16-year-old son says he is keen to get his licence, but it terrifies me to think of him behind the wheel. What should I do?

There is no one-size-fits-all answer to this question. If you live in a city with a decent public transport system, I'd wonder why your son is in such a hurry. However, if you live in an area poorly served by trains or buses, and there is simply no other way for your son to get to work, or to visit his friends other than relying on you, then it might make sense. In fact, the variation in minimum driving ages between the states and territories reflects just that – Victoria's is 18 years and the Northern Territory's is 16 years, 6 months. (Interestingly, the minimum age for a learner's permit is still 16 in most states and territories; however, if a driver obtained their learner's permit after 1 July 2007, they must log 120 hours of practice before they can obtain their provisional licence.)

If you decide to go ahead, use a professional driving instructor if you can: they know what they are doing and have huge cojones! Of course, if you live on a farm, have an old ute and millions of acres to roam around on, teaching him yourself is fine. Free lessons are available through the Australian government-funded program Keys2Drive. Once he gets his learner's permit, you are expected to be his supervising driver for 120 hours. To help you through this sometimes traumatic experience, there are six things to bear in mind:

1. Insurance. Make sure your policy covers a learner driver who is being taught by a parent, as a minor bingle or two is usually par for the course.
2. Get a safety check on your vehicle. Fix squeaky brakes, wonky steering, crappy tyres, etc., because a car that is ship-shape will make the driving experience easier and safer.
3. Take a road rules refresher. You may think you know all the rules, but you'll be surprised at what details you've forgotten.
4. Decide on a manual or an automatic. If your household has both a manual and an automatic vehicle, keep in mind that if he tests for his P1 licence in an automatic, he cannot then drive a manual until he gets a P2 licence twelve months later (unless he is driving with an unrestricted driver in the passenger seat). If you do decide to teach your son to drive a manual car, one dad advised me to keep the window down so your son can hear the engine revs.

5. If you are teaching him yourself, find a good place to start off, such as a quiet, local street, a deserted country road, an empty car park or an industrial estate on a weekend. As he becomes more experienced, gradually introduce him to light traffic.
6. Establish a checklist for each driving session, and take it slowly. Before he even turns the ignition, explain the process of driving and talk him through the main functions on the dashboard, the gears and the pedals. Teach him a 'cockpit drill' – checking and adjusting the seat and mirrors – and make sure he does it every time. It is especially important to talk about blind spots. You have 120 hours. Take it slowly, and help consolidate the basics first.

The accident statistics for Australian drivers under 25 are very scary, particularly during the first six months after they get their licence. Many parents are so focused on getting their teens through the learning process and practical exam that they drop their guard when their teenager is finally qualified to drive. *Going Solo* is a free booklet available online from the Monash University Accident Research Centre (monash.edu.au/miri/going-solo-brochure.pdf) with advice for parents on helping their young drivers through this critical period. These are the high-risk situations to avoid:

- driving with peer passengers
- driving at night
- being distracted (hands-free mobile phones, CD players)
- driving in poor weather conditions
- driving on high-speed roads
- driving when tired.

Drugs

My son is in his second year of high school and is hanging around a crowd I don't really care for. These kids seem to spend a lot of time at the local shopping centre, which I take as a bad sign (it's the kind of shopping centre that has a reputation for petty crime). I've actually heard from other parents that one of the kids is smoking and has taken drugs and I'm scared that my son will be influenced by their bad habits. I really want to talk to him about the dangers of drug taking, but I'm worried that I will alienate him. How should I deal with this?

Adolescence is a time of experimentation, and young people may take drugs as they struggle to establish their independence in a society where alcohol and other drugs are associated with being an 'adult'. However, you are right to be concerned about your son, as drug experimentation is more likely to become a problem if started early in high school or if a young person hangs out with others who are using drugs. The good news is that while peers can influence his choices, so can you. The research shows that teenagers who have a close attachment to a trusted adult (a family member, teacher or coach) are less likely to make poor choices when confronted with the chance of using drugs.

You can also reduce the risks by doing the following:

- Involve him in sport, art, music, dance or drama – these activities will help him to develop a strong sense of self and give him opportunities for healthy risk-taking (e.g. through performing).
- Make clear your values and attitudes about drugs – no lecturing, please! The best thing you can do is to model the responsible use of alcohol yourself.
- Establish clear and consistent ground rules. Explain that your role is to keep him safe, and his job is to experiment, and that together you need to find a compromise between the two. Decide on the rules together, and what the consequences should be if the rules are broken. For example, that you should know where he is, who he is with and when he is expected home. You'll need to be flexible and adapt the ground rules as he starts to show that he is ready for more responsibility.

- Explain how to assess risk. You can talk about other people's behaviour and its consequences (for instance, in movies or on the news). For example, 'If he hadn't been speeding, he wouldn't have lost his licence. Now he's going to lose his job as well.'
- Keep the lines of communication open. If you harass the stuffing out of him, he's not going to feel like telling you where he's going, let alone who he'll be with.

My (just) 17-year-old daughter came home from a party last week and was clearly stoned. Although she didn't break curfew (she came home before midnight) and she wasn't out at a pub or anything, I'm still worried. How should I deal with this?

Adolescence and risk-taking go hand in hand. This is because teenagers are trying to work out who they are, and this involves pushing boundaries, exploring their identity and testing their abilities. It's part of their journey to becoming independent young adults. Your daughter may have chosen to try marijuana for a number of reasons, which may have included one of the following.

- sheer curiosity (everyone seemed to be so happy that she wanted to experience it too)
- peer pressure (everyone else was doing it and she did not want to feel different or left out)
- sensation-seeking (she wanted to experience the thrill of doing something that her parents disapprove of)
- distraction (she may have wanted to avoid feelings of frustration about school or work, sadness or anger about friendship or relationship difficulties, or low self-esteem and/or depression)

While rates of cannabis use in Australia have reduced markedly over the past decade, it is still widely used by young people, and the possible impacts on adolescent development remain an important issue. According to the 2010 National Drug Strategy Household Survey, rates of cannabis use by males and females aged 14–19 have converged over time and are now almost on par (15.9 per cent for males, 15.5 per cent for females). This convergence is similar to the pattern seen for tobacco smoking and alcohol consumption. Adolescent use of cannabis has been linked to a range of developmental and social problems. A review of current literature suggests that cannabis use from an early age impacts memory, attention and learning ability, leading to poorer educational outcomes and problematic behaviour. It also places the person at risk of impaired emotional development, increased risk of becoming more dissatisfied with their life and increased risk of depression.

If you suspect your daughter has tried smoking pot as a means of distracting her from facing deeper issues, you must attend to these as early as possible to prevent any related drug use from escalating. You can get heaps of great information by logging on to australia.gov.au/drugs or calling 1800 250 015.

Eating disorders

My daughter is 15 and is obsessed with her body weight. She is very thin, and is very strict about what she will and will not eat. She is fine with vegetables, but never eats bread or pasta, rarely finishes her dinner and never eats dessert. Although she takes her lunch to school every day, I'm never sure if she eats it. I've tried to talk to her about how important it is for her to eat well while her body is growing, but she only gets angry with me and gives me a lecture about the evils of sugar and carbs. I am really worried that she is developing an eating disorder. What should I do?

The first thing you need to do is to open up a dialogue with your daughter so that you can get her to see a GP. I realise you have already tried to talk to her, but you must persist. Anorexia has the highest mortality rate of any mental illness, yet is still poorly understood. It's predicted that between 8 and 20 per cent of victims will die as a result of the disease – half of them by their own hand – and that a further 30 per cent will remain chronically ill for the rest of their lives, battling complications such as heart failure, osteoporosis, digestive diseases, chronic anxiety, psychosis and depression.

To start a discussion with her, the Eating Disorders Foundation of Victoria recommends using 'I' statements to tell her about the behaviours you have noticed. For example:

- 'I'm feeling anxious because I've noticed that you seem to be very concerned about how you look, and you seem to be giving yourself a pretty hard time at the moment. Is there anything I can do to help?'
- 'I'm really concerned about how much exercise you are doing. I am finding it hard to talk with you because we seem to end up fighting whenever I bring it up. What can I do to help?'
- 'I'm very worried about you. You don't seem very happy. Is there anything that you would like to talk to me about?'
- 'I've noticed that you don't seem to be enjoying time with your friends any more, or spending time doing things that you used to love doing. I would really like to help you to feel better about yourself.'

Here are some of the things you must *not* do if you want your daughter to get well:

- make comments about her appearance or weight ('You are so skinny')
- name other people who are also worried ('Your father and I . . .')
- try to force her to eat
- try to trick her into eating
- use judgemental 'you' statements such as 'You are completely unreasonable', 'You need help', 'You aren't eating enough', 'You are bulimic, anorexic or you have an eating disorder', 'You are being silly', or 'Just get over it and eat'.

Tell her you are worried about her, and that you would like her to see the doctor for a check-up. Offer to go with her to the appointment if she wants you to.

A diagnosis of anorexia nervosa is usually made if your daughter weighs 15 per cent less than she should for her height and age, and if she has particular beliefs related to her food intake, weight and shape. The doctor will ask about weight history, family problems, attitudes to food, dieting and weight loss behaviours, and about the way she thinks she looks, or feels she should look. Diagnosis will also involve a comprehensive medical examination with blood tests and/or an electrocardiogram which records the electrical activity of the heart over time.

People who have anorexia usually fit the following criteria:

- weigh much less than is healthy or normal
- are very afraid of gaining weight
- think they are overweight even when they are very thin
- obsess about food, weight and dieting
- strictly limit how much they eat
- exercise a lot, even when they are sick.

Here is some other behaviour you may notice:

- taking a long time to eat, yet consuming very little
- missing mealtimes
- denying feeling hungry
- amassing recipes and preparing food for others while finding reasons to avoid eating
- accumulating or hoarding food
- wearing shapeless clothes
- feeling fearful or anxious before eating and guilty after eating
- grumbling about feeling bloated or full after eating a tiny amount of food.

If your daughter does have anorexia, the first thing you must accept is that when she looks in the mirror, she does not see the same gaunt figure that you see. Treating anorexia is very difficult because most sufferers deny that they have a problem. Even those who are near death will insist that parts of their bodies are overweight. Part of the challenge for clinicians is working out whether the symptoms that occur with an eating disorder are a result of the disorder, or a cause of it. Extreme weight loss itself causes personality changes, depression, anxiety, mood swings, obsessive thinking, irritability, feelings of inadequacy and social withdrawal. Current methods of managing eating disorders in adolescents and young adults can vary from one hospital or clinic to another, but generally attempt to deal with the underlying psychological causes. Although many eventually have a favourable outcome, professional treatment involving family therapists, dieticians, psychiatrists, psychotherapists and physicians is often lengthy and expensive with a substantial risk of relapse. A different method developed in Sweden (the Mandometer method) focuses on altering the disordered eating patterns of the patients with a practical measurement and reward system. It has a relatively high success rate but is very lengthy (9–14 months) and expensive.

My daughter is 16 and seems to eat an enormous amount without putting on any weight (some nights she has second helpings of main course, and will often go back for thirds at dessert!) I didn't think too much of it until I heard her retching in the bathroom one night after dinner and began to notice lots of chocolate bar wrappers in the rubbish. She does play netball, but isn't excessively sporty or obsessed with exercise. Is she simply hungry because of all the growing her body is doing?

It is quite possible your daughter is suffering from bulimia. Bulimia nervosa (known commonly as bulimia) is an eating disorder characterised by episodes of binge eating, followed by compensatory behaviours such as self-induced vomiting (known as purging), fasting, the use of laxatives, enemas and diuretics, and overexercising. It is estimated to be twice as common as anorexia – 1 in every 50 women and 1 in 500 men.

The first thing you need to do is talk to your daughter about what you've noticed. Start by saying you are only raising your concerns because you genuinely care about her. Come straight to the point and have examples to back up your concerns. For example, 'I've heard you throwing up in the bathroom/I've noticed chocolate wrappers in the bin. I am concerned for you. I would like us to try and get some help.' If you can collect some of the wrappers and show her, it will be more difficult for her to deny the situation. Focus on your own feelings of love and concern for her and use 'I' statements. This will lessen the chance that she'll see your comments as a character assassination. Try to focus on behaviours and feelings rather than eating and weight. Your daughter is more likely to recognise that she has been unhappy, withdrawn or miserable and may be highly protective of the eating and associated behaviours.

There are two types of bulimia nervosa: purging and non-purging. Purgers use self-induced vomiting and other ways to rapidly remove food from the body before it can be digested, such as laxatives, diuretics and enemas. They may also exercise or fast, but it is more a secondary form of weight control. Non-purging bulimics (6–8 per cent of cases) use excessive exercise or fasting after a binge to offset the calorific intake. Unlike anorexia, bulimia can be very difficult to identify because young people with bulimia tend to be of average weight (or only slightly above or below). Their eating and exercising patterns may not be as rigid, either, making it harder to diagnose. With bulimia, the binge–purge cycle may be repeated several times a week or, in more serious cases, several times a day causing serious medical conditions such as chronic gastric reflux, peptic ulcers and dehydration (from the frequent vomiting). Other common problems include electrolyte imbalance, which can lead to cardiac arrhythmia, cardiac arrest and even death, as well as inflammation of the oesophagus. The repetitive insertion of fingers or other objects into the mouth and throat can causes lacerations to the lining of the mouth or throat. Frequent contact between teeth and gastric acid, in particular, may cause severe caries and the erosion of tooth enamel along with swollen salivary glands.

People with bulimia nervosa share the same fear, guilt and shame about food and fat as those with anorexia nervosa, but they are two separate disorders with different symptoms. People with anorexia starve and exercise themselves thin. People with bulimia eat unhealthy amounts of food and then vomit or purge themselves. People with anorexia or bulimia tend to start at normal weights, but then suffer from poor nutrition as well as the mental and emotional effects of having an eating disorder. Some people with eating disorders may have a combination of anorexia and bulimia. Both anorexia and bulimia are treatable. People with eating disorders need professional help from doctors and psychiatrists. It may take years to learn to control an eating disorder, and the love and support of friends and family are essential for recovery.

Gender

Our son is 11 and from very early on was never interested in the activities that other boys his age were into. He hated sport, and wasn't interested in cars and trucks or construction toys like Lego, preferring to play the piano or play dress-ups (he especially enjoyed being female characters). He's never really had any male friends and tends to prefer the company of girls. When he was bullied at the local primary school, we decided to send him to a private school, and even though it has been a struggle financially, we're glad we did as he hasn't been bullied there at all. We love him dearly and have always allowed him to be himself, but I know my husband is secretly hoping that this is just a phase, and I think my son is beginning to sense that. How should I handle this?

First up, you and your husband need to be united in your support of your son. He needs to know that you both love him unconditionally – that you will love and care for him no matter what choices he makes. As you have already discovered, his being 'a bit different from the norm' has already resulted in him being bullied, and sadly, research has found a link between nonconforming gender behaviour and abuse. In 2012, researchers at Boston Children's Hospital found that children who don't fit traditional gender stereotypes were at significantly greater risk for physical, sexual and psychological abuse and were more likely to develop post-traumatic stress disorder (PTSD) in young adulthood. The researchers also noted that childhood gender nonconformity was reported across all sexual orientations; of the 9000 young people studied, 85 per cent who were gender nonconforming as children identified themselves as heterosexual in adulthood.

Gender identity (the identification of ourselves as male, female or transgender) often gets confused with sexual orientation (who you want to have sex with). When a child starts identifying with the opposite gender, there is no way to determine whether they will go on to experience gender dysphoria (previously known as gender identity disorder), where they feel a profound discomfort (confusion, anxiety, stress) with their biological sex and a strong identification with the gender of the opposite sex. Dutch researchers have found that children may show signs of gender dysphoria (GD) as young as three but only 16 per cent of children with GD will still have it in adolescence or adulthood. They conclude that the most likely outcome of childhood GD is homosexuality or bisexuality.

In the latest Diagnostic and Statistical Manual of Mental Disorders (the DSM-V), the criteria for gender dysphoria are:

1. A strong desire to be of the other gender or an insistence that he or she is the other gender (or some alternative gender different from one's assigned gender)
2. In boys (assigned gender), a strong preference for cross-dressing or simulating female attire; in girls (assigned gender), a strong preference for wearing only typically masculine clothing and a strong resistance to the wearing of typically feminine clothing

3. A strong preference for cross-gender roles in make-believe or fantasy play
4. A strong preference for the toys, games or activities stereotypically used or engaged in by the other gender
5. A strong preference for playmates of the other gender
6. In boys (assigned gender), a strong rejection of typically masculine toys, games, and activities and a strong avoidance of rough-and-tumble play; in girls (assigned gender), a strong rejection of typically feminine toys, games, and activities
7. A strong dislike of one's sexual anatomy
8. A strong desire for the primary and/or secondary sex characteristics that match one's experienced gender.

When children with GD hit puberty, they can become extremely distressed due to revulsion towards unwanted physical changes in their bodies. For those children, anxiety, depression and rates of self-harm are very high and ongoing psychological support is very important. In addition, pre-pubertal adolescents with persistent GD may be given hormonal treatment (GnRH) to suppress puberty, followed by cross-sex hormone therapy to promote physical development in the affirmed gender. Current evidence suggests that when a strict, multidisciplinary assessment and clinical protocol is followed, hormone treatment to suspend the development of puberty is associated with a good outcome and a low rate of regret.

The prevailing opinion within the national and international medical community is that the treatment for GD starts with a comprehensive psychological assessment (note – assessment only, not therapy to 'change' or 'correct') followed by hormonal and surgical treatments if recommended. When children insist that their gender identity doesn't match their anatomy it can trigger a painful and confusing odyssey. It is almost always very isolating because of the lack of understanding and the stigma. But the ultimate factor has to be your son's happiness and his ability to function at school. Children with GD experience a disconnect between their anatomy and their gender and if this is not addressed they can experience great distress. Ultimately, being allowed to live like a little girl is an important part of his/her treatment called social transitioning. So start by getting an expert assessment and with educating your husband.

Gifted children

My 7-year-old son is intellectually gifted but is constantly getting into trouble at school. I've even been called in to the school for 'parent interviews' because his behaviour is so disruptive. My partner and I have always made sure that he has plenty to challenge him at home, but we are quite strict with him. Do you think we need a different approach?

Giftedness is most often defined in terms of intellectual abilities, including reasoning, verbal memory and other areas of general intelligence (IQ). However, this is a somewhat narrow definition, as gifted children may also demonstrate outstanding or advanced creative abilities (original thinking, problem-solving), social and emotional abilities (sensitivity, empathy) and physical abilities (fine motor skills, agility). They may also display heightened perceptual awareness, and be particularly sensitive to sights, smells, touch, hearing and taste. As a result, they may experience ordinary life events very differently to others.

Your son is no doubt latching on to new ideas and picking up concepts much faster than his classmates, so it may be that he is, quite simply, bored. Some people argue that everyone gets bored and that gifted kids should just learn to deal with the boredom. However, this is manifestly unfair, as adults have a range of ways to deal with boredom (taking a break; finding a new job) that are not available to kids.

You are doing all the right things for him – having him tested when you suspected he had above-average abilities, keeping him engaged and interested at home, and making sure there are firm boundaries in place. (Gifted children can be incredibly creative and persuasive in pursuing their goals, but feel very insecure if they are able to manipulate adults, so setting and enforcing limits is very important.) In this instance, then, the problem is with the school.

Presumably you have notified the school of his special abilities, yet the fact that he is receiving constant detentions indicates that his teacher (or the school in general) is unable to recognise and appropriately respond to the needs of gifted children. In this situation, you will need to advocate on his behalf. The constant punishment he is receiving, combined with the lack of stimulating learning experiences can, in the long term, lead to boredom, alienation, social difficulties, depression and underachievement. Giftedness is largely a measure of potential. It is up to the people in your son's environment to develop that potential, and this includes his teachers.

Grief

My son is five and his beloved pet fish has not been moving around much these past few days – it's definitely on its way out. Is my son too young for me to have a chat to him about death?

If you are concerned about discussing death with your children, you are not alone. *Many* parents are reluctant to talk about death, particularly with youngsters. However, death is an inescapable fact of life. We must deal with it and so must our children. If we are to help them, we must let them know that it's okay to talk about it. Trying to protect children with vague or inaccurate explanations can create anxiety, confusion and mistrust, so just explain that when people and animals get sick or old they die so that they don't have to suffer any longer. This is a good opportunity to talk about your own beliefs about death or, if you aren't religious, to briefly explain what some of the other religions believe. As a result he will have a good understanding about the cycle of life. Let him know it is normal to miss pets after they die and encourage him to come to you with questions or for reassurance and comfort. After the fish has died, he may want to bury it, make a memorial or have a ceremony, which is an important part of learning how to grieve. It is best not to immediately replace the dead pet, as it won't give him time to process what has happened.

There are some wonderful picture books that can help a parent talk to their child about the death of a pet. See if your local library has *The Dead Bird* by Margaret Wise Brown, *Badger's Parting Gift* by Susan Varley or *The Tenth Good Thing about Barney* by Judith Viorst.

There has been some turmoil in our family recently with a job loss and two grandparents dying, and I've noticed that our 10-year-old daughter has become quiet and withdrawn. She is an only child, and was very close to both her grandparents. However, my wife and I are completely overwhelmed by our own grief (we've each lost a parent) and the stress of our financial insecurity. How can we help our daughter through this?

This may well be the first time your daughter has experienced a profound sense of loss and she needs your help. Loss triggers a deep sense of insecurity ('I am not safe') in children and they can become so overwhelmed by strong emotions (most often anger: 'Why is this happening?') that they withdraw. You can help her express her grief through drawing or painting ('Let's paint a picture about Nanna'), storytelling or music. Ask her to make a memory box for each grandparent, or encourage her to write a poem about each of them. This can provide a sensory bridge to the expression of emotion. Don't analyse or interpret her work – let her tell you about it. Psychological healing time is different to chronological healing time. Children will often break their feelings up into manageable amounts, as it's difficult for them to tolerate ongoing, intense pain. Therefore, it is not unusual to see a variety of emotions unfold in a short span of time as they slowly work through their grief.

My husband passed away two and a half years ago. My daughter and he were best friends, and she believes that never in a million years could anyone replace him. She lives with me and her twin sister and is miserable. I can't talk to her at all, and even her sister can't relate to her. I have a boyfriend and she says things like, 'It makes me feel sick knowing that Dad's not in your heart any more, Mum.' She really misses her dad and is disappointed in me. What can I do?

With the death of a loved one, people can initially be very sympathetic, but after a short while (a month or so) may expect us to 'get over it' and move on. However, the loss of a parent is profoundly traumatic for a young person, and it may take a lot longer than two and a half years for your daughter to come to terms with her father not being part of her life. It's completely normal for her to miss him and to be angry that he is gone; however, it sounds as if she is projecting some of that anger on to you. You need to explain to her that just because you have a boyfriend, it does not mean that her father isn't in your heart any more. She needs to appreciate that everyone resolves their grief in different ways.

Elisabeth Kübler-Ross identified five stages of grief: shock and disbelief ('This isn't happening'); bargaining ('If only I hadn't . . .'); anger ('It shouldn't be like this!'); sadness ('Oh this hurts so much . . .') and acceptance ('It happened; I'll be okay').

While it is healthy for your daughter to be able to express her rage, it is not good for her to hurt others in the process. She is completely stuck in the anger stage of her grief, and needs help to move on. Call Kids Helpline on 1800 551 800 to find a grief counsellor near you.

Hair and make-up

My 11-year-old daughter wants to wear lipstick and mascara to a party. I don't wear any myself, and although I'm not against other people wearing it, it worries me a bit that she already feels she should paint her face to 'go out'. Should I discourage her?

Good lord, have a look at Lady Gaga and take a reality check. Your daughter is just 'trying on' an aspect of female identity. This doesn't mean she's going to sell herself into prostitution. The desire to wear make-up often represents a young girl's eagerness and excitement to become a 'grown up', and explore her attractiveness to peers, but for parents like you, it can bring up fear, stress and anxiety relating to their child maturing and becoming interested in boys! It may also represent your daughter beginning the emancipation process where she separates herself from her parents and begins to focus more on her peers, which is always a bit challenging for some parents. Of course, if she insists on wearing make-up to school (most schools don't allow a lot of it) then you might have a problem. Ask her why she feels she needs to wear it, and tell her it's fine to do so for the occasional party, but it's not on for every day. Carol Tuttle, author of *Dressing Your Truth: Discover Your Personal Beauty Profile*, says she recommends starting with lip gloss and mascara between the ages of 10 and 12, progressing to foundation or cover-up at 13–14 and eyeliner and eye shadows at 15–17. One serious piece of advice: you need to picks your battles, and it is far better to take a firm stance on boys, drugs, alcohol and getting her homework done rather than on her wearing a bit of lippy.

My son is 16 and came home last week with spiked, purple hair. We freaked out. This week he's wearing eyeliner. I'm getting used to it, but my husband can't even look at him. How do we handle this?

Logan Pearsall Smith once wrote, 'Don't laugh at a youth for his affectations; he is only trying on one face after another to find a face of his own.' One of the main tasks of adolescence is to answer the question 'Who am I?', so I suspect your son is trying on different 'faces' to see if one fits. It is a process many young people engage in as they explore their own values, ethics, spirituality, racial and ethnic identity, sexuality and gender. Fortunately, at the same time that he is busy learning what makes him unique, he has a powerful need to fit in to his social group. How long his hair and make-up routine lasts depends on his peers. The next time he comes home with a new look, just ask him how his day was and try to resist the temptation to ask him when the carnival begins!

Homework

When I was younger, I was really good at school and always keen to get stuck into my homework. My 15-year-old daughter, on the other hand, is the opposite. She says she finds it hard to concentrate in class and always leaves her homework until the last minute. She's going into Year 10 next year and there's a lot more work ahead of her. How can I get her to do her homework without it becoming a nightmare for both of us?

It's a shame you haven't addressed this problem earlier, but don't worry, all is not lost. Here are some simple tips that can make homework much easier for your daughter.

1. Make sure she gets at least 8.25 hours sleep each night (sleep is the most important study tool).
2. Before she starts her homework make sure she has fed her brain. She has 100 billion brain cells with a trillion connections, all of which work much better if she has provided them with some energy. Great brain foods include carbohydrates, eggs, avocado, blueberries, yoghurt and flax seeds.
3. Ensure she has some water to sip as the brain is 80 per cent water and this will ward off dehydration.
4. She should work in blocks of 30–50 minutes (never longer) with fifteen-minute breaks.
5. Encourage her to do her homework in the same physical place and as close to the same time as possible every day.
6. Provide a study space with good lighting and ergonomically designed furniture that is away from distractions like TV, pets and noisy siblings.

7. Give her some gum to chew while she is working (researchers at the University of Northumbria found that it aids focus and concentration).
8. Make sure she switches off her smart phone and closes social networking sites on her computer if she is doing her work digitally.

Our local primary school does not set homework for any grade (not even in upper primary), yet I know from friends that other schools in our area do. My son is in Year 6 and I've heard that the high school he's going to next year does set homework for Year 7. I'm worried that it's going to be a big enough challenge for him coping with the transition to high school, let alone managing homework as well. Is there anything I can do to help him?

The debate about homework has been going on for more than a century and is still a touchy subject for parents, students, teachers and education researchers. Way back in 2007, the Australian Council of State School Organisations called for a review of the setting of homework, arguing that there was no evidence that primary school students benefitted from the practice. Since then, some schools have reduced the amount of homework and/or changed the type of homework required, while others continue to set an avalanche of homework from years 3 to 12.

So what does the evidence say? Most empirical research into homework focuses on how well it does the following:

- improves student learning and achievement
- helps students to develop the skills of independent, self-directed learning
- involves parents in the educational activities of their children in ways that are beneficial.

Australian researchers Richard Walker and Mike Horsley have conducted extensive reviews of international research on the effectiveness of homework and have concluded that in terms of academic outcomes homework is not beneficial for primary school kids, is of limited benefit for junior high-school kids, but is reasonably beneficial for senior high-school kids. They note that the quality of the homework is much more important than the quantity, and suggest that the best kind of homework focuses less on drill and practice and more on making choices and developing autonomy. Also, the best scenario for kids occurs when parents support their children's autonomy and essentially try to provide guidance and assistance rather than being interfering and controlling.

So if homework is a fact of life for your child, resist the urge to get over-involved. Your son will fare better if you don't do his homework for him or push him (or punish him if he doesn't meet your expectations for its completion). Instead, provide an organised study area, with good light, away from distractions. Like all children, he'll need a break and physical play after school, but also a fixed place and regular time for homework. This will help him develop good study habits for the upper secondary years, when homework gets more intense and marks matter more.

Injuries

Parents I know scold their 6-year-old when he hurts himself and cries. They shout, tell him to stop crying and call him a sook. I want to hug him and say it's okay. I feel that if we are so harsh on kids they'll grow up bitter and resentful. Am I wrong?

No, you are not wrong. Shouting at a child who has hurt himself and calling him a sook is a harsh and antiquated parenting style, and is tantamount to child abuse. The adults are literally punishing the child for expressing his feelings, and this is not only cruel, but when reinforced repeatedly, can have serious long-term consequences for the child's emotional development. These parents might mistakenly think that they are helping the child become stronger and more resilient (it's more than likely that they were parented this way), but instead they are teaching the child that feelings are bad, and must be pushed down (hello anxiety, depression and self-medication with alcohol).

Minor bumps and bruises are common in the course of play and sport – it's how kids learn new skills. While most falls and scrapes are not serious, they can be very frightening for a child. This is because children are overwhelmed by strong emotion – they literally become more upset about being upset. Clearly, shouting will make them feel even more terrified, and is likely to make them cry even more, not less. Kids need our help to learn that feelings are okay, and to teach them how to express them safely. The best approach is to hug the child. This helps to calm them, and reinforces the parental bond. When they are calmer you can teach them how to cope with pain and how to avoid harming themselves again.

In-laws

When my wife and I go out, we are fortunate enough to be able to drop our children (aged seven and 10) with her parents for the night. However, they spoil the children rotten – showering them with gifts and basically letting them get away with anything. The other night, for example, the kids were eating ice cream at 10 o'clock at night! It's becoming a real problem because the children expect the same treatment at home and they respond very badly when we don't bend to their wishes. It's a tricky situation, because if I talk to my wife about it, she gets a bit defensive and thinks I am attacking her parents. How do I handle this without ruining my marriage and my kids?

Start by getting your partner on the same page. Tell her that over-indulgence is one of the most pernicious forms of child abuse. As parents, your job is to prepare your children for how the world actually works. In life, you don't continuously get what you want. Explain that your children will be better equipped to deal with reality when they are teens if they've experienced it when they are little. Life rewards action, so once you are united in your understanding of what's best for your children, both of you must approach the in-laws together. That way they will know you are both serious, and that you are together on this.

Begin with a positive message – telling them how wonderful it is that your children are lucky enough to have caring, loving grandparents who want to be involved in their development and training. Then, in the same way that you convinced your spouse, explain to the in-laws that all of you need to work together to guide the children's behaviour and expectations. Tell them that if you each have conflicting approaches, it is only going to hurt the children in the long run. Set clear guidelines about any future visits and tell them that they need to respect your wishes. In-laws can be amazingly useful in giving parents respite – but they are not supposed to create behavioural problems in your children.

I think you should continue to limit and monitor your kid's time with their grandparents. There is also a great book I often recommend called *The Complete Idiot's Guide to Dealing with In-Laws* by Laurie E. Rozakis, though perhaps avoid reading this in front of your partner.

Magazines

My 14-year-old daughter wants a subscription to a teen girls' magazine. I'm worried that they'll be full of wafer-thin models in outrageously expensive clothing that will just mess with her head. Should I say no?

The 2012 Mission Australia survey asked young people who they turn to for advice when they need help and unsurprisingly the generation born with a mouse in its hand turned most to the internet (78.3 per cent), followed by parent/s (59.4 per cent) and finally magazines (55.1 per cent). Some parents may be reluctant to allow their daughters to read teen magazines such as *Dolly*, *Girlfriend* or *Total Girl* for fear that the content may upset or adversely influence them.

However, you may be interested to learn that *Girlfriend* has been running 'reality checks' since 2006. These are media literacy tools that graphically indicate when an image has (or hasn't) been retouched; when readers have been used in a shoot; and how much time and effort has gone into getting it 'perfect' (i.e. it took four hours, 123 shots and a professional hair and make-up team to get this one shot). *Girlfriend* now only uses models in one shoot per month (main fashion) opting instead to use readers who represent the demographic more accurately. In addition, it is currently running 'Project YOU', a campaign designed to help boost self-esteem, increase confidence and offer young people the opportunity to experience wellbeing. This campaign was introduced by the current editor, Sarah Tarca, in response to readers telling the magazine that overcoming poor self-esteem was the biggest challenge they faced, which also comes through strongly in the Mission Australia data.

Many parents ask me at what age their offspring should be permitted to read the magazine – expressing consternation about whether the content is suitable. First, age does not always indicate maturity but, second, I believe that *Girlfriend* staff members are hyper-vigilant to ensure that the content is appropriate. My bookshelves at home are overflowing with *Girlfriend* magazines and they easily outstrip text books, psychology journals and my holiday reading. Every 'despairing' young woman writing to me, each direct or heart-wrenching, hilarious, strange or even downright ludicrous question that comes my way, is a moving reminder of what is so amazing about adolescents.

My 10-year-old daughter wants to read Girlfriend. *Do you think it is appropriate for her?*

If I had girls, I probably wouldn't allow them to read the magazine before puberty, as the issues are really more for older girls and young women. A better alternative for tweens is *Total Girl*. Interestingly, its publisher, Pacific Magazines, ran an experiment publishing a boys' magazine called *Explode* in 2004 – it lasted five weeks before being canned. It seems boys don't read magazines for boys!

Manners

I recently took a Skybus from Tullamarine into Melbourne. The bus was so crowded that I had to stand in the aisle. While I was standing there, I saw a father ask his 7-year-old son to sit on his knee so that an older passenger could take the boy's seat. 'I don't want to' the boy said stubbornly. To my amazement, the father did not insist and the child had a comfortable journey while his elders pitched and reeled around him. As a father of two I was horrified to witness this child's selfish behaviour. I really wanted to say something, but did not want to cause a scene. Was I wrong to judge this father?

No, you are not wrong! He should be lined up against the nearest wall and shot with hot goat poo! Both my grandmother, Lily, and my mum, Charlotte, would have been horrified by what you describe. Kids learn about manners from the example set by their parents and other adults in their lives, and even if he couldn't get his son to stand up, *he* should have stood for the older passengers! Teaching by example is the most effective way for children to learn to be considerate of others, especially in the early years. In her great book *A Guide to Australian Etiquette*, Ita Buttrose, twice voted Australia's most admired woman, identified cases of precisely the same sort of moral chaos you witnessed in supermarket aisles, elevators and on walkways. Both Ita and I are at the point of despair over the paucity of manners as our fellow Australians – and not just the young ones – are dragging one set of knuckles on the ground as they return to the cave, while blathering moronically on mobile phones. Ita tells the story of a group of children at a holiday camp finding it 'strange to sit at a table to eat their meal' because they were used to sitting on a couch or the floor to eat while watching television. A good place for parents to start, of course, is with table manners. When teenagers know the rules (napkin on the lap, appropriate cutlery, no reaching across the table, keep the dinner conversation polite, criticism of the meal at the table is unacceptable) they can choose to conform to the rules and be considered mature and thoughtful, or not. Ita Buttrose says good manners give a person increased self-confidence and the ability to be at ease in most situations.

My friend's 7-year-old daughter has appalling manners. She never says please or thank you and helps herself to whatever she wants without asking. My friend is a single mum, but I still think she should teach her children good manners. Am I being a hard arse?

I hate to break it to you, but children actually learn courtesy through imitating their parents and teachers. If your friend's daughter is not respectful of others, she's not seeing other people behave that way. It may be that your friend is so flat out being a solo parent that she's had to choose her battles. Why don't you become a role model for her daughter?

I take my two boys (aged three and five) to a local playground several times a week. One afternoon, my 5-year-old was accidentally hit by another child of about the same age. The mother was extremely embarrassed, and scolded her son, insisting that he say sorry to my son. I told her not to worry about it because it was an accident, but she was very red-faced and insisted that her son apologise. We couldn't leave until the little boy had mumbled 'sorry'. I actually felt bad for the little fellow, and wondered if I would do the same if the situation were reversed. Is she doing the right thing?

Telling a child under seven or eight to say sorry (before empathy has kicked in) is like teaching your budgie to say 'I love you'. Young children are still very egocentric – most don't even understand that other people have feelings – so angrily forcing them to apologise when they don't *feel* sorry is just confusing. Of course we *want* children to develop remorse, regret, compassion and care for others. But we also want them to first be aware of how they feel, and then to be honest about those feelings. Saying sorry before they feel any remorse does not teach kids genuine compassion – it only teaches them how to stop adults from showing scary emotions.

When your child has hurt another, you first need to help her become aware of what the other child might be feeling by questioning how she would feel in the same situation. (What do you think it would feel like to be pushed onto the ground?) By the age of 10, children should be able to apologise without being prompted, but their words also need to be supported by action. Just as an 'I love you' is a throwaway line without authentic love, a 'sorry' is pointless without real remorse. Professor Andrew Whitehouse of the Telethon Institute for Child Health Research at the University of Western Australia argues that teaching young people to say 'sorry' is only the first step in mending their gaffes, and that this word needs to be followed by acts of penitence: cleaning whatever was spilt, offering to mend or pay for whatever is broken or simply passing a tissue to a hurt child.

Meal times

When my children were little, I made the mistake of letting them eat dinner in front of the TV – mainly to get them to eat and to be quiet at dinner time. Now that they're 10 and 12, I want to get them into the habit of eating at the table with us. How can I make the transition easier for everyone?

You are right to want to change. Apart from the obvious benefits of being able to model proper table manners, meal etiquette and social skills, dining together provides opportunities for communication and building relationships. In 2012, The National Center on Addiction and Substance Abuse at Columbia University reported that teens who had frequent family dinners (5–7 per week) were 1.5 times more likely to report having an excellent relationship with both their parents. The study also found that teens who reported a 'less than very good' relationship with their father were:

- almost 4 times likelier to have used marijuana
- twice as likely to have used alcohol
- 2.5 times as likely to have used tobacco.

And compared to teens who said they had an excellent relationship with their mother, teens who had a less than very good relationship with their mother were:

- almost 3 times likelier to have used marijuana
- 2.5 times as likely to have used alcohol
- 2.5 times likelier to have used tobacco.

The researchers also found that families who eat together less frequently tend to eat less healthy food, talk less and report more conflict and tension during meals.

As your family is not used to eating together regularly, start small. Sit down with the kids and explain why you are introducing the new routine, and, with their input, select two or three days and write them on the calendar. As the weeks progress, you can begin to have more and more regular meals.

Include the kids in the preparation of the meal and in the decision about what foods will be offered. Of course, parents have final say about what foods are prepared, but allowing children to participate encourages commitment to eating, develops confidence and is just more fun.

Try to limit the conversations to positive or neutral topics. Do not let the conversation get out of hand or allow family members to criticise one another. Keep it light and fun. Create an environment that leads to healthy communication.

Let everyone know when dinner is served and when they must be home. Show children good etiquette and table manners. And eat slowly. Remember, this is an opportunity for the family to spend time together. Do not make it about the food; make it about the family.

If the children are particularly resistant (and they may well be), set up a reward system. Every time they sit down at the table, eat nicely and participate in the conversation they can get extra time on the computer, more TV time, stay up later, get extra pocket money or a token system where ten tokens equals a trip to the movies or a rental DVD or some other treat.

Mobile phones

I'm thinking of buying my 10-year-old daughter a mobile phone as sometimes I can be late for pick-up and it would be great to be able to let her know. What's a good age to get a child their first mobile phone?

At the risk of being called a digital Neanderthal, I believe that there is no need for primary-school aged children to have a mobile phone unless there are compelling safety/travel issues. If you are picking up your daughter every day, she is in safe hands. If she was walking home or catching public transport for a short stretch a phone would be important – but only a really basic model without the bells and whistles. By the time children reach high school, however, the pressure on many parents to buy a phone increases. As long as a child is responsible enough to look after an electronic device (which includes remembering to keep it charged and to take it to school every day), a prepaid phone is probably not to going to land them in too much trouble. The last time the government researched mobile phone usage among children was in 2009. At that time 76 per cent of kids aged 12–14 had one and 2 per cent of children aged 5–8. In May 2013, the Australian Communications and Media Authority (ACMA) released a report showing that 89 per cent of people aged 18–24 years had a smart phone and 83 per cent of this age group downloaded an app in the six months to May 2013. By comparison, 22 per cent of people aged 65 years and over had a smart phone but only 9 per cent downloaded an app in the same period.

My 13-year-old son makes his way to and from school by himself, so I prefer him to have a phone for safety. However, he refuses to take the phone we bought him, claiming he is too embarrassed to use it because it's not a smart phone. I feel under great pressure to buy him one for his birthday. What are the pros and cons of these phones for young teens?

The smart phone has infiltrated the way we communicate on a daily basis. Like any revolutionary technology, there are both advantages and disadvantages to your son owning a smart phone. Yes he will be able to update his Facebook page, check his email account and stay connected to his circle of friends. But smart phones are more expensive to buy outright and he may be tempted to stay glued to its glowing screen 24/7 if you don't set limits. According to the ACMA, nearly half a million teens were online with their mobiles in June 2013: 71 per cent streamed movies, music, TV or videos; 42 per cent accessed social media platforms; 33 per cent looked at news, sport or weather; 28 per cent downloaded or uploaded photos and 20 per cent played games. If possible, it's best to buy the most recent model of the brand you can afford. Get your son to help with the research, and come up with a compromise if he wants one you cannot afford. A prepaid plan is best, as it is then up to him to manage his data allowance. Or he could simply use his phone for texting when he is away from home, and connect to your internet at home when he wants to go online. If you are looking at iPhones, log on to prepaidiphone.com.au, which provides a guide to all iPhone prepaid mobile phone plans from all of the service providers. One word of caution: the dark side of constant innovation is the constant rendering of older units as obsolete. As each generation of smart phone comes out, older systems become increasingly under-supported. This necessitates users purchasing a new phone every two years or so just to keep up with current technology.

Moving house

My Year 9 daughter is having real troubles with her new home group teacher. We have recently moved states and while she seems to have settled in to her new school and made friends, her home group teacher refuses to allow her to come home when she says she feels unwell. My daughter says the teacher accuses her of 'pretending' to be sick and simply ignores her. How should I deal with this?

Moving states is a huge adjustment for a teenager, and even though she's made friends, which is very important, her transition to this new school sounds less smooth. You need to be your daughter's advocate, so make an appointment with the teacher and find out what is going on. All schools have a duty of care to their students. Assuming your daughter's perceptions are right, it sounds as if her teacher thinks she's feigning illness – instead of seeing her as a young person doing her best to cope with a major transition and struggling psychologically. When you talk to the teacher, take a friend for moral support and stay calm. Tell the teacher that you expect your daughter to be treated as a human being, and that if she is ill, it should be taken seriously and the school's sick kid protocol followed (which may well involve a phone call to you). Tell her you want to develop an action plan to help your daughter. This may involve her seeing the school counsellor or a psychologist. Follow up your meeting with an email and an agreement to meet again in a few weeks. If, in a few weeks, nothing changes for your daughter and the teacher is still maintaining a judgemental attitude, make an appointment with the deputy principal and tell her that you feel that your daughter's teacher is being unreasonable.

We are moving to a new home in a different suburb next month. We have a 4-year-old girl at kinder, and a 7-year-old boy. Our son is very anxious about the move. How can we help him adjust?

Moving house is often easier for young children who are not all that familiar with their local community, or who don't have friends or neighbours they will miss. However, if your son has a strong connection with friends at school or is more sensitive to change, there are some things you can do to help him adjust.

- Give him a little address book and help him write in his friends' telephone numbers, email and snail mail addresses.
- Keep a 'special bag' handy for each child that contains their favourite toys and books. If they can easily access these throughout the moving process it will help them to feel a bit more settled.
- Allow children to help pack up their room so that they will understand that their toys and clothes are not disappearing.
- Take them to see the new home as many times as possible.

Music lessons

My son has been learning the piano since he was six years old and appears to be quite talented. He is always chosen for recitals at his school, and his music teacher is very enthusiastic about his potential. This year, however, he has begun to complain that he wants to give it up. He's almost 12 and to me it seems such a shame for him to throw away all that talent. We have also spent a substantial amount of money on his lessons, his piano and all the AMEB gradings, so I am probably not being very objective about it all. My husband insists that he continue, but I'm not so sure. Any advice would be greatly appreciated.

The trick here is to determine whether your son really *doesn't* enjoy piano, or whether he does like it, but sometimes would prefer to kick a footy rather than practise piano. Few psychologists would advise you to make him stay with piano if he's truly not interested, but given his skill level, it is unlikely that he abhors it. I suggest you do some surreptitious surveillance for two or three weeks and then answer the following questions:

1. Does he ever initiate a practice session himself? Many kids need to be prompted but occasionally will play spontaneously because they like it. If your son *never* plays without you nagging him until his ears bleed, that's a red flag.
2. Once he is at the piano, does he sometimes lose track of time and practise for longer than usual? If he remains dour, hostile, brooding and resistant for most of the practice session, that's a red flag.
3. Is there another activity that he is passionate about, and to which he insists he would be ready to dedicate himself, but which you have resisted because of your values, prejudices or beliefs?

Depending on your answers, you have a couple of options. You could allow him to take up another activity he loves in return for sticking with the piano for an agreed period. Michelle Obama allows her daughters to play two sports each, one they picked and one she chose for them, precisely because she wanted them to learn how to work harder at things they found difficult. I think there's a real value in old-fashioned perseverance. And with all the talk of 'life skills' these days, I don't think it's a bad idea for children to start learning the value of commitment early on, even when they find something onerous.

If, however, your observations reveal that your son genuinely hates the piano, think about why you want him to be a musical maestro. Are you concerned that he will regret not continuing with lessons when he is older? Do you resent the money you have invested in his lessons? Is this more about you? You need to work out whether it is worth damaging your relationship with him by forcing him to continue with something that is clearly not floating his boat.

New baby

My daughter has just turned five and seems to have entered a phase where she is constantly whinging about everything. Could it be because we have a new baby (seven months old) and she feels she is not getting enough attention? What can we do?

Yes, I suspect the green-eyed monster has descended. But this is quite normal in younger children who don't have the cognitive or emotional maturity to comprehend why they are no longer the centre of attention. But there are specific techniques psychologists recommend to resolve the problem.

- Be patient – it can take some time for a 5-year-old to understand that while Mummy and Daddy have a baby to take care of, it doesn't mean she is loved any less. She needs many positive interactions with you and the baby to feel safe and secure.
- Talk to her – explain that the baby needs Mummy and Daddy a lot because babies can't yet do all the things that she can do.
- Never punish her for expressing jealousy or resentment. Not only does this reinforce the message that the baby is more important (exacerbating the jealousy) but it also tells the child that she is 'bad' or 'naughty' and unworthy of your love and respect.
- Include her in the care of the baby, giving her little tasks that she can cope with such as helping with dressing or choosing toys for her to play with. Giving her the opportunity to act like a loving older sister (under your supervision) will help strengthen the bond between them.
- Regularly schedule 'special time' with your 5-year-old, either as a couple (if you have a babysitter) or individually. It can be something simple like a walk to the park, cooking something special or reading together.
- Read her *Babies Don't Eat Pizza* by Dianne Danzig or *Aren't You Lucky!* by Catherine and Laurence Anholt.

Nightmares

My daughter seems to have nightmares every week. She says she is often trapped somewhere and can't find her way out, or she is being chased by something and can't move. I know most children have nightmares from time to time, but my daughter is nine. Should she have outgrown them by now?

Nightmares can be frightening for a child and may be concerning for the family; however, rest assured that they are transient events and in the vast majority of cases are developmentally normal for children. A nightmare is a bad dream that usually involves some imagined danger or threat and often involves disturbing themes, images or figures such as monsters, ghosts, animals or bad people. Nightmares can start when a child is about two years old, and usually reach a peak between the ages of three and six years, tapering off thereafter. Your child may have only a few scary dreams a year, or be troubled by nightmares much more often. About one-quarter of children have at least one nightmare every week.

The cause of nightmares isn't known, but it is thought to be the brain's way of processing the ordinary stresses and strains of growing up. Children who have experienced a significant change such as starting school, moving to a new neighbourhood, parental divorce or remarriage may have nightmares. Nightmares generally occur in the second half of the night and if children wake up they are able to recall the events. These features distinguish nightmares from night terrors, which occur in the first half of the night and are associated with little or no recall and a confused state of awareness.

It sounds as if you are doing the right thing with your daughter – listening to her and taking her fears seriously. Tell her that it's normal to dream every night and that everyone has bad dreams occasionally. However, if she is overly distressed by her nightmares (i.e. you need to go to her during the night) or she begins to have recurring dreams, you might need to consider what might be triggering them. Is she watching frightening shows on television or reading scary books?

Or is there anything troubling her? Stressful events that could trigger a spate of nightmares include a new sibling, moving house or starting school. In such cases, talk about the bad dreams together and reassure her that this is a passing phase. If it is a recurring nightmare, help her to explore its meaning through drawing, writing or play acting. Thinking about the nightmare creatively – especially when the child comes up with a happier ending or 'makes friends' with the nightmare character – can help to defuse the power of the dream. If none of these approaches work, seek professional advice. See your doctor for information and referral.

Our son is five and every now and then has these terrible nightmares where he literally screams the house down. When I go in, he can be sitting up in bed, often panting and obviously distressed, but he doesn't seem to know I'm there. I just wait a bit and when he is calmer, I tuck him in. When I ask him about the dreams, he says he can't remember even having them. It is becoming a real worry. Should we take him to see a therapist?

This sounds like night terrors rather than nightmares. Night terrors are sleep disturbances during which a child may sit bolt upright in bed or thrash about, crying, moaning or mumbling, often with their eyes wide open, but without being properly awake. They are less common than nightmares (1–6 per cent of children have night terrors once a month, while 25 per cent of children have nightmares at least once a week) and typically begin in the toddler and preschool years but sometimes start later. An episode of night terrors can last anywhere from five to forty-five minutes, though the next day the child will have no memory of it. This is different to nightmares, where a child wakes up afterwards and remembers details of the nightmare. Also, night terrors usually occur in the first few hours of the night, during the deepest phase of sleep, while nightmares occur during the REM (or dream) stage of sleep, usually after 2 a.m. The good news is that night terrors usually disappear by adolescence (if not before) when the child's neural circuitry develops.

The cause of night terrors is not known, though they have been linked to erratic or insufficient sleep (which, in turn, may be related to stress or illness). Certain medications or caffeine also can contribute to night terrors. Also, children are more likely to have night terrors if someone else in their family does too. However, night terrors do not mean that a child has a psychological problem.

There is some indication that night terrors can result from being overtired, in which case interventions such as creating a bedtime schedule can increase the chances of restful sleep. In some cases, a child who has night terrors will require additional comfort and reassurance during the day and before bedtime.

My 12-year-old has been having terrible nightmares and wakes up screaming every night. It's only happened in the last couple of weeks, ever since my husband was injured in a car accident. He did have the occasional nightmare when he was younger, but this seems different. Should I take him to my GP?

Your son may have a condition known as nightmare disorder or dream anxiety disorder, characterised by frequent and intensely terrifying dreams where his survival or safety is threatened. While many children have nightmares, those with nightmare disorder experience them with greater frequency and vividly remember them. Upon waking they are alert and oriented within their surroundings and show symptoms of anxiety such as increased heart rate and sweating. They may have trouble falling back asleep for fear that they will experience another nightmare. This disrupted sleep can in turn create other problems, such as poor immune function, problems concentrating and adverse effects on mood and behaviour, so it is important to confirm the diagnosis. Your GP will be able to organise a referral to see a psychologist.

In the meantime, continue to offer your son love and support. I presume his screams wake you up and that you often then go to him. Cuddle and reassure him calmly and gently. Appreciate that he is feeling genuinely terrified, and be prepared to stay with him until he has calmed down. If he is particularly frightened, you may need to soothe him with a favourite (but relaxing) activity, such as reading a book together. If he wants to talk to you about the nightmare, let him. Encourage him to come up with alternate endings for the nightmare that are happy or funny.

During the day, try to alleviate sources of stress at home and school, and help him to get the best chance of a good night's sleep. Exercise has long been known to help with sleep, so if he doesn't play sport, encourage some other form of regular exercise every day, straight after school if possible. Diet is also important – leafy greens and coloured veggies, lean meat, nuts and seeds are all good. Mindfulness meditation is becoming popular as an adjunct to conventional medical and psychological therapies, so try the free app Smiling Mind, which has a section for children. Also, show him how to counteract frightening thoughts with images of happiness, safety and bravery. When he is fearful, help him think of situations that make him feel happy and in control – for example, he might benefit from thinking about a favourite activity or playing with his favourite pet.

In some cases, clinical hypnosis has been found to be an effective treatment, probably because it increases relaxation.

Obesity

My grandson is nine and is very overweight. He told me once that some of the children at his school tease him about being fat. When he stays with me, he is obsessed with food, and is always in the fridge and pantry, even though I know he's eaten plenty at each meal. I tried to talk to my son about it and he became quite defensive, insisting that the family eats healthily and that the boy is just going through a phase. However, my daughter-in-law is also very overweight, so I had to bite my tongue. How can I help my grandson without offending his parents?

In 2007–08, it was estimated that almost a quarter of Australian children aged 5–17 years were overweight or obese (17 per cent overweight, 6 per cent obese). The Australian Institute of Health and Welfare reports that once children become obese they are more likely to stay obese in adulthood and have an increased risk of developing diseases associated with obesity including coronary heart disease, type 2 diabetes, some cancers, knee and hip problems and sleep apnoea. In the short term, however, overweight children are more likely to be teased by their peers and develop body image problems. Once children are overweight, it requires a lot of effort and commitment for them to return to a healthy weight, and in this they need adult support. Until your son is willing to face the issue of his wife's weight issue, he will not be able to assist his son. However, that does not mean you cannot educate your grandson about healthy eating when he's in your care. I don't mean lecturing the poor kid, just modelling healthy eating yourself, and giving him tips here and there when the occasion arises. For example:

- Have water or low-fat milk to drink instead of fruit juice or soft drinks (fruit juice is very high in calories – you're better off getting the fibre and other nutrients by eating the whole fruit).
- Keep fresh fruit and healthy snacks within easy reach (and keep any high-calorie foods out of sight, or better still, don't buy any).
- Show him how to make fruit smoothies with low-fat yoghurt and fresh or frozen blueberries, raspberries, banana or mango.
- If you have a veggie garden, get him to pick the ingredients for a meal; or make a small veggie or herb garden together.
- Cook something together using lean meat and fresh veggies.
- If your grandson feels uncomfortable participating in sporting activities, help him find something fun and not competitive, such as bike riding or bushwalking, and go with him.
- When your grandson is cruising around for food in between meals, explain that the kitchen is 'closed' and distract him with an activity outside.
- Above all, practise what you preach!

Pets

My 7-year-old daughter is obsessed with getting a dog. I'm not keen on the idea as we don't have a big yard and I work three days a week so the dog would be at home alone. We've had a guinea pig and two mice, which I mostly took care of due to her being so young. She insists she's old enough to help take care of it, but I'm not so sure. What's your advice on pets?

A dog is a wonderful companion for a single child and a great source of joy and love for everyone in the family, but they can be expensive to keep and they require a *lot* of care. Dogs need exercise, discipline and affection – in that order – and if they don't get enough exercise, they can develop destructive and unruly habits (excessive barking, destroying plants, clothing, furniture, etc.). Dogs also need to be trained properly (to walk on the lead, do their business outside, etc.), which is very time-consuming, especially if you get a puppy. In your case, the dog would be alone for three days a week and would need a long walk in the morning and evening on the days you work. If you can't manage that, you may need to employ a friend or relative to help out with the dog's exercise on those days. Also, realistically, your daughter is not old enough to take a dog walking by herself, so even though she may be in charge of tucker time and pooper-scooping, it's going to be up to you (or your partner) to do the walking for the next few years at least. Of course, walking the dog with your daughter would be a great way to get one-on-one time and a bit of exercise, too. If you decide to get a dog, consider adopting one from a shelter. Every hour, about twenty-five abandoned or rejected pets are euthanised. Their owners clearly did not give the decision to own a pet as much thought as you have.

My children are five and six, and dearly want us to get a cat. I like the idea that cats are relatively independent, and that the children are old enough to help with feeding, brushing and so on, but with another baby on the way, I'm not sure I can handle this.

I can see how getting a pet might help your children cope with the arrival of a new sibling, but ultimately you need to work out yourself whether the benefits of a furry friend are outweighed by the costs. In your case, a cat is a far better option than a dog, but kittens are still a handful. There's the daily feeding, house-training (the joys of changing litter trays), vaccinations, flea treatments, worm treatments, etc. Have you thought about two guinea pigs? They are great for recycling veggie scraps and very easy to look after. Just make sure they are the same sex!

Phobias

My 8-year old daughter is terrified of thunderstorms, so much so that she has to get into our bed and cannot get back to sleep. I can feel her shaking – what can we do?

While some people will be tempted to rush to a diagnosis of astraphobia, which is the fear of thunder and lightning, I am hesitant to do so. The truth is that such fears are extremely common in children and full-blown phobias should not be diagnosed in children unless they have persisted for six months or more (which can be tricky to diagnose given that thunderstorms tend to be seasonal and limited to one or two months of the year). If a combination of reassurance and distraction fails to help your daughter cope, go to your local library and find her some general anti-anxiety books like *Go Away, Mr Worrythoughts!* by Nicky Johnston or even specific thunderstorm books such as *Thunder and Lightning: They're Not So Frightening* by J.D. Schmith. If, after this, her fear is still severe and she is inconsolable, it is important to seek treatment. The good news is that this is treatable using a type of talking therapy called cognitive behavioural therapy (CBT). With a good child psychologist, she can be taught soothing messages to repeat during storms, replacing her negative self-talk, or she may be taught breathing techniques or visualisation exercises that she can use to calm her fears. Early diagnosis and prompt treatment is associated with a better outcome.

My 6-year-old son completely freaks out at the shopping centre when he sees Santa Claus. Last year he threw a huge fit and refused a photograph with him. I'm trying to be understanding, but it seems so odd. What can I do?

If this fear is restricted to the fat man in the red suit then he may have a simple case of Santaphobia – yes, an abnormal, persistent fear of Father Christmas does exist. Truthfully, it is rarely recorded in authoritative lists of phobias, but when Christmas comes around, some children, despite their excitement, can show signs of fear and anxiety when confronted with Santa. There are a number of reasons for this fear. For a child, Santa is huge, both physically and symbolically. Many parents do not realise that a fully costumed Santa can be an intimidating presence, a literal giant when compared to a 6-year-old. When involuntarily dumped on Santa's lap, they look up at a mass of white hair, red nose and glasses, while a reverberating 'Ho Ho Ho!' emanates from somewhere within the big, hairy, red giant – no wonder your son is scared! The beard functions like a mask, concealing from the child any recognisable, 'normal' facial features. One solution is for him to watch other children with Santa a few times on the day before, or a couple of hours beforehand, so he gets used to him.

My 14-year-old daughter seems to have a phobia of needles. She was okay with them when she was little, but in the last couple of years, seems to have developed a completely out-of-control panic about any type of needle – vaccination, blood tests, acupuncture or even piercings or tattoos (which is probably a good thing, I know). I'm concerned that this will cause all sorts of problems for her in adulthood. Is there anything I can do to help now?

Trypanophobia, like all phobias, can have both a genetic component and/or an environmental trigger. An unusually large percentage of those with needle phobia have relatives with needle phobia (who has it in your family?). Indeed, from an evolutionary perspective, it makes sense to be afraid of having your skin pierced because during most of human history, a scratch could be potentially fatal due to infection (they didn't have antibiotics back then). I'm guessing, though, that your daughter may have had a past negative experience that she hasn't told you about. She could have had a bad experience with an injection (the nurse having trouble finding a vein, etc.), or she might simply have seen someone else have one (e.g. seeing someone faint at school). Sometimes even hearing negative information about needles can trigger a phobia.

It's important to take her fears seriously and not belittle her. Many adults with needle phobia talk about how they received negative reinforcement such as teasing or insults for their needle fears when younger. Talk to her about the anxious thoughts she might have, such as 'It's going to hurt!' or 'I can't cope with this!' And encourage her to challenge those thoughts and replace them with more positive thoughts: 'It's not going to hurt that much' or 'I can cope with this!'

If she is still extremely panicky at the thought of having a needle, seek professional help. Phobias respond extremely well to psychological treatment. A therapist can help her realise that her thoughts about needles or pins are distorted and teach her deep breathing or relaxation exercises to help reduce the fear.

Play dates and sleepovers

My daughter (who is eight) often ambushes me after school with a friend by her side and requests an after-school play. I hate having to say no in front of another child, but I nearly always do. (I think I've caved in once.) My daughter already has piano on one night and soccer practice on another (and my son has his after-school activities as well), so I've told her that she has to play with her friends on the weekends, not during the week. I've explained that we need to have this rule because she gets overtired and cranky the next day, and also that it's inconvenient for me to have to collect her during peak hour traffic (making dinner late and leaving me cranky!). However, sometimes I watch all the other kids happily heading off with other mums and I feel like she might be missing out. Am I being too strict?

No, you are not being too strict. It's your right to say 'yes' or 'no' to unscheduled play dates, though I acknowledge that you can end up feeling like the Grinch who stole Christmas when you decline. Remember, though, that they have already seen these friends *all day.* They can go to a friend's house on the weekend. The reality is that by the time your daughter gets home from school there are about four hours left until bedtime. Call me old-fashioned, but I'd prefer you to spend that time together as a family. It seems some parents feel they have to schedule something almost every single day. I applaud you for establishing a firm no-play-dates-during-the-week policy. I know many families who have adopted this policy and their children are doing fine, still have friends and they are all happy.

My 7-year-old son had his first sleepover at a friend's house on the weekend and came home utterly exhausted. He was irritable and rude to everyone and eventually dissolved into tears. The next day he woke up with a viral infection, no doubt caused by being so run-down. He loves his friend, and I don't want him to stop having sleepovers, but should I say something to the mum?

Yes, you should say something. When a child visits another family the parents in that family act *in loco parentis*, Latin for 'in the place of a parent'. Whoever was supervising the children on that sleepover had a responsibility to ensure that your 7-year-old went to bed at a decent time. Speak to the mother (or father) face to face and ask about their views on children's bedtimes. You may well find that they are quite happy to keep their children up until midnight. If this is the case, tell them that your doctor recommends that 7-year-olds need around 10–11 hours of sleep otherwise they are physically, psychologically and mentally wrecked and explain that your child was at home sick for several days after the weekend. I suspect that this is all you will need to say. Then if your son is invited to a sleepover at their home again, ask them to put the children to bed at a reasonable hour.

Pocket money

My son came home from school yesterday (he's in Year 5) and informed me that one of his classmates gets $20 a week pocket money and another child gets $50! I'm a single mum, so I haven't been able to afford to give him more than $5 a week. How should I handle this?

Pocket money is a huge concern for kids and one of the first ways they learn about spending and saving – unquestionably a skill they need for life. For older children, pocket money gives them a feeling of independence.

Many parents give their kids a weekly allowance that's dependent on them doing jobs around the house, as well as extra cash as a reward for additional chores or excellent behaviour. The problem is that children learn to help around the house and behave well for financial reward, not because they think it's the normal and right thing to do. Withdrawing pocket money as a punishment also creates conflict and resentment – not what we're going for as parents.

One way to handle this pocket money issue is to give your son a certain amount each week that's completely unrelated to behaviour or any expectation that he must 'earn' it. The philosophy behind this approach is that when children reach a certain age, they are old enough to have a bit of money to spend for themselves. They can choose to save it or to spend it immediately, which helps them learn about the pros and cons of spending and saving. Although the money should not be withheld as punishment, some argue that it is reasonable to withdraw pocket money when particular expectations are not met. Another option is to combine the two approaches: half of the pocket money is given unconditionally and the rest if chores are completed.

If your family finances or ethics mean you'd rather not give pocket money, that is perfectly fine and a significant lesson for your children.

Porn

My 14-year-old son is a good boy and does well at school. But one day, when I thought he was doing his homework on the computer, I caught him watching porn. He was embarrassed and angry, and told me to bugger off and mind my own business. My husband has made it clear that he doesn't want to have these kinds of conversations with his son, so it's up to me. What should I do?

Pornography can be defined as exploitative and unrealistic depictions of sexuality with the intent to cause sexual excitement. It is often infantile in the way it portrays male and female sexual roles, which may have a detrimental effect on your child's developing sexuality and intimate relationships. Watching video of other people having sex at a young age and prior to having one's own experiences of sexual relationships is particularly problematic as it sets up unconscious expectations of what sexual experiences 'should' be like (with pornographic photographs or literature at least some imagination is still required and some naivety remains). When a young person begins to experiment with their partner, the images they have seen (especially if repeated hundreds of times) can have considerable influence on what they find erotic and enjoyable, and what they expect from, and how they interact with, their sexual partner.

A 2012 UK parliamentary report found that 80 per cent of 16-year-old boys had regularly accessed online porn, and that 1 in 3 10-year-olds had seen explicit material. This is deeply concerning, as research has found that boys (and men) who view porn are more likely to denigrate women and see them as deserving of maltreatment. The more they view porn, and the less they actually meet and engage with real girls and interact with them as equals, the angrier they become, and the more likely they are to develop a 'creep' mentality, wanting to control, dominate or hurt women.

There is nothing wrong with your son being curious about the human body and the act of intercourse – like it or not he is a sexual being and this curiosity is an important and natural part of his development. However, pornography, with its undertones of domination, humiliation and hurt, and dearth of intimacy or love, is not the way to learn about sexuality. As difficult as this might be, you must talk calmly and reasonably to your son about pornography. Tell him the following things:

- Porn actors are flesh-and-blood cartoon characters. Most have had surgical work, and have been styled and photographed in exaggerated ways. No one really looks like that.
- Porn sex is the 'fast food' version of sexuality. In the real world, people don't relate to each other this way. They have complex needs, and sex is usually just one part of their relationship.
- It is harmful to keep looking at it, and that you don't want him to continue to do so.

Whether or not he listens to you will depend on the strength of your relationship. Be honest about how concerned you are. If, however, there is insufficient trust in your relationship, you may need to investigate server-based filtering options offered through your ISP or set up filters on his computer. These technologies can be helpful, but keep in mind that they're not foolproof and are no substitute for parental supervision. I'd also recommend that he never take his phone into his room – that he charge it in the kitchen or lounge room each night. It also goes without saying that any kind of computer in the bedroom is asking for trouble. By failing to police this, parents just increase the risk of their child developing an interest in nastier and more violent forms of pornography. Over the years, I have seen some boys so addicted to porn that they were emotionally incapacitated and unable to relate to normal healthy girls. No parent can completely control what their children see, but you can help shape how he interprets what he sees. You must do everything you can to keep the lines of communication open. He will still know how to talk to women by being able to talk to you.

Presents

I am quite strict about not spoiling our kids with lots of gifts (other than at birthdays and Christmas), but when my parents visit each week they always bring something and the kids now expect it. Am I setting them up to be brats if I allow it to continue?

You are not necessarily setting them up to be brats because proportionately they will be spending more time with you than their grandparents. Your rules and values will be more of a shaping influence on your children in the long term, notwithstanding the fact they will remember the love they received from devoted grandparents. Constantly overindulging your children with gifts is not healthy, particularly if, as you say, your children come to routinely expect presents. So no, I don't think you should allow it to continue. I would make two points to your parents, being as tactful as possible. First, explain that you're worried that your children will learn that material possessions are an expression of love. Second, that providing instant gratification may lead to undesirable traits when they are older. Assuming that your parents are reasonable people, they would want to make any modifications necessary to rectify the situation. My recommendation would be that they don't bring gifts every time, but instead bring them something small every third visit. They need to know that your children will love them just the same and that when they limit gift giving, it is more special when the child does receive something.

My 11-year-old son is writing a rather long Christmas list. No doubt his friends are getting what they want but we simply can't afford all the latest gadgets. How can I explain that to him without disappointing him?

This is a common problem for many working parents, especially when kids hit 10 or 11 and the peer pressure kicks in, stirred up by the relentless advertising on TV, radio and print media. I suggest that this situation presents an opportunity for you to teach your son some financial and shopping skills – not to mention the realities of life. Find a quiet time, sit him down and tell him that the family can only afford to spend a certain amount on Christmas presents this year. Life is full of disappointment and giving children the opportunity to experience it is the only way they will learn to get over it. It's crucial that they learn that they have 'enough', in the same way you have had to accept that your income is 'enough'. So set a budget and then show him how to use the internet to do some comparison shopping. That way he can redraft his list, choosing several gifts that are within a lower price range, or he can elect to get just one of the expensive gifts on his list. Encourage him to do some chores around the house or neighbourhood so he can save some money to buy some of the gadgets himself – maybe in the Boxing Day sales. It is really important that children remember there is more to Christmas than just presents. He who has not Christmas in his heart will never find it under a tree!

When should I start encouraging my kids to think of buying gifts for others instead of themselves? I was hoping that they would just learn to be thoughtful by watching us be kind and generous, but they're seven and nine, and so far it's just 'me, me, me'.

By around the age of seven, give or take a year, most children are beginning to make up their minds about what is right or wrong, partly because they have developed the mental cutlery to do so, but also because they are beginning to identify with your values. Human beings are hardwired to be kind – our survival as a species depended on us building strong relationships with each other – but we still need lots of opportunities to practise. When you see your children behaving in considerate or kind-hearted ways, don't pass up the opportunity to commend them for it. Be sure to explain to your child what was so thoughtful about the behaviour and how good it made you or the other person feel. This will likely inspire them to act that way in the future.

Puberty

I'm a single father and my daughter is 10. I know I need to have 'the talk' with her soon, but I really don't know how to go about this without embarrassing us both. Do you have any tips?

It's great that you are prepared to talk about puberty with your daughter, and you're not alone in feeling a bit apprehensive about it. Fortunately, Australian state school curricula include an excellent sex education program that begins in Year 5. Of course, how well this is run depends on individual teachers, and, in my view, this in no way lets you off the hook. All parents should talk to their children about the changes of puberty as early as nine years of age (girls can start menstruating as young as eight, and some before they have other signs of puberty, such as breast development). Lucky for you there are some brilliant sex education materials to help you and your daughter. The Hormone Factory is a great website developed by La Trobe University. Log on first at thehormonefactory.com in order to familiarise yourself with the content and then hop on with her. Also get her a copy of *Girl Stuff* by Kaz Cooke. Buy some tampons and sanitary pads so she knows what they look like and, as the time approaches, equip her with a 'pad pack' for her school bag.

My son is 14 and, except for the occasional bout of moodiness, is showing no signs of entering puberty. Most of his friends are well on the way: their voices are breaking and they are taller, broader and generally much swarthier. I know this bothers him, but he doesn't talk about it. How can I help?

Puberty is a time of great change for any teen, even when it follows a 'normal' course. It involves changes to almost all aspects of a young person's life: academic demands increase, social relationships become more complex, independence to some may seem daunting and the physical changes of puberty can be challenging. In your son's case, where puberty comes late, it can cause further difficulties. Family and friends need to be supportive of the young person as he comes to terms with 'being different'. Some boys may experience behaviour and self-esteem issues as a result of being left out of sporting teams or being teased about their lack of development. Encourage and support him to pursue activities that help him to feel competent and capable, as this will boost his self-esteem.

Public transport

My 11-year-old son is keen to catch the bus to school by himself. I'm more than happy to drive him to school and, although it is an inconvenience (it adds half an hour to my morning drive), I would prefer to continue doing so. However, he insists that many children his own age are catching public transport. When is a good age to allow kids to catch buses and trains by themselves?

This is one of those situations where assigning a particular age is unhelpful as age does not define maturity. Parents should ask three questions before taking the PT plunge:

1. Does he have a track record of making good decisions or is he easily led into unsafe situations?
2. Does he hang out with sensible kids or is he susceptible to dodgy peer pressure?
3. Is he a sensation-seeker by temperament or more risk averse?

If he and his friends are sensible kids and not easily led astray, then public transport is a great way for him to begin to take on more responsibility. It's going to be during peak times anyway, when most other commuters are just heading to work. However, if you are feeling really anxious, why not start gradually? You could allow him to catch the bus once a week for a couple of weeks, increasing the frequency as he proves that he is able to cope.

I have a 12-year-old (almost 13) who wants to catch the train into town with two of her friends on Saturday morning. She keeps telling me that her friends have done it once before, and know their way around, but I'm horrified by the idea. I want to support public transport, but some of the drunk and mentally ill people I've seen on trains truly scare me. And then I picture the three of them wandering about in the city and my imagination goes crazy. I don't mind buses or trams, because at least there's a driver who can see what's going on with their passengers, but we've only got trains where we live. Help! What should I do?

Some parts of the media are very good at reporting bad news, particularly gruesome stories about children who are abducted, abused and murdered – so it is understandable that parents like you are worried. But statistics show that these are actually *extremely* rare events. The best you can do is to reduce the risks. My advice is to educate her about being street smart, and here are some ways to do this:

1. Show her how to use Google Maps and street directories so she really knows her way around.
2. Teach her how to handle unexpected situations, such as missing a train, or what to do when a stranger approaches her.
3. Get her to practise 'reading' people (looking for aggressive body language as well as obvious signs of inebriation, mental illness, etc.).
4. Emphasise that she must never talk to strangers.
5. Make sure that she carries a fully charged phone *with* credit.
6. Tell her the safest department stores to shop in.

Then, start with small experiences – perhaps not all the way to town, but a shop in the next suburb. As she shows you her competence, allow her increasing amounts of freedom. Most psychologists think that children should be allowed independent experiences as it builds resilience and confidence. Letting her take risks can be scary, but it's necessary if she's going to become a responsible, independent young person. The danger is that in attempting to keep her safe, you may be neglecting to teach her how to make her own way in the world.

Reading

My partner and I love reading, and we have a house full of books; however, my 9-year-old son is just not into reading at all. He resented doing his home readers in prep, and although he can read, he won't go near any of the books people buy him. He's far more interested in sport. Do you have any tips?

You might wonder why I have included a section on reading given my strong anti-hot-housing message. The fact is that reading is absolutely critical for boys, since the part of their brains that processes language develops later than girls', and needs as much help as it can get.

While you should not discount the presence of a developmental problem such as dyslexia (which can impair his ability to read), the main reason boys don't read is that they are not interested in the books they are given. Here are some tips for finding the right books and encouraging reading:

1. Find out what genre interests him the most (non-fiction, humour, adventure, mystery, the occult, science fiction, etc.). You will get an idea from his favourite TV shows, movies or video games.
2. Take him to a bookshop and browse the shelves together, or order some books or comics online. You'll be amazed what publishers produce to try to entice reluctant readers, such as extensive *Star Wars* readers, children's books written by famous sporting heroes etc. Check out the websites at Penguin (puffin.com.au/content/349355/books-children) and Scholastic (scholastic.com/parents/books-and-reading/book-lists-and-recommendations/ages-8-10).
3. Read together – it's a brilliant way to connect with your son, and at nine, he's not yet too old to share a bedtime story. You

could take turns selecting something to read, and it could be anything from a magazine, to a video game manual or a favourite storybook from early childhood.

4. Never belittle his reading interests, even if you think they stink.
5. Ask him questions about what he's reading. Boys like to talk about things they read, but can be reluctant to initiate a conversation so sit with him and ask him what's happening in the story, or which is his favourite character, or to show you a funny part (or a gross part).
6. Let him read on a tablet or Kindle if printed books don't float his boat (many boys can become inspired by the technology).
7. Encourage him when he has finished reading something. 'Good job! Keep it up!'

If none of this works, as a last resort you could do what Harvard economist Roland Fryer Jr did. He paid second-graders $2 every time they read a book – 85 per cent improved their reading by the equivalent of five full months of extra schooling, and continued to improve the year after that, even when they weren't being paid any more.

I have a 7-year-old son struggling with reading and I think this is impacting on his classroom behaviour as he is often in trouble. I try to sit with him to do his school reader, but it's so torturous for him that I usually end up reading it for him. He is in a reading recovery group at school, but it doesn't seem to be helping. What should I do?

Your son is not alone. In 2011, *The Sydney Morning Herald* reported that between 20 and 25 per cent of Australian children have difficulty understanding and using language on school entry. Arrange to speak to his teacher. Talk to his reading teacher and see what she thinks. It's possible that he has dyslexia, which is a persistent difficulty with reading and spelling. The Australian Dyslexia Association estimates that dyslexia affects at least 10 per cent of the population, and possibly a great many more are undiagnosed. However, it is important to realise that it has nothing to do with intelligence. Some amazingly talented and gifted human beings have it (or had it), such as Albert Einstein, Pablo Picasso, Steven Spielberg, Richard Branson and Steve Jobs, just to name a few. So arrange for an assessment from an educational psychologist who will administer a series of standardised tests to find out where his reading difficulties are coming from. If he does have dyslexia, it just means he learns things in a different way, and needs to have teachers who understand how to teach him. Ask your school principal if the reading recovery teacher is trained to work with children with dyslexia or other learning disabilities. If there is no support at your school, contact the Australian Dyslexia Association for more information. In general, a child with dyslexia will learn better by hearing, seeing and saying the words on the page (this is called multi-sensory learning). Blio and MeeGenius are two great apps your son can use with e-books, where he not only sees the words (they are highlighted as he follows along) but hears them being read by a human voice (rather than a computer-generated one). The apps are free but you must purchase the books.

Self-harm

My daughter (she's 13) had been very quiet and didn't seem her usual self – she hadn't been to see any of her friends for a week. When I asked her if everything was okay at school, she insisted she was fine. And then last weekend I noticed that she had some nasty scabs on her arm. When I asked her about them, she said she'd been carrying a glass at school and fallen and cut herself. This didn't sit right with me – the school usually sends an incident note home for something like that – so I called the office to find out what had happened. They told me they had no record of any accident and suggested that my daughter see the school counsellor. I was quite surprised, but they didn't explain why, and I can't get anything out of my daughter. What is going on?

It sounds like your daughter may be going through a rough time. Is she being bullied? Has she been through some other traumatic event at home? The reason I ask is because the cuts on her arm may well be her way of managing powerful feelings. She could be engaging in self-harm as a way of articulating difficult emotions (deep sadness, self-hatred, anger, loneliness and guilt). In Australia, as many as 12 per cent of all teenagers engage in self-harm, most of them young women, though the number of young men who self-harm is increasing.

Many clients tell me that when they hurt themselves they feel a release that helps them to manage overwhelming feelings, albeit temporarily. The harm is inflicted in a secretive manner and often continues for some time without anyone finding out. The most common forms I see include (in order of frequency):

- cutting
- burning
- taking overdoses of medicines
- swallowing harmful substances
- biting or hitting
- banging their body against hard objects
- pulling hair
- scratching and picking at sores.

Some patients have confessed to me that they self-harm because one or more of their friends began to engage in the behaviour and they felt a desire to join in. Once they started doing it, they said it became addictive. The harm distracted them from emotional pain (grief or guilt), relieved tension, and indirectly let others around (including parents) know how distressed they were feeling.

Discovering that a child is self-harming can be very distressing for parents. If it turns out that your daughter is engaging in self-harm, it is normal for you to feel shocked, sad, confused or angry. However you feel, try to stay calm and let her know you are there for her. She needs your love and support. Listen if she wants to talk, but don't force or pressure her. Try to avoid jumping to conclusions or trying to find solutions. If she doesn't want to talk to you, don't take it personally or feel that you have failed as a parent. Children often don't talk to their parents about self-harm because they are trying to protect their parents. Displaying understanding may help to develop your child's confidence to discuss this with you at a later time. Suggest that she write you a letter or email about her thoughts and feelings, have a chat to another trusted adult or contact Kids Helpline on 1800 551 800. Help her find other ways to cope with her feelings. Positive activities like listening to music or talking to friends and family may help her to channel her feelings and avoid self-harming. Help her build confidence by suggesting activities that could help focus her energy or catch her imagination. Don't force tasks on her, but getting involved in art, music, dance, drama or sports may help boost her self-esteem.

Your school has done the right thing referring your daughter to the school counsellor, though I would also take her along to your GP. Your doctor can treat any injuries and advise on harm-minimisation techniques (such as how to keep piercing and cutting implements sterile) until the reasons for the self-harming behaviour are identified and brought under control. Either professional will be able to refer her to a psychologist.

Some parents believe deliberate self-harm is attention-seeking behaviour that is best ignored. This is unwise for two reasons. First, a 2005 study published in the *American Journal of Psychiatry* found a thirty-fold increase in risk of suicide among self-harmers compared with the general population, and second, for some young people self-harm can become the default position for coping, despite the potential for permanent physical damage and the destruction of family relationships.

Sexting

My son (16) was sprawled on the couch glued to his phone the other day and I happened to glance at the screen as I walked past and I noticed a rather inappropriate photograph of one of his mates. (My son was laughing so hard he didn't notice me until it was too late.) I mentioned that I thought the photo was a bit too much (his friend was flashing what we used to call a 'brown eye'), but my son insisted it was just a joke and that I should lighten up.

No, don't lighten up. This is 'sexting', which involves taking explicit, naked or intimate pictures of oneself or others and sending them on to friends or someone else via mobile phone. Teenagers often do this in a locker room, bathroom or dressing room and send the images to others as a joke. However, everyone who receives the images has the ability to save, forward and post them on a social networking site. Once in the online world it's almost impossible to remove them, let alone control who sees them, and this could lead to embarrassment, humiliation and even sexual assault. It's also illegal. If your son is found to have sexual or explicit photos of someone under 18 years of age on his phone or computer, or if he forwards them on (even if he's deleted it), he can be charged with a criminal offence. What most people don't realise is that even if your son had actually posted a photo of himself and *agreed* to the photo being sent, it is still a criminal offence. Even pictures that have been photo-shopped to make a young person look naked, or cartoons of young people having sex are classified as child pornography. In Australia, a person under the age of 10 years is immune from criminal responsibility, but over 10 you are culpable for your actions. The maximum penalty for making, sending or having child abuse material is 15 years in jail.

Sexual abuse

My daughter has told me that her cousin is always touching her inappropriately. They are both 12 and whenever she tells him off, he calls her immature. She says he is always staring at her breasts, and once he pulled her on top of him. She says he also 'pervs' on her when she's changing. She says that he scares her. What should I do?

You are the adult and you have a duty of care to your daughter. Your nephew is displaying highly inappropriate and potentially criminal conduct. This cannot be dismissed as adolescent curiosity – it is a repeated pattern of harassment that puts your daughter at risk. So the first step is to protect your daughter by minimising (or preventing) contact with your nephew. You also need to educate her about standing up to such behaviour from anyone in the future. Tell your daughter that she did the right thing by talking to you, and that if her cousin (or anyone else) attempts to touch her in this way without her consent she should shout, 'No. I don't want you to do that!' and report the behaviour to a trusted adult. As for your nephew, you must inform his parents about his behaviour, no matter how tricky this will be for you. The boy needs to get a professional assessment and a treatment plan. This is not just about him and your daughter – he is potentially a danger to others outside of your family.

Here are some national online and phone support services for sexual abuse or assault:

- **1800MYLINE** (1800 695 463) offers 24/7 telephone counselling for young people having relationships difficulties, especially where to 'draw the line' on disrespectful behaviour.
- **1800RESPECT** (1800respect.org.au/) offers phone counselling (1800 737 732) or online counselling about sexual assault or domestic violence, as well as a user-friendly website with fact sheets and links to services in your area.
- **Family Relationships Online** (familyrelationships.gov.au) provides all families (whether together or separated) with access to information about family relationship issues.
- **Lifeline** (13 11 14) offers 24/7 crisis support and suicide prevention services.

I have recently learnt through a close friend (a parent of one of my daughter's friends) that my 16-year-old daughter is being pressured to have sex with her 17-year-old boyfriend. My husband and I are very strict with her, and never allow her to stay overnight at her boyfriend's home or him to stay here. I can't talk to my husband about this as he would be absolutely livid. I am very worried about her, but don't know what to do. Do you have any advice?

Sadly, this is a familiar tale. Through my work with *Girlfriend* magazine, I have learnt that boys who want to experiment sexually with girls who are not yet ready or comfortable with the idea will often resort to four coercive tactics:

1. 'If you really loved me you would let me do it.'
2. 'I'll have to break up with you if you don't.'
3. 'You led me on, and if we don't have sex I'll be in severe pain.'
4. Or they use alcohol or drugs so the girl is too inebriated to resist.

This is one of those conversations you absolutely must have, for her sake and for yours. Find a place to talk where you won't be interrupted and put aside your own fears and judgements – this is about your daughter. As a mum it is a great privilege to have a conversation with her about whether she is ready to have sex for the first time. The key here is to make sure she understands her right to say 'no' – something that has been enshrined in our cultural history for nearly fifty years. It remains one of the outstanding achievements of the women's movement alongside outlawing rape in marriage and teaching women to resist unwanted advances. Here are some useful questions to kickstart the conversation.

- Does she feel comfortable with her choice of partner?
- Has she talked with the other person about what kind of relationship they both want?
- Does she feel pressured to have sex (by her friends or her partner or both)?
- Does she feel more anxious than excited?
- Does she feel safe with the person she's thinking about having sex with?

- Does she know about the risks of sex, like pregnancy and STIs?
- Is she comfortable talking about contraception and safe sex with her partner?

If she's struggling with these questions, and you get a strong sense that she is not ready for a sexual relationship with this boy, then you need to talk to her about how she can assert herself so that she does not get pressured into doing what she does not want to do. The Fourth National Survey of Secondary Students and Sexual Health found that for young women the experience of unwanted sex increased significantly between 2002 and 2008. In 2002, 28 per cent of young women reported having unwanted sex and in 2008 this figure had increased to 38 per cent. You can help her to avoid becoming part of these statistics by encouraging her to be assertive. Here are some responses she could make to the first three pressure tactics:

SCENARIO 1

Coercive partner: 'You would do it if you really loved me.'

Your daughter: *'If you really loved me you wouldn't try to make me do anything that I don't want to do.'*

Coercive partner: 'I guess we have different ideas about love.'

Your daughter: *'Good point. I guess I don't really love you.'*

SCENARIO 2

Boy: 'I will break up with you if you don't do that with me.'

Girl: *'You can't make me do something by using threats.'*

Boy: 'I guess we just broke up.'

Girl: *'Wow. I've just realised that I want to break up with you, too. I don't feel special with you.'*

SCENARIO 3

Boy: 'You've just got me aroused and now you won't do it. This will make me sick. I *need* to have sex.'

Girl: *'You can't force me by making me feel bad. I still don't want to do it. There is nothing wrong with not having sex, it can't hurt you.'*

Boy: 'But I feel so bad. Boys have stronger needs than girls. I can't help it.'

Girl: *'It's not true that men have stronger sexual urges than women. That's just an excuse. I will feel worse if I do something that I don't want to.'*

If your daughter continues to struggle with this, 1800MYLINE (1800 695 463) is a 24/7 telephone counselling service for young people having relationships difficulties, especially where to draw the line on bullying or abusive behaviour.

Sex and sexuality

The other day my 6-year-old daughter asked me where babies came from, but I had to fob her off ('I'll tell you later') as we were on a bus, and I didn't feel like tackling that one with an audience! What should I tell her?

When she asks you again, be ready to answer her. Even when you find the topic or question embarrassing, your child needs to know that there is always a reliable, honest source she can turn to for answers – you. (Wouldn't you rather be her number one news source for sex ed, rather than her peers or the internet?) You don't need to make a speech. Listen to her questions, and keep your answers simple ('Babies grow in their mother's womb, which is inside their tummy'), and then wait for her to prompt you with further questions (e.g. 'But how do they get in there?'). Always use the correct names for body parts, and don't giggle or appear overly serious – you don't want her feeling ashamed or embarrassed about her curiosity. Talk openly, and let your child know she can ask you about anything. As she gets older, and the questions become trickier (e.g. 'What's a dildo, Mum?'), be honest if you are unsure of the answer, or even if you feel uncomfortable with the question. And by all means ask her where she has heard these words or terms in the first place!

My 16-year-old son has been spending a lot of time with a 15-year-old girl he insists is just a friend and has asked to have a sleepover at her house. It seems her parents are okay with the idea. Should I let him?

Assuming you have spoken to her mum and confirmed that she is okay with this adventure then your decision really depends on how well you know your son. Is he a sensible kid who carefully considers risk, or is he impulsive with a track record of acting before thinking about the consequences? Kids learn most about relationships from their families, so if you have encouraged open discussion with your son about important life issues such as relationships, sexuality, birth control etc., he is more likely to be honest with you about his choices.

The idea that our children will become sexually active is a confronting thought to many parents, but burying our heads in the sand will not help. The most recent edition of the Survey of Secondary Students and Sexual Health found that the majority of Year 10 and 12 students (78 per cent) have experienced some form of sexual activity, with more than a quarter of Year 10 students and just over half of Year 12 students experiencing sexual intercourse.

Even if you believe that your son's relationship with this girl is platonic, it won't hurt to remind him that some relationships can become physical, and, if this happens, he needs to remember that she is 15 years old and below the age of consent.

My daughter is 13 and is seriously obsessed with One Direction. Does this signal a general obsession with boys and should I talk to her about sex?

Don't get too freaked out by your daughter's boy-band fixation. This stage will pass. Having a crush on a pop star or stars is a safe way for her to explore feelings of sexual attraction, to identify with a particular group or subculture, and to begin developing her taste in music. It doesn't mean she's ready to hop into the sack with the first Bieber-esque boy she meets. In any case, it's a good idea to be open with your daughter about sex and sexuality. Sit down with her and tell her that she can ask you anything she wants about relationships, boys, sex or whatever. Answer her questions as honestly as you can. (Most Australian schoolchildren in public schools begin sex education in Year 5, so by Year 7, she may well know more than you!)

My son is 17 and has told me that he thinks he is gay. He wants to know how he can confirm his sexuality and whether to tell all his friends at school. He has a younger brother at the school and I am worried about what impact his older brother's public disclosure might have on him. Can you advise on both counts?

First, I'd tread carefully about shouting the news from the rooftops. We still live in a homophobic world and I think you are right to worry about the impact on his brother. The fact is that people will react differently based on their own beliefs, expectations and values. Some will have no problem with your son's sexuality, and others may reject him, which can be incredibly stressful for the whole family. A 2014 study by the Young and Well Cooperative Research Centre found that 16 per cent of the 1032 young people who identified as lesbian, gay, bisexual, transgender, intersex and questioning (LGBTIQ) had attempted suicide and 33 per cent had harmed themselves as a result of widespread homophobic and transphobic harassment and violence in Australian society. Tell your son that he doesn't have to go through this alone, that there are people in every state and territory to talk to. The Gay and Lesbian Counselling Service (1800 184 527) is open daily from 7 p.m. to 10 p.m. (AEST) and can put him in touch with local sexuality and gender support services. There's also Qlife (qlife.org.au), which offers a counselling and referral service for people of diverse sex, genders and sexualities. You might also like to contact PFLAG (pflagaustralia.org.au), an organisation that provides resources and hosts events for parents, family and friends of same-sex attracted people.

I recently learnt from a friend whose 12-year-old daughter attends the same school as my younger children that one of her daughter's friends was giving blowjobs to boys behind the sheds at the school. I was horrified! Is this really what goes on? My twin girls are only in Year 4, but I'm still worried about them being in a school where this kind of thing is happening. What should I do?

You are right to be horrified. There is no doubt that the early sexualisation of children is changing the experience of childhood, yet there has been little public discussion of its implications. We are seeing the shrinking of the years that constitute childhood, and in my opinion some parents have either been complicit in this or have elected to turn a blind eye. At 12 years of age, the young girl should be enjoying a time of freedom, exploration and imagination, free from adult concepts, yet sadly hyper-sexualised messages are everywhere – in movies, TV, beauty pageants (don't get me started), clothing, make-up, toys, advertising, magazines, video games and the internet – all entrenching and mainstreaming sexualised messages at every level of our culture.

I'd be worried about any primary school student engaging in such sexual activity and I think the most useful thing for you to do is to speak to the school about the young girl's behaviour, and for the school to notify the child protection authorities. Very often such behaviour is displayed by young women who have been sexually abused.

The second thing you can do is to help your own daughters to develop self-respect. Here are some tips on how to do that:

- Tune in to what they are watching and listening to and ask them what they think about the way girls are portrayed.
- Encourage your girls to participate in activities that prioritise skills and abilities over physical appearance.
- Help them find people to admire who have become heroes not because they are pretty, rich or thin, but because they have demonstrated more positive values.

- Praise and comment on your daughters' ideas, imaginations and behaviour rather than their looks and clothes.

Shyness

My 7-year-old son is painfully shy. Is there anything I can do to help him come out of his shell or will that just stress him out even more?

There is a wide range of shy behaviour that is completely normal. Not every child can be the life of the party, and some children need more time than others to get used to a new situation. An overly shy child, on the other hand, avoids many social situations, such as joining in games, going to birthday parties or playing in the park when there are other children about. This is when shyness becomes a problem, as it blocks the child's ability to move ahead developmentally – to build relationships with people outside the immediate family, including peers, teachers and other adults.

If your child is slow to warm to a new situation it is important that you don't shame him or label him as a 'shy kid' in front of others. Instead, show him empathy – tell him about your own experience with shyness, explaining how you felt and how you managed it.

Parents can help shy children by encouraging them to practise meeting new people or joining in a game through role-play. 'Hi, I'm Adam. Can I join in your game?' They can do this by acting out the roles themselves or using puppets.

Also, give him plenty of opportunities to interact with new people. Some shy children show more confidence with younger children, or when they meet new people in the safety of their own home. Praise even the slightest improvements in his confidence.

As his confidence grows, take him out of the home to meet new people. An after-school group activity such as swimming or music is a good idea – the more practice shy children get interacting with unfamiliar people the faster the shyness will decrease. However, the exposure will work best if it is gradual, so don't start with a solo concert performance!

If his shyness persists to the point where it stops him from doing what he really wants to do or is making him unhappy, consider talking to your family GP or local child psychologist.

Sibling rivalry

I have two girls, aged five and seven, and I am heartily sick of their constant bickering and fighting. If I don't intervene, it can escalate to the point where they scream, pull each other's hair and even start hitting. It's driving me insane! What's the best way to handle this?

Research tells us that siblings under the age of five can fight as often as once every ten minutes, so it's no wonder you feel like you're in the *Rugrats* version of *Fight Club*! Sibling rivalry is completely normal and is an important way for your children to develop social and emotional skills such as empathy, emotion regulation and conflict resolution. Children aren't born knowing how to handle disputes, but all children can learn the skills they need to reduce conflict.

The first thing you need to do is to observe your own responses when they fight. Do you jump in and try to solve the problem for them? It may be that they're not getting enough opportunity to try to resolve their own disputes and have learnt to rely on you to rescue them. So next time they are getting close to clobbering one another, remember these tips:

- Stay calm, speak with a low, even tone and stand near your children (don't scream out from another room).
- Never ask who started it, who had it first or who hit whom or you will get sucked in to the battle. Children often feel very distressed and will desperately try to make you take on the role of umpire. It is important to avoid this, as it not only robs the children of the opportunity to learn skills such as negotiation and self-calming, but also makes it hard for you to remain

neutral. Instead, try using the following types of statements:
'I know you want me to sort this out but it is your disagreement and I believe you two can sort it out yourselves.'

- Acknowledge their feelings and ask them to think of ways they can handle the dispute:
  'I can see you are both angry and unhappy about this. What do you think you could do to fix it?'
- Ask them to try to sort it out themselves, but give them a few suggestions:
  'I need you both to sort this out. You could try taking turns or find something else for one of you to do, or use a timer so that you know when it will be your turn.'
- Ask them to sort it out, suggesting a logical consequence if the conflict continues:
  'I didn't see what happened, so you will have to work this out yourselves. If you can't work it out then neither of you will be able to have/do this until you can.'
- Read them *The Knife and the Fork Go Dancing* by Traudi Allen. It focuses on the benefits of peaceful conflict resolution and cooperation with others.

If you model good social and emotional skills your children will naturally pick these up. However, if your children's fighting is often physically aggressive or is causing you great anguish, you might find it advantageous to consult an experienced professional such as a paediatrician or psychologist.

My daughter is 12 and lately has been accusing us of showing favouritism to her 9-year-old sister. My husband goes overseas a lot and he always brings them both back presents but the 12-year-old always says that her sister's are better, and that her sister is allowed to do more than she was at her age. Please help. I don't know how much more of this I can take!

It is a fact of life that as each child is born, the disciplinary rules of the family tend to become a bit more relaxed, which is why your eldest thinks her sister is allowed to do more. Try to make time to do special things with each daughter separately, so they each get a sense of their individuality. Also ask the 12-year-old to focus more on her own behaviour and less on her sister's. We teach people how to treat us, so if your daughter wants people to treat her as a mature, sensible older sister, she needs to behave in that way.

My youngest (I have three boys) is very competitive with his elder brothers but because he is younger he often doesn't beat them in whatever they are playing or doing. This seems to fuel his determination (and anger)! How do I encourage him to be less competitive?

This is a common problem for boys with older brothers. Try not to worry too much—the disappointment he experiences will help him to accept that some things are beyond his reach, at least for now, and he will learn to concentrate on the things that matter most to him. Here are some more tips:

- Sit down with him and do some research into the lives of people he admires, so that he can see that everyone has successes and failures along the way.
- Encourage him to try less competitive activities so that he can relax and not always feel that he has to be better than everyone else.
- Praise him for effort more than achievement.
- If the rivalry gets too physical, state a 'no-violence' rule with logical consequences for breaking it (e.g. the game ends; use your pocket money to pay for your brother's torn shirt, etc.), and break up any altercations without escalating the conflict or taking sides.

Sleepovers

My daughter is pestering me to allow her to go to a friend's house for a slumber party. Her friend is turning nine but my daughter is still eight and there will be quite a few children there (six, not including the siblings). I don't know the parents all that well, but they seem nice enough. My daughter says they have a huge house, so there is plenty of room. I'm not sure this sounds like a good idea. What do you think?

I don't have a problem with your 8-year-old attending a slumber party, as long as you know the family and see them as responsible. I see this sleepover as a 'rite of passage', which extends way past primary school age and into early adolescence. The first positive sleepover experience will be an important psychological milestone for her, demonstrating to her and you that she can handle a little independence. Best of all, sleepovers consolidate friendships and the research shows conclusively that people with strong and broad social relationships are happier, healthier and live longer. Here are my key tips for sleepovers:

1. Before her first sleepover at a friend's house, make sure she is comfortable spending the night at a grandparent's house or with other close relatives – this will acclimatise her to being away from her own home.
2. Tell her she can call you at any time if she feels uncomfortable.
3. Friday nights are better than Saturday nights, especially during the school term, as she'll need a couple of nights of sleep to recover.
4. Assuming you did know the family well, I'd ask who else is sleeping over and check out safety issues, such as the types of movies, television and video games allowed.
5. Resist the temptation to call her to find out how things are going, but be there to take a call from her.
6. Establish basic rules such as lights-out time and prohibitions against leaving the house.

My son is 14 and hangs out with a couple of kids who are much older. He's always demanding a sleepover at one particular kid's house who is a real lout. It's causing increasing conflict between us. Should I let him stay there?

First, I do not believe it is in the interests of your son to associate with peers who are older; in fact, I consider this a risk factor. Second, no teenager, especially a 14-year-old, should be demanding anything from their parents. The tail should *never* wag the dog. Third, when it comes to the teenage years, sleepovers are a different ballgame. It is very tough for parents to supervise and monitor what their kids are doing as they get older and the temptation to sneak out at night is significantly higher. Well-meaning parents often end up combing the streets late at night rounding up teens who have escaped the house. So while I am all for negotiating and compromising with teens, there are some issues that are not up for debate and this is one of them. Stick to your guns. Sleepovers end at high school. Also, encourage him to socialise with peers his own age.

Smoking

My partner smokes, and although he has tried to keep it a secret from the kids (he smokes outside and, until recently, only did so when they were at school or in bed), they are completely onto him. The children are now 12 and 13, and I'm worried that his habit is going to influence them in a negative way. He is in denial about the risks, so what should I say to them?

Unfortunately, you are right about the negative influence of a smoking parent. Research has found that the three most powerful influences on whether young people smoke tobacco are parents, peers and promotion. Luckily, however, you are a non-smoker, so you will also have some influence. Ask your children to imagine breathing in flea powder, nail polish remover and floor cleaner all at once, and explain that this is what people who smoke are doing. Tell them that cigarette smoke contains over four thousand chemicals and 69 of these are known to cause cancer. Explain that even if you don't smoke you can still get sick from these poisonous chemicals just by breathing in other people's smoke. Sit down with your kids and have a look at the Kids Health website about smoking (kidshealth.org/kid/watch/house/smoking.html).

The 2008 Victorian Secondary School Students Survey estimated that 6 per cent of male and 7 per cent of female 12–15-year-old students were smokers. Among 16–17-year-old students, 12 per cent of males and 15 per cent of females had smoked in the week before the survey. Alarmingly, research also indicates that the average age of adolescents taking up smoking is around 16 years old.

I think my 16-year-old daughter has started smoking. I found a cigarette in the washing and last night she came home smelling of cigarettes. No one in our family smokes, so I have no clue why she has started. How should I handle this?

Tobacco smoking is the single largest cause of preventable illness and death in Australia, killing more than 15,000 people every year. This is estimated to be about 78 per cent of all drug-related deaths. One in two lifetime smokers will die from their habit, half of those in middle age. Smoking causes a range of cancers, as well as heart disease, stroke and emphysema. A Victorian survey shows that 17 per cent of men and 13 per cent of women aged 18 years and over smoked in 2011.

The bad news is that most lifelong smokers start out as occasional smokers, but don't panic. And don't confront her about what you found in the washing or accuse her of anything. First, have a general chat about drugs and alcohol – The Other Talk (theothertalk.org.au/) is a great website to help parents with this tricky topic. When you talk to her about this, you will be able to gauge her attitude to risk-taking, and her comfort level with such topics. Above all, let her know you are there for her to talk to any time.

After a few days or whenever you think she's ready to talk about smoking, start out by telling her about your own or a friend's experience with tobacco. Then ask her if any of her friends smoke. If she doesn't fess up, casually ask her if she's been having an occasional smoke. If she comes clean, stay calm and reasonable. If you become angry and judgemental, she's more likely to rebel and go off and smoke anyway. That's what teenagers do. She's at that age where she's finding her independence and her own way in life. Talk about health issues, which will probably bore her, and the reasons why teenagers smoke, such as wanting to look cool, copying other kids, etc.

If you suspect that this is going to be where she digs her heels in, you might try a strategy one of my colleagues developed. The first time he knew his daughter smoked a cigarette he promised her $1000 if she didn't smoke another before her 21st birthday. He says it was one of the best investments he ever made, as none of his children smoke. Another parent I knew made his 18-year-old smoking son wash his own clothes and bedding separately, pay for his own tobacco with his own money and banned him from smoking anywhere in the home or backyard.

Social networking

My 11-year-old son desperately wants a Facebook account. He says most of his friends already have them and that he knows all about cyber safety from school. I'm not interested in any of the social networking sites myself, so I'm not sure what to do. It all looks too confusing to me. Do you have any advice?

An 11-year-old boy should not have a Facebook account because he does not have the intellectual, emotional or psychological maturity to handle a digital footprint. The social networking site requires all users to be at least 13 years old before they can create an account (in some jurisdictions, this age limit may be higher). Creating an account with false information is a violation of their terms, and this includes parents registering on behalf of someone under 13. Facebook states that it will promptly delete the account of any child under the age of 13 reported to them through the online form found at this link: facebook.com/help/contact/209046679279097. If you know his friends' parents, it is worthwhile letting them know that their underage children are using the site.

When your son is 13, you should log on to the Department of Broadband and the Digital Economy and download the Australian government's 'Easy Guide to Socialising Online', which provides information on social networking sites (communications.gov.au/easyguide). It is important for him to have the knowledge, skills and strategies to be able to use such sites in a safe, smart and responsible manner. Much of this material can also be obtained from the Cybersmart website (cybersmart.gov.au) run by the Australian Communications and Media Authority. All parents should utilise parental controls. A recent study commissioned by the European Commission provides a ranking of parental control tools, including free tools. Access the review at http://sipbench.eu/

My 14-year-old daughter is not interested in doing anything other than watching YouTube and talking to her friends online. Apart from going to school, she does not play sport, spends most of her life in her room and doesn't seem to be going anywhere or doing anything else. She's not unhappy, but I'm worried that this isn't good for her. What can I do?

Contrary to what many readers of this book may think, a 2011 report by the Young and Well Cooperative Research Centre has found that there are significant benefits associated with the use of social networking sites (SNS), including facilitating supportive relationships, helping identity formation, promoting a sense of belonging and increasing resilience. That's not to say there isn't a downside. I think SNS have fundamentally changed the nature of teenage peer relationships. Not only are relationship break-ups very public, but a profile can include an unrestricted record of every relationship mistake they've ever made. It can also be harder for young people to let go or get over an old relationship, as they can still see what their ex is up to. There's an academic downside as well. A 2010 survey of the top HSC students in New South Wales revealed that all students with a perfect score had one thing in common – they restricted social networking to one hour a day!

Balance is the key here. At 14, your daughter needs to find her signature strength – something that she loves to do that gives her drive – Ken Robinson calls this 'the element'. Finding this will help free her from the need for approval that plagues many 14-year-old girls and diminishes their confidence. You need to keep asking her 'What do you really love to do?' and 'How can I help you to do that?' You also need to widen the net of parental responsibility to include relatives or other female friends in whom your daughter might confide. Girls of this age often develop the Princess Bitchface Syndrome (a pattern of behaviour where they regard their mother as a malevolent witch) and do not feel they can discuss certain subjects with Mum. Psychologist Steve Biddulph calls this the 'aunties army'.

Sport

Our 10-year-old boy is sport mad! He's into everything! At the moment it's footy in winter and cricket in summer, plus he's had stints at soccer, squad swimming and basketball. He's not great academically, so we're happy for him to have something that makes him feel good about himself. The problem is that our 6-year-old daughter (who's been doing gymnastics since she was three) now wants to play netball. It's been pretty hectic juggling our schedules to get to all the training and games every week, and the thought of adding one more to the mix is really daunting. Because my son has been encouraged to follow his sporting interests, it doesn't seem fair to stop my daughter doing the same, but I'm just feeling a bit overwhelmed. How should I handle this?

I'd be overwhelmed, too! It's great that your children are developing their 'islands of competence', which is very important for their future social and emotional wellbeing, but children also need family time and this is a great opportunity for them to learn that there is such a thing as 'enough'. You are entitled to a quality of life and some nice romantic time with your partner. You should not be spending all your spare time as a glorified taxi driver. Either limit each child to one sport, or car pool with other trusted parents to reduce the burden.

My husband is pushing my son to play football even though I know he doesn't want to. It's stressing them both out. What should I do?

Your hubby's enthusiasm for sport is not entirely misplaced as the benefits of playing team sports are colossal. Team sports foster confidence, comradeship, and a healthy and active lifestyle. Studies show that kids who play sport are less likely to become obese, abuse substances or do poorly in school. Learning to compete also prepares a child for the demands of teenage and adult life, including the ability to cope with winning and losing. On the other hand, some men are too heavily invested in their child being the next great full forward for Hawthorn and pressure their non-sporty offspring to achieve what they wanted when they were young. Here's what I suggest:

- Ask your husband why he is so keen for your son to play footy, and try to get him to understand that the decision needs to be based on your son's needs, not his.
- Encourage your husband to consider that it might be equally valuable for your son to play another team sport of his own choice.
- Sit down as a couple and ask your son what sport he would like to play and whether any of his friends would be playing it.
- Discuss logistics (how much time would be involved in training and playing, and which parents would be involved in transport and attending sessions and games).

- If he is interested but hesitant, encourage him to have a go at that particular sport.
- If your son is very keen on trying his chosen sport, it is reasonable to insist that he commit to finishing the entire season. (You don't want him bailing out on his teammates in mid-season or giving up when the activity becomes more strenuous or demanding – there's no resilience-building there!)

Starting school

I don't know how to deal with my clingy daughter. She's almost five years old, but I can't go anywhere without her holding on to me and she cries if I leave her with a babysitter. I know it sounds pathetic, but I couldn't even take her to 4-year-old kinder as it was so stressful for both of us. Now I am really worried about her starting school next year. Am I going to have to let her cry and walk away?

This is a common and distressing problem but happily has a simple solution. Going cold turkey (where you just walk away and let her cry) is not the way to go as you run the risk of triggering her fears of abandonment, plus you'll also be a mess. Instead, you can use a technique known as systematic desensitisation, which is a type of behavioural therapy used in the field of psychology to help effectively overcome phobias and other anxiety disorders. Begin by taking your daughter somewhere she loves, ideally with lots of fun things to do, and while she is absorbed in an activity, gradually move away from her so that you are still in sight, but not in actual contact. Then gradually build up to staying in the area but moving off to talk to other adults. Once she adjusts to this, bring in the babysitter and choose your moment to leave briefly. She'll probably be a bit upset, but just say goodbye and walk away. When the babysitter has texted that your daughter has calmed down, you can return. The message she will learn is that calm behaviour brings Mum back.

My son likes to take his teddy bear everywhere. He will be starting school in two months and I don't want him to get teased, or to lose his bear. Should we try to wean him off his furry best friend?

It is very common for children to have 'transitional objects', which take the place of the mother–child bond. Research shows that these objects not only provide a sense of security for the children attached to them, but also help them adapt to new situations. At the end of the day no teacher is going to mind a child bringing a teddy or other comforter to school if it helps them to settle in. You can try to wean him off his teddy over the summer but do not panic if you do not succeed. The trick to weaning him off his furry friend is to encourage him to cope without his bear in short bursts such as a fifteen-minute trip to the shops. Don't mention the bear and if your son asks for it, explain that you left him at home because you didn't want to lose him, then distract your son with another activity, such as pushing the trolley or selecting the grocery items for the shopping trolley. Gradually increase the length of time that he copes without the bear. However, it is not the end of the world if he starts school with his teddy. Chances are that the distractions of school will take over during the year and he will no longer need his bear.

My child has hated every day of his first week at primary school and keeps telling me he doesn't want to go. What can I do?

Every child occasionally grumbles about school, but 1–5 per cent dislike it so much that they don't want to attend. There are three common reasons for this: loneliness, separation anxiety and learning difficulties.

- Loneliness: If your son is feeling lonely, it may take a little while for him to warm to the people in his new environment. In the meantime, you can bolster his social skills by setting a positive example. Always greet people warmly. Speak respectfully to your partner when you have a disagreement. When a conflict occurs between your son and another child, ask them both how they are feeling and brainstorm solutions for resolving the conflict. Talk about feelings with your partner, and appreciate each other's strengths and differences.

- Separation anxiety: How you say goodbye is critical to children's confidence. A firm 'Have a great day, and I'll pick you up at 3.30!' is more confidence-inspiring than 'Don't worry. I can be here in ten minutes if you need me.'
- Learning difficulties: Some children dislike school due to physical or cognitive problems. For them, hating school is really about the frustration they feel at being a step behind, no matter how hard they try. Make sure that your child's vision and hearing have been checked, and if necessary, also check for the presence of learning difficulties or disabilities.

Give your child a few weeks to settle in. Ensure you know who to contact for any situation, and the school's preferred means of contact. If your child is consistently having problems, social or educational, make an appointment to see his teacher. An experienced teacher will have both the experience and objectivity to guide you towards finding a solution.

We have just moved house and my 6-year-old daughter is frightened of starting school. Is this normal?

Moving house is already a huge change for a young child, so starting school on top of that is a double whammy. You need to be very patient with your daughter. Most schools run orientation sessions to ease children's transition to primary school and ensure a smooth and settled beginning in their new, exciting environment. However, if you've missed those, contact the school to see if they will organise one for you and your daughter. Start by making a number of practice runs to the school, so she gets used to the ride there. Call the school and ask for a daily schedule of activities to discuss with your child. Try playing on the playground and looking into the classroom windows. Find out where the toilets are and how and when they can use them. Explain about recess and lunch time and practise packing a lunch box. Most importantly, be excited and interested as your child will pick up on and follow your cues.

Step-families

I'm having trouble with my 15-year-old stepdaughter. We don't fight, but I can't get her to join in outings and family time with her two step-siblings (my 12-year-old son and 15-year-old daughter) and she just won't pull her weight doing chores. I don't want to alienate her (or upset her father, my new husband) by trying to force her in any way. Do you have any tips on how to handle this situation?

Most stepmothers initially have some trouble connecting with teenage stepchildren. Stepfamilies do not work like a biological family because most stepfamilies are built on loss. There are a number of current and past relationships to be negotiated and emotional baggage can also intrude. If you don't want to alienate her, then follow this five-point plan.

1. Allow your spouse to take the lead with disciplining her.
2. Respect her privacy and ensure she gets plenty of time to herself.
3. Never speak ill of her mother.
4. Urge your partner to spend time alone with her, as young people in this situation are often frightened that their relationship with their biological parent will be overshadowed by the one their biological parent has with their new partner and stepchildren.
5. Make time for you and your new partner, away from the kids. This is crucial as research shows most stepfamilies work best if the marital couple works as a team.

You can't fast track this relationship. There is no such thing as 'instant love'. No stepmother can expect instantaneous close loving relationships between all family members. Stepfamily members might grow to love each other given time, but this might never happen. Encourage an environment of respect and understanding.

I am about to get married to a man with two daughters (aged 11 and 8) whom I adore. However, I'm not sure they feel comfortable around me yet. What can I do to encourage their respect and love?

As far as difficult jobs go, becoming a step-parent is up there with air-traffic controller and brain surgeon. You are about to preside over a minefield of hidden hurts, half-concealed traditions and occasional tugs-of-war. The secret of survival is to be patient and realistic, as there is a lot more to this than 'just add children and stir'. You can't 'make' your stepchildren (or indeed anyone) respect you. You can only be respectful and loving towards them – the rest is beyond your control. No one can walk into a ready-made family, with a history of its own, and become an instant 'mother'. The term often used is 'blended not bonded'.

The most successful stepfamilies are those where the parents make their new relationship the priority and are then able to nurture and guide their children from a solid, secure base. Don't get stuck in unrealistic expectations of what the family should be like. As far as the girls are concerned, never play the disciplinarian (biological parents correct their own offspring), get yourself into their world and enjoy it, and try to become a poster parent for a positive attitude. And don't ask them to call you Mum – you're not their mother, and you never will be. They're conflicted enough, and pushing them to use 'Mum' will only confuse them even more.

I am seeing a man whose 10-year-old son lives with him on the weekends. As much as I try, I can't get him to trust or even like me. It's breaking my heart. What can I do?

Ten-year-olds can be wary of intimacy and he may have divided loyalties, which makes relating to other adults in his father's life awkward. This will be a long-term project – kids need at least two years to get to really know and accept a stranger. A good rule of thumb is that the level of affection they'll accept from you is the same as what they'd accept from a teacher. Be friendly, be interested in his life and encourage him to invite a pal when going out together with his father (this may ease his anxiety). Regular outings will increase the odds of him feeling you're a part of the furniture. Don't presume love, affection or authority and remember to accept the child's limits. Given time and understanding your patience will be rewarded with respect and sometimes even love.

Suicide

I keep reading that Australia has the highest youth suicide rate in the world. Is this true? And if it is, how would I know if my 16-year-old daughter is at risk?

First of all, Australia has never had the highest youth suicide rate in the world (a World Health Organization report places Australia at 26th on a list of ninety countries). Second, international comparisons of suicide rates are always problematic due to varying clinical definitions of suicide, and cultural taboos that lead to underreporting. According to the latest figures released in March 2014, the number of suicides among Australian teenage boys aged 15–19 has actually dropped from 122 in 1997 to 70 in 2012. Disturbingly, however, the number of suicides among teenage girls has risen from 33 to 59 in the same period.

Suicide is a complex human behavioural response that cannot easily be predicted, but research by several groups, including the Centre for Adolescent Health, has identified several primary risk factors for suicide and suicidal behaviour. They include mental illness; severe self-harm; and drug and/or alcohol abuse.

Mental illness is a strong risk factor for suicide. People with depression, anxiety, bipolar disorder or schizophrenia are seven times more likely to commit suicide. It is important, therefore, to be alert to signs of depression. These may include:

- loss of interest in things they used to enjoy
- withdrawn, upset or irritable behaviour or more marked personality changes
- violent behaviour
- running away from home, truancy from school
- changes in eating and/or sleeping habits
- poor concentration
- lack of care with appearance, schoolwork, etc.
- drug or alcohol abuse.

Self-harm includes cutting, burning, overdosing on medicines and swallowing harmful substances as a way of distracting oneself from unbearable emotional pain. One study has shown that people who engage in self-harm are thirty times more likely to attempt suicide.

A substantial proportion of young people who are suicidal give some warning that they are intending to take their own lives. Direct statements from young people thinking of ending their own lives might be:

'You would be better off without me.'
'I wish I was dead.'
'I just want to go to sleep and never wake up again.'
'Life is not worth living.'
'I wish I could disappear forever.'

Adolescents intending to kill themselves also often ask questions about death or heaven, write songs or poetry about death, or read books about death and dying. Morbid themes may appear in their artwork or the music they listen to or they may become obsessed with movies or shows about murder, death or suicide.

While suicidal thoughts are fairly common in adolescence (up to a third of adolescents have thought about suicide at some point), research and clinical practice suggest that it is relatively unusual for young people to think about suicide seriously enough to actually set a date, develop a plan and make an attempt. If you notice your child or another young person displaying any of the behaviours I've mentioned, the best thing to do is to simply ask them how they are feeling, and ask if they may have had thoughts about harming themselves or ending their lives. Research has found that they are often relieved to talk about it. If you suspect a child is in crisis, seek help immediately by calling emergency services. Other resources are as follows:

Lifeline
13 11 14
Provides 24/7 crisis support and suicide prevention services for adults over 25.

Kids Helpline
1800 551 800
kidshelp.com.au/teens/get-help/phone-counselling.php
Provides 24/7 counselling and support for young people aged five to 25.

Youth beyondblue
1300 224 636
youthbeyondblue.com/
Provides 24/7 phone counselling and support for young people, and online chat services from 4 p.m. until 10 p.m.

beyondblue
1300 224 636
beyondblue.org.au
Information on depression and mental illness for parents.

Headspace
1800 650 890
eheadspace.org.au/
Online and telephone support for young people 12–25 and their family and friends.

Sane
sane.org/information/factsheets-podcasts/211-suicidal-behaviour
Fact sheets about suicide.

Black Dog Institute
blackdoginstitute.org.au/public/depression/inteenagersyoungadults.cfm
Fact sheet about depression in young people.

Swearing

My 5-year-old has begun to use profanities and I'm not sure what to do. I didn't want to make a fuss as I thought it might just make the f-word an issue (everything else I scold him for he just seems to want to do more!). We don't use this kind of language at home (except for an occasional 'bugger') so I have no idea where this is coming from. How can I discourage him from swearing?

Undoubtedly one of the funniest moments for any parent is when a toddler or young child innocently uses a swearword for the first time. They are usually imitating adults, or a playmate who has enlarged his or her vocabulary and kindly shared it with the rest of the kinder group. You are doing the right thing by not making a fuss. Being horrified, angry, bursting into laughter, smiling or acting surprised all act as powerful reinforcers! So adopting an impassive poker face is the first step. Next, encourage clean but fun substitutions like 'shizzle' or 'abracadabra' and give him praise, cuddles and positive attention for using the alternative words. Lastly, if swearing becomes a repeated pattern of behaviour you need to set limits calmly – don't describe their meaning or why they're not to be used. Instead make it clear which words are not on. Ensure this is a short conversation, quickly moving to a different subject or activity so that you minimise the attention his swearing behaviour gets. It may be necessary to create a household rule to address repeated cursing. For example, 'We use appropriate language in our house, even when we are angry. If anyone swears, they must put some money in the swear jar (or take time out).' A 5-year-old may need reminding about what constitutes 'appropriate' and a warning before you follow through with the consequences. Above all, watch your own language!

Talking back

My two teenage children are at the stage where they argue with me about everything. They question everything I say and do. It is very upsetting. What is your advice on how to handle this?

Your teenagers are in the process of mastering the art of communication, so may sometimes come across as belligerent, rude, snappy, senseless or unreasonable. Often the problem is that they simply cannot express what they are thinking and feeling appropriately. Some teenagers can be very egocentric, believing that they are the centre of the world, and they may have a hard time seeing the views of others. This is not a product of poor upbringing or a sign that you missed something in your parenting along the way. It is instead a product of the developmental stage of adolescence that includes self-centredness. The top tips for communicating with teens are:

- Keep calm – try not to yell, scream or shout.
- Choose your battles – only argue over things that matter (i.e., are to do with their health and wellbeing).
- Keep it upbeat and never use sarcasm or put-downs – this just triggers defensiveness and shuts down communication.

- Look for a negotiation or compromise – show them that you value being kind above being right.
- Let your teenagers know that you cannot (and will not) speak to them when they are yelling, but always respond calmly and rationally when they stop yelling.
- Praise them whenever they are able to express themselves effectively.

We teach people how to treat us by how we treat them. It sounds as if they have identified a few of your buttons and are enjoying pushing them. Don't get sucked in to their teenage turmoil.

Tantrums

My 6-year-old son pesters me to buy him a treat every time we go to the supermarket. I used to be able to get away with buying him a Freddo frog or some other small snack as a reward for his good behaviour, but now he's fixated on the toy aisle, and sometimes throws a tantrum on the floor if he doesn't get what he wants. I try to breathe deeply and speak to him calmly, but it's just so embarrassing to have a crying and screaming school-aged child that sometimes I end up caving in. I know this is why he keeps doing it but I don't know what else to do. Please help!

Tantrums are usually considered the purview of the toddler, but older children can also lose control of their emotions, and the terror of these strong feelings escalates the whole experience. Some call these hissy fits or wobblies.

Every time he throws a tantrum, take time out – don't yell or scream, simply remove him from the situation. Look for the closest exit, leave the supermarket trolley and head for the nearest bench. Sit there quietly. Don't try to talk to him or lecture him or discuss what happened. Just wait until the storm is over. When he is calm, ask him if he is ready to go back in. This teaches him self-soothing – how to regulate his own emotions. Repeat the process every time he throws a wobbly. Consistency is the key. Eventually he will realise that there is no point in throwing a floor show as he'll just have to sit on the stupid bench *every time*.

You are basically teaching him the skills that he needs to be out in public; in other words, to follow the rules of socially acceptable behaviour. It helps to remind him of these rules every time you go out, such as 'Walk beside me' and 'No shouting or screaming'. It may also help to give him specific tasks connected to each public place you go. For example, when you take him shopping, his job might be to push the trolley, read items from the list, find items from his own small list or scan items if you have a self-serve register. Having rules for children to follow at the supermarket – and having them recite the rules before each shopping trip – is a particularly effective method. The research (yes, this has been studied!) says that praising good behaviour, involving them in the shopping experience and rewarding them after a tantrum-free trip works well.

Tattoos

My 17-year-old daughter and I are at loggerheads over the fact that she wants to get a tattoo with her boyfriend's name on her shoulder. How can I convince her that a tattoo is for life and her boyfriend may not be?

Tattoos used to be the province of sailors, bikies, criminals, circus people, carnival folk, thugs and bad guys, and used to be associated with risk-taking behaviours among minors such as sexual intercourse, binge drinking, smoking, cannabis use, fighting, gang membership, truancy and academic failure. But how things have changed. It's Gen X, Gen Y and Gen Inked! Studies show that 1 in 4 young Australians have tattoos and your daughter is part of the first generation in which tattoos are considered mainstream.

Kids get tattoos for a raft of reasons—to emulate celebrities, express their individuality, memorialise a loved one, or to simply get attention.

Others are the result of a drunken mistake or youthful impulsiveness. A 2013 study of 500 Australian adults found that 12 per cent had tattoos. Nearly 1 in 3 regretted getting a tattoo, and 1 in 7 had commenced or looked into tattoo removal.

There are several ways to handle this. You can ask her to wait until she is 18 so that she is absolutely sure she still really wants a tattoo (and still has the same boyfriend). In the meantime, she could do a trial run with a henna tattoo or find another way to express her love and commitment to her boyfriend, such as getting a piece of jewellery (a ring, bracelet or necklace) engraved with his name.

You could Google 'old people with tattoos' and show her some of the images. Ask her to consider what it might mean to live with this tattoo for the rest of her life, how it would look at her wedding, her graduation, when she's going for a job, etc.

Suggest that she wears her favourite clothes every day for two weeks – going to bed in them, going to school in them, visiting friends in them, etc. Then have a discussion with her about our need for variety. Ask her what her favourite songs were five years ago, and what she likes now, or what her favourite outfits were when she was five. This can help her understand that our tastes change, and that what we like now may seem ridiculous in years to come.

If she is still determined to get a tattoo, encourage her to consider one that is more discreet and to do her research on tattoo artists – the explosion in DIY tattoo kits available on the internet and the subsequent proliferation of backyard operators raises serious health issues. If she wants a good tattoo she is going to have to pay for it, and she may even have to wait several months for the best artist.

Tutoring

My son is almost nine and is struggling with maths at school. He says his two best friends are in the 'top' maths group and that he is in the 'dumb' group. I've asked him how he feels about that, and he just shrugs and says he doesn't mind, but I'm not so sure. He's already had a hard time learning to read, and his school was not very proactive when it came to helping him catch up. In the end, I had to borrow a set of readers from the library and we worked through them together at home. He seems to be enjoying reading now, so I feel it was worth it. But now I'm worried about the maths, as his close friends are really into science and maths, and I'd hate for him to be left behind. Should I arrange a maths tutor for him?

It's great that you care about your son's school experience, but he is only nine and he has got a lot of developing to do. He is still a work in progress. I think it is important to rule out the presence of any learning difficulty or learning disability in your boy and your school should be able to refer you to an independent educational psychologist. Meanwhile, your main job as a parent is to help him with the important task of figuring out who he is. If you can help your son find his 'spark' – something that he loves to do, that gives him a sense of purpose – it will help free him from the need for approval that haunts many early adolescents and diminishes their confidence. Why not ask him 'What do you really love to do?' and 'How can I help you to do that?' He might choose a sport, music, drama, drawing or dancing. Allow him to try one thing at a time, and see what blows his hair back. If it transpires that he does have a learning problem in the maths arena, then by all means arrange (in association with the school) some form of remediation.

TV

I'm worried that my grandchildren are watching too much TV. My son-in-law is the main carer (my daughter is the one who works) and he leaves the television on all day. The children eat breakfast in front of the TV before they go to school and then have dinner in front of it as well (my daughter has a long commute to work so doesn't get home until 7 p.m.). This can't be good for them. How can I bring this up without offending everybody?

Researchers have long known that too much TV is a bad idea, but no one has actually been able to demonstrate a cause-and-effect relationship between too much TV and negative outcomes such as poor grades in school. This is because television itself is not evil, but when it displaces family time around the dinner table, at the park or in the backyard, children lose crucial opportunities to learn how to build and maintain relationships. The research is clear now that young people with strong, broad social relationships are happier, healthier and live longer. Constant TV watching (like constant internet browsing) is not going to facilitate close relationships with family and friends.

A new study by researchers at the School of Medicine at Johns Hopkins University surveyed 350 third-graders at six primary schools in northern California and found that more than 70 per cent of the students reported having a television in their bedroom. These students scored between seven and nine points lower on standardised mathematics, reading and language arts tests than did their peers. This study provides even more evidence that parents should either take the television out of their child's room, or not put it there in the first place. This study doesn't prove that having a television in your grandchild's bedroom will decrease his or her test scores, but it does add to the increasing evidence that it's not a good idea.

Another, more recent, longitudinal study from New Zealand has found that young adults who watched more TV during childhood and adolescence than their peers had an increased likelihood of a criminal conviction, a diagnosis of antisocial personality disorder and more aggressive personality traits. The associations held fast even when the researchers controlled for IQ, socioeconomic status, previous antisocial behaviour and parental control. This doesn't mean children who watch TV will end up in jail, but screen time has to be balanced with human-being time.

In your situation, depending on your relationship, and your daughter's willingness to take advice, I'd initiate a conversation about your concerns. You could start by downloading a fact sheet from the American Academy of Child and Adolescent Psychiatry, which covers the issue and discusses some alternative activities to TV watching (aacap.org/App_Themes/AACAP/docs/facts_for_families/54_children_and_watching_tv.pdf).

Sadly, your influence is somewhat limited because you don't live with them, but there is no harm in trying.

Vegetables, dessert bribery and other food stuff

I'm trying to encourage my 10-year-old son to make his own breakfast, but he won't even eat breakfast unless I put it in front of him. Someone said I should just stick to my guns and if he doesn't make his own, he doesn't get any. But that sounds wrong. He wouldn't be able to concentrate at school, would he? He's already starving when he comes home from school, and he always eats a bowl of cereal after he's had dinner and dessert!

You are right – without breakfast he would not be able to concentrate or focus at school. Breakfast is the most important meal of the day from a neurological point of view – our brains run on glucose and we need carbs to make it. In 2012, Professor Jenny O'Dea surveyed the breakfast habits of 8003 children and compared them against their NAPLAN academic results and found that children who ate breakfast performed better academically than those who consumed nothing at all. Sadly for you, the greatest impact was observed in boys. You need to choose your battlegrounds, and I wouldn't worry about teaching him to make his own breakfast at present – making sure he eats a nutritious breakfast is far more important.

My 8-year-old son refuses to eat any vegetable except carrots and potatoes. We've tried to encourage him to try sweeter veggies like lettuce, sweet corn, snow peas, tomato, red capsicum, sweet potato and pumpkin, but he says he hates them all. Even when he was three, he would only eat steamed dim sims or chicken nuggets. In desperation, I used to puree broccoli and parsnip in a 'chicken and potato' soup, but he has since discovered my ruse. Someone told me I won't be able to do anything to change his habits now because I didn't offer him enough variety when he was a toddler. What can I do?

It may be that your son is what nutritionists call a 'super taster'. These kids can often detect a single piece of onion in a casserole! Most are male and we've no idea why this is so. Nutrition expert Dr Rosemary Stanton once told me the story of a 7-year-old boy she'd encountered who, when blindfolded, could identify different types of apples by the tiny slivers that were placed on his tongue. She said she'd tried mixing two different types of apple and placing them on his tongue at the same time, but he could always tell them apart. His mother had always found her son's fussiness annoying, but when she learnt that this was a special skill, she gave him a big hug and said she hadn't realised he was so clever. They agreed to play some tasting games at home, and soon he had tried many more foods.

Refusing all vegetables is the most common picture with these kids. There is a theory that this may have its genesis in infancy when they were being given mushy veggies at a time when they were developmentally ready to chew. It's also possible that you didn't persevere with getting him to try new foods in his toddler years. Some studies show toddlers need to taste a food up to ten or twelve times before they accept it. They are often happier eating raw veggies, too, so picking one (carrot sticks perhaps or cherry tomatoes) might be a way in.

The worst thing to do is to try to force the issue, as stress around meal times is known to contribute to unhealthy relationships with food. Bribery with dessert won't work either – it just makes veggies the bad guys and sweets the good guys and lays the groundwork for later food addiction. The best plan is to keep offering veggies, and to model eating them yourselves, without making a big deal out of it. Just make veggies a fact of life. Get him to help you chop vegetables for stir-fry dishes and salads. Make tacos or pizzas where he gets to choose and assemble his own ingredients. Let him help you choose fresh vegetables when you're shopping (tell him his job is to find the best-looking tomatoes, etc.). Plant a vegetable garden with him, or even just put a small cherry tomato plant or lettuce in a pot in a sunny spot in the yard. Encourage and praise him when he tries a new vegetable, even when he doesn't eat much of it.

Should we use dessert to bribe our kids to eat their dinner? My husband insists that it is the only way to get our kids to eat their veggies. He says it is something that his family always did when they were kids, but I'm not so sure. I've heard that it can set up bad habits. What advice can you give?

There are a couple of points to address here. The first one is the idea of getting children to finish their dinner or 'clean their plate'. Most healthy young children eat when they are hungry and stop when they are full, so it's not a good idea to mess around with their internal cues by encouraging or bribing them to eat past the point that they naturally feel 'full'. Instead, provide moderate portions at meals and encourage your kids to eat until they are comfortably full. Teaching your kids to be in tune with their own cues for satiety will help them to develop a positive relationship with food so that they avoid overeating as they grow older. The second aspect is about bribery. Unfortunately, encouraging children to eat their meat and veg by promising a sweet treat teaches our kids that nutritious foods are less appealing because their consumption requires a reward and that dessert is the 'prize'. Multiple studies have shown that, in the long run, preference for foods decreases when kids are given rewards for eating them. Don't get me wrong – it's fine to have dessert, but don't make it conditional on eating veggies and don't make a big deal out of it. Studies at Penn State University have found that when kids are restricted from eating treats of any kind, their desire to eat them *increases*, and they're likely to overeat them every chance they get.

Video gaming

My 13-year-old son is begging me to allow him to play MA15+ games on his Xbox online. He says his friends are all playing them, and I believe him because I can hear him talking to them on his headset. The games seem scary and violent to me, but I am an older mum, so maybe I'm not up with the times. He wants to play Grand Theft Auto, *and I forbid that, but he says he could play a war one and turn off the gore. What should I do?*

Video games are a fact of life. Research conducted by Bond University for the Interactive Games and Entertainment Association in 2013 found that 9 out of 10 Australian households own at least one video game device, with 6 in 10 homes having three or more devices. The same study also found that 76 per cent of gamers are aged 18 and over, with the average age being 32. We can play video games on desktop computers, TV consoles, tablets, laptops and smart phones. It can be a huge headache for parents trying to keep up with the technology, let alone the content of the games. Fortunately, the Australian Classification Board (classification.gov.au) provides ratings to help parents decide which games are appropriate for their children. And you are absolutely right to forbid your son to play the latest incarnation of *GTA*. It is restricted to adults aged 18 and over. You wouldn't allow him to see an R-rated movie, so why should a game with the same rating be any different? Even passionate and experienced gamers have blogged about the gratuitous violence and implicit sexism in this game. As for the MA15+ games, I'd stick to your guns (pardon the pun), especially if these are MMOGs (massively multiplayer online games) where he has no idea who he is playing with.

However, this does not mean that all video games are evil. According to Australian research, video games offer a range of creative, social and emotional benefits for gamers, even those who play violent first-person shooters. Dr Daniel Johnson, director of the Games Research and Interaction Design Lab at Queensland University of Technology, and his colleagues conducted an extensive review of the literature in 2012 and found clear evidence that video games have a positive influence on players: improving their mood, boosting vitality, creating a sense of competency and autonomy, and increasing self-esteem and resilience. In a recent study of 429 recreational gamers aged between 12 and 52 (31 per cent were university students), the lab found that the impact of video games on wellbeing has little to do with the type of game played or how often it is played and more to do with the player's level of immersion in the game and who they are playing with. It turns out that moderate video gaming with friends actually contributes to the players' emotional stability and reduces their stress levels. International studies have also found that gamers are better able to identify distractions, have quicker reaction times, improved vision, increased empathy and greater spatial orientation and cognitive flexibility. But 'moderation' and 'connection with others' are the key words here. Video games are not all bunny rabbits and rainbows. Studies also show that excessive gaming (playing more than ten hours a week) is correlated with mild increases in anxiety or insomnia. So, let him play games with appropriate ratings, restrict the amount of time that he plays and ensure there is balance in his life.

Wagging school

My son is in Year 8, and I have just found out that he has five unexplained absences this term. They were from last-period classes that I know he hates. (His secondary school has a computerised attendance system, so once I finally worked out how to use it, I could see when he had missed a class.) It's a complete shock to me, as I thought we had good communication and I have always trusted him to do the right thing. What should I do?

Find out what lies behind this behaviour. Ask him what he hates about the classes he is skipping. Listen carefully. Use open-ended questions that begin with what, where, how, when, why – not questions that are answered with a yes or no. Most 14-year-olds want to be heard, and they want help for the things they can't do anything about. By showing him you really are interested in his happiness (and you are not jumping to conclusions and judging him) you are maximising the chances of finding out what is going on. If he refuses to talk, then contact the school psychologist and ask for an appointment. You might be really surprised by what you hear. You may find that you have to set everything aside to make things better.

Walking to school

My daughter is in Year 5, and really wants to walk to and from school by herself. I let my son walk when he was in Year 5 – a fact my daughter reminds me of repeatedly – and although she says that quite a few of her friends are allowed to walk, I can't help worrying about her being alone. To me girls seem more vulnerable than boys, which she says is sexist (!). The walk is about twenty minutes, and she only has to cross one busy road (she can use the pedestrian traffic lights), but there are two less busy roads that she has to cross without lights (though they do have a refuge island). Am I being overprotective?

Yes, you are. Your child is 38,000 times less likely to be abducted than she is to be struck by lightning. But consider this: she has a 1 in 5 chance of becoming overweight and suffering heart disease and diabetes in adulthood. I'd be putting more energy into encouraging her to develop self-respect, emotional intelligence and resilience so that she doesn't learn to put food on her feelings. It's okay to be concerned about safety, but make sure your fears are grounded in facts and not media hype. Bubble-wrapping is not caring for your daughter, it's caring for yourself. Your job as a parent isn't to protect your child from every potential threat in the world, no matter how remote; it's to teach your children how to live in the world by themselves. The world is an amazing place, but sometimes bad stuff happens. All you're doing is giving yourself a false sense of security – the illusion of control – which teaches your children to live in fear of everything. If this is really hard for you, get her to walk with another child, or buy her a phone. Or she could ride a scooter or a bike. Allowing her to do this will help her to develop independence, competence and resilience.

Year 7 transition

My daughter seems very nervous about going into high school. We couldn't afford to send her to the private school her friends are attending, so she won't have any friends from primary school starting with her. Is her fear normal?

High school represents a big step towards autonomy and the whole process of growing up and leaving childhood behind. As such, it can be overwhelming for kids and parents alike. You can help her to adjust by building her confidence, as children with a bit of confidence are more likely to make friends. Ask her if she has any worries and listen to her concerns. Show that you feel positive about her school and 'talk it up'. If you have high expectations for her social and academic achievement, she will sense this and it will stress her out even more. Have a trial run of the route, especially if she takes public transport, walks or cycles. If she misses a school bus home you need to talk through what she will do, especially if you are working and can't pick her up straight away. Remember to get up earlier during the last week of the holidays, so that school starting times aren't a shock to her system. The first few weeks at a new school are probably going to be tricky, just because everything is new. Encourage her to keep in touch with her old friends – just because she's not seeing them every day doesn't mean she can't stay close via social media. Remind her that she's not alone – all of her Year 7 buddies are in the same boat, and she'll be sure to find someone she can click with. Above all, tell her that you are there to listen if anything is worrying her.

My son was quite outgoing in primary school, but starting high school seems to have knocked the wind out of his sails and he has become quite introverted. Should I be worried?

Don't panic, but keep an eye on him. For some young people, starting high school is a stressful transition and they can feel a little shell-shocked as they go from being a big fish in a little pond to a speck of plankton in an ocean! It is full of big adjustments like having to learn a different school layout, missing old friends, feeling shy or nervous about talking to new people, not to mention suddenly having to deal with multiple teachers, all with different personalities and approaches. Almost everything is bigger, different, harder and more frightening. Encourage him to talk to people, to keep in contact with old friends, and to get involved in school activities like music, art, sports or drama, which will help him connect with others who have similar interests. Tell him that things will eventually fall into place – he just needs to be patient. If, after a few weeks, he is still withdrawn, arrange for him to have a chat with the school counsellor, doctor or other trusted adult.

Year 12

My son is in his final year of school and is studying for his mid-year exams. It's great that he's so focused, but he is extremely stressed. He studies until the wee hours and because he's trying to stay awake, his diet is full of caffeine and sugar. He looks terrible. What can I do to help?

Sleep is the single most important study tool going around. Research shows that if your son gets between 8.25 and 9.25 hours a night, not only will his memory and academic performance improve, but his stress levels will drop. (If you're not convinced of the importance of sleep, consider that sleep deprivation is associated with poor physical health including increased risk of diabetes, obesity and depression.) To help him sleep, the caffeine has to go, and he needs to be getting at least thirty minutes of exercise every day.

The next most important study tool is diet. Glucose is the sole source of energy for the brain and comes from carbohydrates. The best carbs are the complex, slow-release ones in grains and veggies, not the simple carbs in sugar, which mess with insulin levels and mostly end up stored as fat. In addition, eggs, yoghurt, fish oil, avocado, flax seeds and blueberries all help with focus and concentration.

Encourage your son to get into a routine of studying at the same time in the same place, away from distractions, for no more than fifty minutes at time. Believe it or not, chewing gum can also help (there's even research to prove it), as can sipping water every twenty minutes or so.

Your job is to help him realise that he is not his ATAR and that life will still be worth living irrespective of his final score. This can take some doing when the whole community seems to be so focused on exam scores. A 2006 study of 700 Victorian Year 12 students found that nearly 1 in 5 had considered suicide or self-harm because of exam and homework pressures. The fact is, there are many different ways for young people to get where they need to go. There is always a side door to achieve life's goals. History is replete with highly successful figures who either never completed high school or whose final years were less than distinguished. They matured later.

This is not to say we shouldn't support our children in their final school year, just that we should worry less about the quantity of work a student is engaging in and, instead, focus much more on their emotional wellbeing.

My daughter has started Year 12 and seems quite stressed. She sets very high standards for herself and studies for hours every night and on weekends. She doesn't seem to be going out much or seeing her friends. Her father and I were the complete opposite when we were young, so we are at a loss about what to do. What's your advice?

The latest Mission Australia youth survey involving 14,461 young Australians aged 15–19 found that school or study problems continue to be among the top three issues of personal concern for students (the others being stress and body image). It's hard to tell whether this is a product of peer pressure, hysterical parents or schools taking an enormous eggbeater to the supposed importance of Year 12. Having spoken to thousands of final-year students I have discovered that this 'beating up' of the last years of school has become something of a national pastime, fuelled by the media and a genuine, if misplaced, belief among friends and relatives that this somehow provides motivation to the beleaguered student. The perpetrators of this inanity seem to have three main themes: one, that this will undoubtedly be the most stressful year of the teenager's life; two, that they can say goodbye to a social life as success can only come from relentless toil; and three, that the student's results will determine the rest of their life. In other words, their final score will be the sole determinant of their success or failure as a human being.

Aside from the fact that these observations are ridiculous, in many students they induce a sense of anxiety and dread that is profoundly unhelpful. The last years of school have always been stressful, but now there is increasing evidence that such stress is considerably magnified because of the hype and blah. A 2008 study by Karen McGraw and her colleagues found that more than 20 per cent of female HSC students have depression, 30 per cent show symptoms of acute anxiety, and 60 per cent of female students attribute most of their stress to final-year exams (the figures are slightly lower for male students).

Explain to your daughter that her final-year score does not measure her intelligence or her individual skills and abilities. In simple terms, the ATAR is basically a measurement of who can remember and apply the most knowledge in an exam situation. It most certainly doesn't define her as a person. Tell her that she can only do the best that she can do.

She also needs to realise that feeling disconnected from her peers will only exacerbate her stress levels during exam times. Karen McGraw's 2008 study also found that students who have lower levels of family, peer and/or school connectedness are more likely to display higher levels of stress, depression and anxiety during exams. Your daughter needs to balance the amount of time she spends studying with down time with family and friends. Year 12 is a year of hard work and huge commitment, but it's also a very social year with many chances for her to step outside the education bubble and let her hair down, especially with all the 18th birthday parties that seem to be held almost every weekend. With so much going on it can be hard to find a balance between study and life. This means keeping up hobbies and leisure activities, and talking to someone if things feel overwhelming.

My son is in Year 12 and is one of those kids who has the ability to do well, but just can't get motivated. He's never failed any subject, but every teacher remarks that he could do a lot better. He's a confident kid and expects to get into a university, but I'm not so sure he'll make it as he just won't put in the hard yards. One father I know got his son to study by promising to buy him a car. My salary won't stretch that far, but should I be pushing my son more?

While some students will benefit from the odd gentle reminder and encouragement to stick to a predetermined schedule, parents need to avoid getting into the habit of nagging and carping – telling kids they are socialising too much, not doing enough work, etc. This will ensure a year of conflict, frustration and anger, possibly creating feelings of resentment and even hatred in their son or daughter that may or may not dissipate over time.

This is not to say that parents should vanish. Showing an interest in your son's progress indicates that you care – a cup of tea and an encouraging word can do wonders. Positive reinforcement is the key, so when you see a good effort being made, praise him for it, showing that you've noticed his dedication.

As for bribing kids with a car, several years ago, I read about a Las Vegas teenager, Kenneth Gonzalez, who was awarded a Honda Fit by his high school for maintaining a GPA above 3.7 and keeping his attendance record spotless (no unexcused absences). Not all graduating seniors with good grades and perfect attendance got a car, but they were eligible to go into a raffle awarding a car as the major prize (with $8000 scholarships as lesser prizes). The school argued that its 'don't-screw-up-and-maybe-you'll-win-a-car' approach encouraged students to work harder because they were working towards something tangible.

Now this sounds good in theory, and maybe some kids got higher scores than they would have otherwise, but did this mean they were necessarily happier as adults? The problem with bribery is that young people don't learn to do the right thing because they believe it's a good idea, but because they are seeking a reward. Plus, they don't get to experience the natural consequences of not doing the right thing. Your son is making choices that may well influence his life in the short term, but they are his choices, and he will learn far more from making them himself than if you attempt to force his hand.

RESOURCES

RELATIONSHIPS

Relationships Australia
relationships.org.au
1300 364 277
Offers information and relationship counselling for all Australians. Fees vary slightly across different states and territories. Rates are either charged as a fixed rate or else determined on a sliding scale based on gross household income and number of dependants. There is a surcharge on most after-hours appointments.

Family Relationships Online
familyrelationships.gov.au
1800 050 321
Provides all families (whether together or separated) with access to information about family relationship issues.

The Line
1800 695 463 (1800 MY LINE)
Offers 24/7 counselling for young people about relationships, especially abusive or violent ones.

1800 RESPECT
1800respect.org.au/
1800 737 732
Offers phone counselling or online counselling about sexual assault or domestic violence, as well as a user-friendly website with fact sheets and links to services in your area.

Gay and Lesbian Counselling Service of NSW

1800 184 527

Anyone outside the local call area of their state or territory capital city who wants to talk to someone about sexuality or gender issues can contact this service between 7 p.m. and 10 p.m. (AEST) to get connected with their local sexuality and gender support services.

QLife

qlife.org.au

1800 184 527

Offers a counselling and referral service for people of diverse sex, genders and sexualities. Online chats are available between 5.30 p.m. and 10.30 p.m. daily.

MENTAL HEALTH

Black Dog Institute

blackdoginstitute.org.au

Has great fact sheets on depression and bipolar disorder and a referral service for clinics in Sydney.

eCouch

ecouch.anu.edu.au/

A self-help interactive program with modules for depression, anxiety, relationship breakdown, loss and grief.

Headspace

eheadspace.org.au/

1800 650 890

Offers online and telephone support, information and referrals for young people 12–25 and their family and friends.

Kids Helpline
kidshelp.com.au
1800 551 800
Offers free calls for kids up to the age of 25 from landlines and all mobile phones (Optus, Virgin, Vodafone and Telstra).

Lifeline
lifeline.org.au/Get-Help/Online-Services/crisis-chat
13 11 14
Provides 24/7 crisis support and suicide prevention services via phone or online chat.

ReachOut
reachout.com.au
Provides support, information and referrals.

Reconnexion
reconnexion.org.au
1300 273 266
Offers phone and online support, information and psychologist referrals for people with panic, anxiety, depression and tranquilliser dependency.

Sane
sane.org
1800 187 263
Offers phone and online help as well as fact sheets about mental health issues, particularly schizophrenia and other mental illnesses with psychosis.

Youthbeyondblue
youthbeyondblue.com/
1300 224 636
Free 24/7 crisis support and online chat between 4 p.m. and 10 p.m.

OTHER RESOURCES

Bullying No Way

bullyingnoway.gov.au/

A comprehensive site with lots of information for children, teenagers, parents and teachers on bullying and what to do about it.

Cybersmart

cybersmart.gov.au

Developed by the Australian Communications and Media Authority (ACMA), Cybersmart provides activities, resources and practical advice to help kids, teens, teachers and parents safely enjoy the online world.

National Drugs Campaign

australia.gov.au/drugs

1800 250 015

Provides information and referrals for parents and teens on drug issues.

Socialising Online

communications.gov.au/easyguide

The Australian Government's 'Easy Guide to Socialising Online', which provides information on social networking sites.

The Hormone Factory

thehormonefactory.com

A digital guide to the 'birds and bees' for kids (or for parents struggling to have 'the talk').

The Other Talk

theothertalk.org.au

Advice, information and support for parents and young people on the topic of alcohol and other drugs.

BIBLIOGRAPHY

Parenting

Buttrose, I., *A Guide to Australian Etiquette,* Penguin Australia, 2011

Cooke, K., *Real Gorgeous: The Truth about Body and Beauty,* Norton & Co, 1994

Edelman, S., *Change Your Thinking,* (3rd ed) Harper Collins, 2013

Gilman, B., *Academic Advocacy for Gifted Children: A Parent's Complete Guide,* Great Potential Press, 2008

Hamilton, D., *Why Kindness Is Good for You,* Hay House, 2010

Manes, S., *Be a Perfect Person in Just Three Days,* Yearling Books, NY, 1982

Rozakis, L.E., *The Complete Idiot's Guide to Dealing with In-Laws,* Macmillan Distribution, 1998

Tuttle, C., *Dressing Your Truth: Discover Your Personal Beauty Profile,* Live Your Truth Press, 2010

Children's books

Andrea, G., *There's a House Inside My Mummy*, Orchard Book, 2002

Anholt, C. & Anholt, L., *Aren't You Lucky!*, Joy Street Books, 1991

Danzig, D., *Babies Don't Eat Pizza*, Dutton Books, 2009

Harris, R. H., *Hi, New Baby*, Walker Books, 2001

Johnston, N., *Go Away, Mr Worrythoughts!*, Nicky's Art, 2008

Lewis, R.A., *I Love You Like Crazy Cakes*, Little Brown, 2000

Schmith, J.D., *Thunder and Lightning: They're Not So Frightening*, Trafford Publishing, 2005

Varley, S., *Badger's Parting Gift*, HarperCollins, 1984

Viorst, J., *The Tenth Good Thing about Barney*, Atheneum Books, 1987

Wise Brown, M., *The Dead Bird*, Harper Collins, 1995

Wishinsky, F., *Maggie Can't Wait*, Fitzhenry & Whiteside, 2013

REFERENCES

ABS, 2008, *National Survey of Mental Health and Wellbeing: Summary of Results*, 2007, cat. no. 4326.023, Canberra.

ACMA, 2013, *Mobile apps: Putting the 'smart' in smartphones* <http://www.acma.gov.au/theACMAengage-blogs/engage-blogs/Research-snapshots/Mobile-apps-putting-the-smart-in-smartphones> retrieved 1 April 2014.

AIHW, 2011, 2010 National Drug Strategy Household Survey report, Drug statistics series no. 25, cat. no. PHE 145, Canberra.

AIHW: Pointer, S., 2013, *Trends in hospitalised injury, Australia, 1999–00 to 2010–11*, Injury research and statistics series no. 86, cat. no. INJCAT 162, Canberra.

Amato, P.R., 2001, 'Children of divorce in the 1990s: An update of the Amato and Keith (1991) meta-analysis', *Journal of Family Psychology*, vol. 15, no. 3, pp. 355–70.

Australian Clearinghouse for Youth Studies, Face the Facts Briefing: *Youth overweight and obesity in Australia* <http://www.acys.info/facts/obesity/FTF_Obesity_briefing.pdf>

Australian Institute of Health and Welfare, 2004, *A rising epidemic: Obesity in Australian children and adolescents* <http://www.aihw.gov.au/workarea/downloadasset.aspx?id=6442471181> retrieved 18 December 2013.

Australian Internet and Social Media Statistics, December 2013 <http://blog.marginmedia.com.au/Our-Blog/bid/99037/Australian-Internet-and-Social-Media-Statistics-December-2013>

Bahr, S. & Hoffmann, J., 2010, 'Parenting style, religiosity, peers and adolescent heavy drinking', *Journal of Studies on Alcohol and Drugs*, vol. 71, pp. 539–43.

Baumrind, D., 1991, 'The influence of parenting style on adolescent competence and substance use', *Journal of Early Adolescence*, vol. 11, no. 1, pp. 56–95.

Baxter, J., 2012, *The housework and homework of 10-year-olds*, presentation at the 12th Australian Institute of Family Studies Conference, Melbourne, 25–27 July 2012 <http://www.aifs.gov.au/conferences/aifs12/baxterslides.pdf> retrieved 27 November 2013.

Belle, D. & Bullock, H., 2011, *The psychological consequences of unemployment*, Society for the Psychological Study of Social Issues' Policy Statement <http://www.spssi.org/index.cfm?fuseaction=page.viewpage&pageid=1457>

British Neuroscience Association, 2013, 'Fetal exposure to excessive stress hormones in the womb linked to adult mood disorders', *ScienceDaily*, 7 April 2013.

Bruck, D., 2006, *Teenage sleep: Understanding and helping the sleep of 12–20 year olds*, Wellness Promotion Unit, Victoria University, Melbourne.

Bullas, J., 'Twenty-one awesome social media facts, figures and statistics for 2013' <http://www.jeffbullas.com/2013/05/06/21-awesome-social-media-facts-figures-and-statistics-for-2013/> retrieved 19 June 2013.

Burns, J., Andrews, G. & Szabo, M., 2002, 'Depression in young people: What causes it and can we prevent it?' *Medical Journal of Australia*, vol. 177, (supplement), pp. 94–6.

Burns, J., Davenport, T., Christensen, H., Luscombe, G., Mendoza, J., Bresnan, A., Blanchard, M. & Hickie, I., 2013, *Game on: Exploring the impact of technologies on young men's mental health and wellbeing; Findings from the first Young and Well National Survey*, Young and Well Cooperative Research Centre, Melbourne.

Byrd, I., 2011 <http://www.byrdseed.com/10-facts-about-social-emotional-needs-of-the-gifted/>

Caldwell, P., Hodson, E., Craig, J. & Edgar, D., 2005, 'Bedwetting and toileting problems in children', *Medical Journal of Australia*, vol. 182, no. 4, pp. 190–195.

CASA, 2012, *The importance of family dinners VIII*, The National Center on Addiction and Substance Abuse <http://www.casacolumbia.org/

addiction-research/reports/importance-of-family-dinners-2012> retrieved 7 April 2014.

Collin, P., Rahilly, K., Richardson, I. & Third, A., 2011, *The benefits of social networking services: A literature review*, Cooperative Research Centre for Young People, Technology and Wellbeing, Melbourne.

Colten, H.R. & Altevogt, B.M., (eds), 2006, *Sleep disorders and sleep deprivation: An unmet public health problem*, National Academies Press, Washington.

Commonwealth Department of Health and Ageing, 2008, The 2007 National Children's Nutrition and Physical Activity Survey.

Cooper, J. et al., 2005, 'Suicide after deliberate self-harm: A four-year cohort study', *American Journal of Psychiatry*, vol. 162, no. 2, pp. 297–303.

Cross, D., Thomas, L., Falconer, S. & Monks, S., 2013, *Cyberbullying and the bystander: Research findings and insights report for the Australian Human Rights Commission*, Child Health Promotion Research Centre, Edith Cowan University, Western Australia.

De Leo, D. & Heller, T., 2004, 'Who are the kids who self-harm? An Australian self-report school survey', *Medical Journal of Australia*, vol. 181, no. 3, pp. 140–44.

De Vries, A., Steensma, T., Doreleijers, T. & Cohen-Kettenis, P., 2011, 'Puberty suppression in adolescents with gender identity disorder: A prospective follow-up study', *Journal of Sexual Medicine*, vol. 8, pp. 2276–83.

DeLoache, J.S., 2010, 'Babies learn from baby media?', *Psychological Science*, vol. 21, no. 11.

Gibbons, R., Hendricks Brown, C., Hur, K., Marcus, S., Bhaumik, D., Erkens, J., Herings, R. & Mann, J., 2007, 'Early evidence on the effects of regulators: Suicidality warnings on SSRI prescriptions and suicide in children and adolescents', *American Journal of Psychiatry*, vol. 164, no. 9, pp. 1356–63.

Gibbons, R., Hur, K., Bhaumik, D. & Mann, J., 2006, 'The relationship between antidepressant prescription rates and rate of early adolescent suicide', *American Journal of Psychiatry*, vol. 163, no. 11, pp. 1898–1904.

Giordano, M. & Ross, A., 2012, *Let's talk about sex: Young people's views on sex and sexual health information in Australia,* Australian Youth Affairs Coalition & Youth Empowerment Against HIV/AIDS.

Golding, J., Pembrey, M., Jones, R. & the ALSPAC Study Team, 2001, 'The Avon Longitudinal Study of Parents and Children', Paediatric & Perinatal Epidemiology, vol. 15, no. 1.

Guy, R., Patton, G. & Kaldor, J., 2012, 'Internet pornography and adolescent health', *Medical Journal of Australia*, vol. 196, no. 9; 546–47.

Haines, J., McDonald, J., O'Brien, A., Sherry, B., Bottino, C., Evans Schmidt, M. & Taveras, E., 2013, 'Healthy habits, happy homes: Randomized trial to improve household routines for obesity prevention among preschool-aged children', *JAMA Pediatrics*, vol. 167, no. 11, pp. 1072–79.

Hancox, R.J., Milne, B.J. & Poulton, R., 2004, 'Association between child and adolescent television viewing and adult health: A longitudinal birth cohort study', *Lancet*, vol. 364, no. 9430, pp. 257–62.

Hetherington, E.M. & Kelly, J., 2002, *For better or for worse: Divorce reconsidered,* W. W. Norton & Co., New York.

Horsley, M. & Walker, R., 2013, *Reforming homework: Practices, learning and policies,* Palgrave Macmillan.

Hyder, T., 2005, *War, conflict and play,* Open University Press, McGraw-Hill Education.

INSERM Collective Expertise Centre, 2004, *Psychotherapy: Three approaches evaluated,* Paris: Institut national de la santé et de la recherche médicale, 2000– <http://www.ncbi.nlm.nih.gov/books/NBK7123/>

Interactive Games and Entertainment Association, 2014, *Digital Australia 2014*, Bond University <http://www.igea.net/2013/10/digital-australia-2014/>

Johnson, D., Jones, C., Scholes, L. & Carras, M., 2013, *Videogames and wellbeing,* Young and Well Cooperative Research Centre, Melbourne.

Juvonen, J., Wang, Y. & Espinoza, G., 2013, 'Physical aggression, spreading of rumors, and social prominence in early adolescence:

Reciprocal effects supporting gender similarities?' *Journal of Youth and Adolescence*, vol. 42, no. 12, pp. 1801–10.

Kelly, Y., Kelly, J. & Sacker, A., 2013, 'Time for bed – associations with cognitive performance in seven-year-old children: A longitudinal population-based study', *Journal of Epidemiology & Community Health.*

Leproult, R. & Van Cauter, E., 2010, 'Role of sleep and sleep loss in hormonal release and metabolism', *Pediatric Neuroendocrinology*, vol. 17, pp. 11–21.

Locke, J., Campbell, M. A. & Kavanagh, D. J., 2012, 'Can a parent do too much for their child? An examination by parenting professionals of the concept of overparenting', *Australian Journal of Guidance and Counselling*, vol. 22, no. 2, pp. 249–65.

Lubman, D., Form, A. & Ryan, S., 2010, 'Parenting factors associated with reduced adolescent alcohol use: A systematic review of longitudinal studies', *Australia New Zealand Journal of Psychiatry*, vol. 44, no. 9, pp. 774–83.

Martin, G., Swannell, S., Hazell, P., Harrison, J. & Taylor, A., 2010, 'Self-injury in Australia: A community survey', *Medical Journal of Australia*, vol. 193, no. 9, pp. 506–10.

McGrath, H. & Noble, T., 2010, 'Supporting positive pupil relationships: Research to practice', *Educational & Child Psychology*, vol. 27, no. 1, pp. 79–90.

McGraw, K., Moore, S., Fuller, A. & Bates, G., 2008, 'Family, peer and school connectedness in final year secondary school students', *Australian Psychologist*, vol. 43, no. 1, pp. 27–37.

Mindframe, The National Health Initiative, 2012, *Self-Harm in Australia* <http://www.mindframe-media.info/for-media/reporting-self-harm/facts-and-stats> retrieved 12 April 2014.

Ochs, E. & Kremer-Sadlik, T. (eds), 2013, *Fast-forward family: Home, work, and relationships in middle-class America*, University of California Press <http://www.theguardian.com/commentisfree/2013/oct/15/american-helicopter-parents-household-chores> retrieved 27 November 2013.

O'Dea, J., 2007, *Everybody's different: A positive approach to teaching about health, puberty, body image, nutrition, self-esteem and obesity prevention*, ACER Press, Melbourne.

O'Dea, J. & Mugridge, A., 2012, 'Nutritional quality of breakfast and physical activity independently predict the literacy and numeracy scores of children after adjusting for socioeconomic status', *Health Education Research*, vol. 27, no. 6, pp. 975–85.

Owens, J., Belon, K. & Moss, P., 2010, 'Impact of delaying school start time on adolescent sleep, mood, and behavior', *Archives of Pediatric & Adolescent Medicine*, vol. 164, no. 7, pp. 608–14.

Patty, W.L. & Johnson, L.S., 1953, *Personality and adjustment*, p. 277.

Perrens, B., Robbins, A., Fildes, J., Ivancic, L., Wearring, A. & Cave, L., Mission Australia Youth Survey 2013 <https://www.missionaustralia.com.au/what-we-do-to-help-new/young-people/understanding-young-people/annual-youth-survey> retrieved 22 January 2014.

Rigby, K., 2010, *Bullying interventions: Six basic methods*, ACER Press, Melbourne.

Rizzo, K.M., Schiffrin, H.H. & Liss, M., 2013, 'Insight into the parenthood paradox: Mental health outcomes of intensive mothering', *Journal of Child and Family Studies*, vol. 22, no. 5, pp. 614–20.

Robertson, L.A., McAnally, H.M. & Hancox, R.J., 2012, 'Childhood and adolescent television viewing and antisocial behavior in early adulthood', *Pediatrics*, vol. 131:3, pp. 439-446.

Robinson, K., Bansel, P., Denson, N., Ovenden, G. & Davies, C., 2014, *Growing up queer: Issues facing young Australians who are gender variant and sexuality diverse,* Young and Well Cooperative Research Centre, Melbourne.

Rosenberg, J., 'Parents forced to go private to treat child learning disorders', *Sydney Morning Herald*, 2011 <http://www.smh.com.au/national/education/parents-forced-to-go-private-to-treat-child-learning-disorders-20110909-1k1vt.html>

Rowe, K., 2003, *The importance of teacher quality as a key determinant of students' experiences and outcomes of schooling* <http://research.acer.edu.au/research_conference_2003/3>

Schiffrin, H., Liss, M., Miles-McLean, H., Geary, K., Erchull, M. & Tashner, T., 2013, 'Helping or hovering? The effects of helicopter parenting on college students' well-being', *Journal of Child and Family Studies*.

Seligman, M., 2011, *Flourish: A visionary new understanding of happiness and well-being*, Free Press, New York.

Smith, A., Agius, P., Mitchell, A., Barrett, C. & Pitts, M., 2008, *Secondary students and sexual health: Results of the fourth national survey of Australian secondary students, HIV/AIDS and sexual health*, La Trobe University, Melbourne <http://www.latrobe.edu.au/arcshs/downloads/arcshs-research-publications/secondary-students-and-sexual-health-2008.pdf>

Wagner, U., Gais, S., Haider, H., Verleger, R. & Born, J., 2004, 'Sleep inspires insight', *Nature*, vol. 427, pp. 352–55.

Wallien, M. & Cohen-Kettenis P., 2008, 'Psychosexual outcome of gender-dysphoric children', *Journal of the American Academy of Child and Adolescent Psychiatry*, vol. 47, pp. 1413–23.

Wasserman, D., Cheng, Q. & Jiang, G., 2005, 'Global suicide rates among young people aged 15–19', *World Psychiatry*, vol. 4, no. 2, pp. 114–20.

Wolfson, A. & Carskadon, M., 2003, 'Understanding adolescents' sleep patterns and school performance: A critical appraisal', *Sleep Medicine Review*, vol. 7, no. 6, pp. 491–506.

Ybarra, M., Mitchell, K., Hamburger, M., Diener-West, M. & Leaf, P., 2010, 'X-rated material and perpetration of sexually aggressive behavior among children and adolescents: Is there a link?' *Aggressive Behavior*, vol. 37, no. 1, pp. 1–18.

Zadik, Z., 2012, 'Obesity, adolescence and sleep deprivation', *Journal of Pediatric Endocrinology and Metabolism*, vol. 25, no. 7–8, pp. 617–18.

Acknowledgements

I am grateful to the numerous young people and families who have come along to the many and varied parent nights that I have been invited to give over the years and who didn't realise how much I was going to learn from them. They have taught me that in a few short decades parenting in Australia has been transformed in ways that previous generations cannot have imagined. This is my eighth book with the scarily talented people at Penguin Books Australia and like the seven that preceded it, nothing would have been possible without their help. Specifically, I am grateful for the wonderful support of the best literary panel beater in the world, Miriam Cannell, and the ever patient, wise and talented Hawthorn supporter Ali Watts, who continues to encourage me to find my voice and indulge my literary fantasies. My heartfelt thanks also to Caro Cooper for her excellent work on my behalf, undoing all the damage that I do to English grammar. Words fail me when it comes to the talented Ron Tandberg, who has illustrated every book I have ever written and brings the text to life with his sandblasted humour. There is an Italian proverb that says 'Little children, headache; big children, heartache'. Hopefully this is a literary blend of Panadol and Alka-Seltzer. My love and thanks to my wife, Therese, whose unwavering support sustains me in all I do.

INDEX